# NO MERCY

**ELEANOR LEARMONTH** has worked as a teacher and freelance journalist in Japan and Australia. She has a reputation as a magnet for natural disasters.

**JENNY TABAKOFF** has been a senior journalist in Australia and Britain for *The Times*, the *Sydney Morning Herald* and AAP. She is the co-author of *Australian Style*.

# NO MERCY

## TRUE STORIES OF DISASTER, SURVIVAL AND BRUTALITY

## ELEANOR LEARMONTH & JENNY TABAKOFF

TEXT PUBLISHING MELBOURNE AUSTRALIA

textpublishing.com.au

The Text Publishing Company
Swann House
22 William Street
Melbourne Victoria 3000
Australia

First published in 2013 by The Text Publishing Company

Cover design by WH Chong
Page design by Imogen Stubbs
Typeset in Bembo by J&M Typesetting
Maps by Guy Holt
Index by George Thomas

Printed and bound in Australia by Griffin Press, an Accredited ISO AS/NZS 14001:2004 Environmental Management System printer

National Library of Australia Cataloguing-in-Publication entry

Author:  Learmonth, Eleanor. Tabakoff, Jenny.
Title:   No mercy : true stories of disaster, survival and brutality /
         by Eleanor Learmonth and Jenny Tabakoff.
ISBN:    9781922147240 (paperback)
         9781922148308 (ebook)
Subjects: Disaster victims.
         Survival.
         Intergroup relations.
         Social interaction.
Dewey Number: 613.69

To my family,
particularly Eric, Nina and Nicky
for their support, encouragement and faith.

*Eleanor*

---

To Stuart.
If I'm ever on a desert island,
I hope it's with you.

*Jenny*

*L'enfer, c'est les autres*

Hell is other people.

JEAN-PAUL SARTRE

# CONTENTS

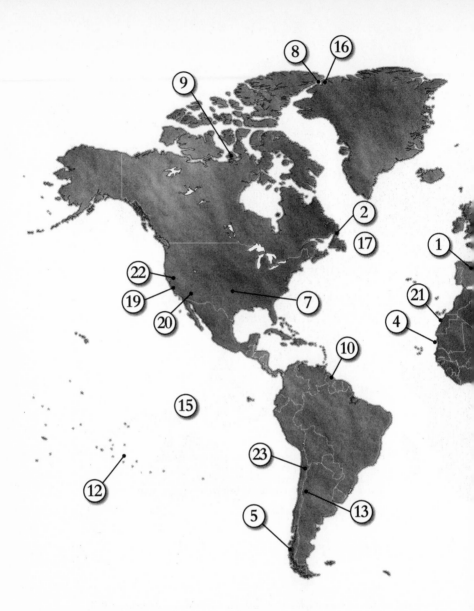

1 Numantia siege, Spain, 134 BC
2 Vinland, Newfoundland, 1100 AD
3 *Batavia* shipwreck, Abrolhos Islands, Western Australia, 1629
4 Raft of the *Medusa*, Mauritanian coast, 1816
5 *Wager* mutiny, Patagonia, 1741
6 *Grafton* and *Invercauld* shipwrecks, Auckland Island, 1864
7 Robbers Cave experiment, Oklahoma, 1954
8 Greely expedition, Cape Sabine, 1883–4
9 Sir John Franklin's lost expedition, King William Island, 1847
10 Jonestown, Guyana, 1978

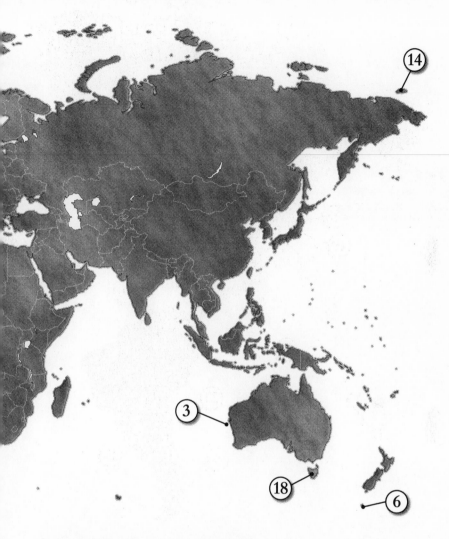

# PROLOGUE

**A GROUP OF** boys find themselves stranded in a beautiful but isolated environment. For a brief period things go well but then human nature starts to assert itself, and their mini-society descends swiftly into antagonism, hostility and violence.

That was the fascinating premise of a book published in 1954.

Actually, two such books were published that year. One was William Golding's *Lord of the Flies*: a work of fiction that was slow to take off with the public but eventually sold millions and became a modern classic. The other, Muzafer Sherif's *The Robbers Cave Experiment*, was factual: a scholarly text that also became highly influential, although much less famous.

*Lord of the Flies* was Golding's fourth attempt at a novel, the previous works having been rejected by publishers. The spark that lit Golding's creative fuse this time was his scorn for the books he had been reading to his own children, particularly R. M. Ballantyne's *The Coral Island*. He found its depiction of boys, living in an island utopia of constructive co-operation, fun and camaraderie, deeply unconvincing. Golding, who was working as a teacher in a boys' school at the time, pictured instead a disturbing, violent dystopia.

In 1953, as Golding worked his way through rejections from seven literary agents and publishers, an experiment was taking place in Oklahoma that would start with a very similar premise. Twenty-two boys were let loose in a deserted scout camp in the Robbers Cave State Park by a team of psychologists headed by Muzafer Sherif and his wife Carolyn. The boys were given food and shelter and almost-complete autonomy, with the researchers there only to observe them. In a very short time they abandoned their civilised conditioning and turned on each other. The result was without question more Golding than Ballantyne.

Any reader unfamiliar with *Lord of the Flies* can find a brief précis at the end of the book, along with a more detailed account of what happened at the Robbers Cave site. However, because Sherif's experiment is less well known, it's worth giving a brief description here.

The overarching aim of the experiment was to generate friction between two groups of strangers, and then bring them together to resolve their differences by forcing them to co-operate. The participants, who thought they were attending a normal summer camp, were eleven-year-old boys.

The psychologists wanted a homogenous group of

intelligent, well-adjusted boys with no anti-social problems, so they carefully selected boys with similar backgrounds from happy, middle-class white families. The researchers pretended to be camp staff and janitors, and melted into the background. The boys were divided into two groups before arriving: the 'Rattlers' and the 'Eagles'.

In phase one of the experiment, each group was left alone for a week of camping, hiking and swimming. Both estab-lished their own hierarchies and group norms, unaware of the other group's existence. Then each group made an unsettling discovery: there were other boys living at the far side of 'their' camping ground. Before the Rattlers and the Eagles had even met, the first signs of rivalry, territorialism and aggression appeared.

The announcement by the staff of a five-day tournament between the two tribes sparked an even greater hostility, and as soon as the groups set eyes on each other the insults started to fly. After losing an early contest the Eagles dispensed with their complacent leader; a more aggressive boy seized power and immediately threatened to beat up anyone on his own team who didn't take the competition seriously. The first day ended with the Eagles seizing and burning the Rattlers' flag; the next day the Rattlers destroyed the Eagles' flag. Brawls erupted and the researchers had to break them up.

Later the Rattlers executed a night raid on the Eagles camp, wearing full war paint to terrify the enemy. They raced into the cabin unopposed: crashing, smashing and stealing. The Eagles' leader rounded on his routed troops, accusing them of being 'yellow', and they subsequently carried out a counter-attack on the Rattlers' camp armed with sticks and baseball bats.

Then, mission accomplished, they retreated and rearmed—this time filling socks with stones.

By this point, the psychologists realised their test-tube friction was degenerating into a juvenile war that was about to get completely out of hand. Nonetheless they watched the arms race escalate over the following days, with the combatants gathering buckets of rocks, fighting, raiding and thieving. Finally, one violent confrontation became so sustained that the researchers were forced to step in, drag the boys apart and remove them to separate locations.

How long did it take for the hostilities to boil over, in an idyllic setting where everyone had plenty of food? Phase two lasted just six days—from the first insult ('Fatty!') to the final all-out brawl. Golding would have loved it.

At one level, Robbers Cave might appear to be little more than boys having a wild time in the woods. And of course these eleven-year-olds were never allowed to sink to the brutal excesses that mark many of the adult episodes highlighted in this book. But there are fascinating parallels between what happened at that summer camp and the behaviour of groups of people stranded together as the result of some catastrophe. The experiment gives an extraordinary glimpse into the genesis of social implosion in groups that find themselves isolated in some way: the 'Lord of the Flies principle' at work in real life.

Over the past two thousand years, fate has occasionally conspired to stage similar 'experiments': take a small group of people, strand and isolate them in a remote location, throw away the rule of law and see what happens.

This book considers numerous such examples of the Lord of the Flies principle in history.

We focus on predominantly adult groups who found themselves stranded and in conditions of extreme stress at dates between 134 BC and 2010 AD, in remote locations across the globe. Several of these episodes will be considered in depth; others will appear as we look at the factors that seem to dictate the survivor groups' behaviour and dynamics. We analyse the twisting path of social disintegration with reference to other failed groups—some famous, others relegated to the dusty, forgotten corners of history.

As a template for social implosion, how accurate is the Lord of the Flies principle? How does the process begin? What causes some survivors to abandon compassion, altruism and the rule of law in favour of selfishness and violence? How quickly can the trappings of civilisation be stripped away? What causes the primitive parts of our superficially modern brains to be unleashed? Does social implosion follow a predictable pattern? And if the occasional group does avoid these pitfalls, what makes it succeed where so many others fail?

As we investigate these tortured communities—struggling to survive not just the environmental conditions but each other—we would like the reader to consider the question, 'What would I do under the same circumstances?'

In *Lord of the Flies* Ralph says: 'I'm afraid. Of us.' Was he right to be afraid?

# THE LORD OF THE FLIES PRINCIPLE

---

1. Groups will inevitably fragment into factions.

2. Leaders frequently become obsessed with maintaining control rather than leading.

3. If the strong are battling to survive, they will not waste care and resources on the weak.

4. Morality, mercy and compassion are the expendable luxuries of civilisation.

5. Individuals will passively sanction evil actions by others to avoid becoming the next victim.

6. The rule of law will decay into a state of nature.

7. In the long run, there is only one rule: self-preservation.

# HELL ON WATER:
## The Raft of the *Medusa*

**LOCATION:** Atlantic Ocean off the Sahara Desert
**NATIONALITY:** Primarily French
**DATE:** 1816
**FATALITY RATE:** 91%
**DURATION:** 13 days

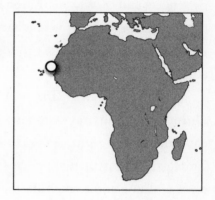

Théodore Géricault's enormous oil painting *The Raft of the Medusa* is famous, but today few people know about the disaster that inspired it. When Géricault chose the subject, the wreck of the *Medusa,* and the ensuing bloodbath, had become a French national scandal. The horrors that occurred on the raft have faded from popular memory, but in the long, dreadful history of naval disasters it is hard to find another incident as disturbing.

The *Medusa* was a well-built six-year-old frigate, nearly fifty metres long, carrying fourteen cannon. On June 17 1816 she set sail from France, the lead ship in a small fleet bound for the west coast of Africa. Their mission was to re-establish

France's colony in Senegal, so the ship was carrying nearly four hundred people—the new Governor Julien Schmaltz and his family, assorted colonists of various types, from bakers to engineers—and soldiers, sailors and all their supplies.

Due to their relative speeds, the ships were ill-suited to travel together and soon became separated. On the *Medusa*, the passengers and crew were unnerved by the loss of a young sailor overboard, perceiving it as a bad omen. Further unease crept in as some on board began to lose confidence in the captain's ability.

Although he was fifty-two years old, Captain Hugues Duroy de Chaumareys was far less experienced than the other captains in the fleet, several of whom were veterans from Trafalgar. Unfortunately, what Chaumareys lacked in experience and common sense he made up for with bombast and self-confidence. Well connected to the reinstalled French monarchy, Chaumareys had spent much of the previous two decades reinventing one episode from his youth early in the French Revolution. With each passing year his part grew larger and more heroic for—like many of the older monarchists of the time—Chaumareys had kept his head on his shoulders by lying as the political winds of the revolution had shifted to and fro. Through decades of upheaval, in which loyalty was often rewarded with death, Chaumareys had learned two invaluable lessons: how to lie and how to save his own skin. As far as sailing went, he knew less than he pretended and hadn't been to sea for over twenty years.

The captain of another ship, the *Echo,* soon noticed that the *Medusa* was off course. Within nine days she was sixty nautical miles off course. Arguments broke out between the experienced crew and passengers as to their position. When the captain found almost everyone disagreeing with him, he turned to the one friendly voice, Antoine Richefort. A vainglorious blowhard, Richefort loudly declared an extensive understanding of the African coast—in particular the treacherous Arguin sandbank, a notorious graveyard of wrecked ships north of Senegal. Charlotte Picard, an eighteen-year-old colonist travelling with her large family, recognised Richefort for what he was: 'a vile impostor' puffed-up with 'pretended knowledge'.

When the ship crossed the Tropic of Cancer on July 1, a vaudeville-style ceremony was held on board. As the captain enjoyed the entertainment, the officer on watch—worried by their proximity to the coast—changed course without permission. This caused more friction between the officers on one hand, and the captain and Richefort. The following day, the alarmed passengers couldn't fail to notice the water change colour; it was obvious they were nearing the Arguin Bank. They again tried to warn the captain and Richefort. With oily smugness, Richefort retorted, 'My dear, we know our business; attend to yours, and be quiet. I have already twice passed the Arguin Bank...and you see I am not drowned.'

Soon fish and seaweed were spotted, then sand. The crew became frantic. Too late, the captain ordered a change in course, but at 3pm the *Medusa* ran aground with a sickening thud. There were no other ships from the fleet in sight and the *Medusa* was about seventy-five kilometres from land—which unfortunately was the vast, scorching, virtually uninhabited Sahara Desert.

Panic was instant. Even veteran sailors fell to shrieking and wailing. Twenty-seven-year-old engineer Alexandre Corréard later described:

> *the extraordinary changes impressed on every countenance; some persons were not to be recognised. Here you might see features become shrunk and hideous; there a countenance which had assumed a yellow and even a greenish hue, some men seemed thunderstruck and chained to their places, without the strength to move.*

Charlotte's sister was struck a severe blow by a military officer who had mistaken the sixteen-year-old girl for one of his men. Others screamed for vengeance and wanted to throw Richefort overboard. The captain was totally silent and frozen to the spot.

Gradually, wiser heads prevailed. Attempts were made to pull the ship off the sandbank. These might have succeeded had the future governor of Senegal agreed to have the ship's fourteen heavy cannon thrown overboard. He refused. The crew and passengers alternated between calm and hysteria. Over two days, Governor Schmaltz decided they must abandon the grounded ship, which was now being pounded by heavy seas. The *Medusa* had six small boats, but they were not big enough to ferry everyone to shore. Various sensible plans were rejected in favour of the construction of a huge raft.

Built from scavenged masts, booms and spars, the raft was designed by Schmaltz who, as Charlotte Picard complained, 'had no design of embarking upon it'. It was about twenty metres long and seven metres wide (a little smaller than a singles tennis court) with nothing but a disastrous knee-high railing around the edge that was designed to stop people falling off. Little was done to give the craft flotation.

While the raft was being constructed, conditions on the *Medusa* deteriorated, particularly at night. Frantic rumours circulated that the ship would be secretly abandoned in the dark. Bands of soldiers and sailors took to looting, then broke into the spirit-room and got rolling drunk.

The ship echoed with the sounds of social disintegration. Men dressed themselves up in lace and stolen finery and ransacked the richer passengers' belongings, misers sewed gold into their clothing, and one man set fire to his possessions. A mutiny was suppressed by a small group of loyal soldiers who threatened to shoot the malcontents. Much later, mining engineer Charles Brédif identified the cause of the crew's anarchy and disobedience as a lack of confidence in the ability of their officers and captain (which in hindsight was a fair call by the crew).

The captain did nothing as lists were drawn up as to who would go on which craft. The general rule of thumb was the higher your status, the safer and less crowded your vessel. The Picard family, with three teenage girls and four young children, were terrified to find themselves assigned to the raft, which Charlotte described as a 'floating tomb'.

The governor stepped into the authority vacuum and twice gave his solemn oath that the six ship's boats would without fail tow the raft to the coast. With the weather deteriorating, it was decided to abandon ship on the morning of July 5.

Chaos ensued. The lists were ignored as any sense of responsibility or duty vanished, instead 'every one pursued the plan he deemed the best for his own preservation'. Food and water in barrels were left on the *Medusa*. A young officer, deranged by fear or alcohol, armed himself with pistols and threatened to shoot anyone who refused to board the raft. Under the weight of the first fifty people, most of the raft sank seventy centimetres under water. To aid flotation, supplies that had been stowed on the raft were pushed into the sea.

Governor Schmaltz, 'busied in the care of his own dear self', commandeered a well-provisioned barge for his family and friends, a large number of possessions and his armchair.

Yet more people were forced onto the overcrowded raft. A concerned Alexandre Corréard shouted up to the *Medusa* to ascertain if the raft had charts and navigational instruments. He was assured by Lieutenant Joseph Reynaud that it did.

Then: 'Is there an officer coming to take charge?'

'It is me; in a moment I shall be with you.' With this audacious lie, Reynaud followed the example of his superiors and fled to the safety of the governor's barge.

The raft now held 147 people, most of them hip-deep in water. It could take no more. Those still on the *Medusa*, including the Picard family, cried out for help and mercy to the boats. Seeing dozens still trapped on the ship, the commander of the longboat, which already had forty-three men on board, courageously took another forty-seven, leaving it dangerously low in the water and leaking.

Meanwhile, Captain Chaumareys, breaking maritime protocol and law, had rushed to one of the safest boats (a barge with a mast) with twenty-five strong rowers. He had taken the precaution of leaving the incriminating ship's log behind.

A fourth boat, a small skiff, approached the *Medusa*. Charlotte's father begged for help. When it was not forthcoming, Picard *père* had the wit to grab a gun abandoned on the deck and threaten to shoot everyone on the skiff if they tried to sail away without his family of nine. The skiff's passengers reluctantly agreed to carry the family to another boat, an eight-metre pinnace.

Other men jumped from the wreck and swam towards the uncrowded barges. The governor's aide-de-camp drew his sabre and threatened to cut off the hands of anyone who tried to board. The terrified men swam back to the wreck, even though the barge had room for at least another dozen men. In the end, seventeen men, many of whom were drunk, were left on the *Medusa*. One furious sailor picked up his gun and shot at the captain in his barge, but another sailor jostled his arm, ruining his aim.

A long chain of boats began to pick up the tow ropes for the raft. The exception was the overcrowded longboat, which was moving down the line and trying to offload men. All the other boats refused to take any, saying, in essence, 'You rescued them, they're your problem.'

Without oars and taking on water, the longboat was almost impossible to control. As it veered close to one of the boats in the centre of the chain, the towrope had to be dropped to avoid a collision. This meant the towline was now in two halves.

This caused a fatal chain reaction. On the governor's barge, the cowardly Lieutenant Reynaud, no doubt with permission from Schmaltz, raised his hatchet and struck the towrope repeatedly, cutting the raft adrift. The other boats quickly followed suit.

Those on the Picards' boat could see the effect this desertion had on those in the raft: 'Horrible cries were heard;

the air resounded with the groans, the lamentations, the imprecations of these wretched beings, and the echo of the sea frequently repeated, Alas! How cruel you are to abandon us!!'

The semi-submerged people on the raft waved and begged as the waves buffeted them. Legs and arms fell through the latticework of the platform, causing terrible wounds. As Charlotte watched the bloody water surging around the raft, she wept with pity and shame that Frenchmen could be capable of such treachery.

On the raft, despair was universal. Most of the platform was under water. They had no oars, no sail, no compass, no charts and almost no food—at the last moment an eleven-kilogram sack of biscuit had been thrown into the water near the raft. Now it was a salty mass to be shared among 146 men and one woman—several mouthfuls per person. It was all gone by the end of the first day.

Even worse, there was almost nothing to drink. With the hot, dry winds of the Sahara Desert blowing across the raft, the survivors had just six barrels of wine and two small casks of water between 147 people. They needed to go east to reach land but, at the mercy of the currents, they were drifting slowly south, a large piece of flotsam on the open sea.

The situation was infinitely better for the governor and captain: the two barges were seaworthy, steerable, uncrowded and well provisioned, and reached safety in just four days. The forty-two people on the smaller, slower craft carrying the Picard family were in a dire physical state when they reached safety eight days later. The other small boats, with varying degrees of seaworthiness, had far fewer supplies per person.

Meanwhile, amid the misery of the raft, Lieutenant

Corréard remembered that one of his engineering team had a small compass in his pocket. Its discovery caused a brief moment of joy—but a few hours later it was dropped into the sea and lost.

There was an attempted suicide a few hours after the raft was cut adrift. Jean Griffon du Bellay, who had been Governor Schmaltz's secretary, threw himself overboard—only to be saved by twenty-three-year-old Henri Savigny, the *Medusa*'s second surgeon. Griffon du Bellay tried again later, but this time his hand instinctively seized the raft, refusing to let him die.

Later that day, Savigny worked with several others to jury-rig a small sail for the raft (using the severed towrope) as well as ropes for people to cling to.

The first night began to fall; all the food was gone and the survivors reported that the weather deteriorated. The curses of the day gave way to prayers as the waves crashed down on the raft, violently flinging it about.

In the inky blackness, some began to hallucinate, imagining fires in the distance. Throughout the night the miserable group fought to stay alive, 'suspended between life and death, lamenting our misfortune, certain to perish'. They cried out farewells to each other and made promises to God.

Daylight revealed a shocking sight. A dozen men had become entangled in the latticework of the platform and were now dead, their corpses embedded in the structure of the raft. Others had been lost overboard. Altogether about twenty had died. Two young brothers found their father trapped in the platform. Believing him dead, they dragged out his body and discovered he was still alive.

Two other boys, unable to bear it, threw themselves overboard. The baker followed suit.

With daylight and calm weather, however, a degree of tranquillity descended on the raft. The day passed largely without incident, although those with flesh wounds suffered greatly from their immersion in saltwater. When it came time to distribute some fluids, it was discovered some of the soldiers had managed to get double or triple their share in the general confusion. Griffon du Bellay, having survived two attempts to kill himself, decided to drink some seawater every day, a decision the rest thought was almost tantamount to suicide.

This brief lull did little to prepare them for the insanity of the second night. Without even a glimpse of the coast or any rescue boats, despondency began to overwhelm many of the survivors. It was another particularly dark night and there was a perception that the sea had become very rough.

Anyone at the edge of the raft was in danger of being swept away, so all struggled to reach the relative safety of the centre. A division began to form within the group: the officers and civilians clustered around the centre found themselves at odds with the sailors and soldiers, who had reached a state of contagious, suicidal despair. The soldiers seized a wine barrel and began to drink. The wine exacerbated their grim mood, culminating in a decision to hack the raft to pieces.

Once this faction realised the officers would oppose their collective suicide, fighting broke out. A tall, intimidating soldier armed with a boarding axe began hacking at the lashings that bound the raft. One of the officers dashed over and killed him with his sword. This was like a spark to a tinderbox. The drunken mob rushed at the officers and another soldier was hacked to death.

Many passengers rallied to help the officers, until this group numbered around twenty. They had plenty to work with: the raft was bereft of anything useful but bristling with weapons—pistols, carbines, sabres, knives, bayonets and axes. After another soldier rushed towards the centre and 'immediately fell, pierced with wounds', the mutineers regrouped at the back of the raft, where they surreptitiously cut at the lashings with a knife. The officers attacked, throwing two of the soldiers into the sea. There was a renewed slashing at the ropes, partially successful; the mast that Savigny had constructed fell, knocking out an officer. The rioters grabbed his unconscious body and heaved it into the sea. He was pulled back by his friends, only to be set upon by the mob who wanted to cut his eyes out with a penknife.

The only female on board (a washerwoman) and her husband were attacked with sabres and bayonets, then seized and thrown overboard. Corréard and another man tied ropes around their waists and dived overboard to save the unfortunate pair. Still the fighting continued, and when the clouds parted, moonlight revealed the platform scattered with the mutilated bodies of the dead and dying.

Exhaustion led to a brief lull. Some of the soldiers even cried out for forgiveness. Then for no reason the battle reignited, the mob driven to a level of aggression that indicated many had abandoned their last links with humanity. Savigny was bitten on the shoulder and legs and another man had his Achilles tendon savagely mauled as those without weapons fought with their teeth and nails. Others attempted to gouge out eyes with their thumbs: 'their senses entirely deranged, they rushed upon us like madmen', according to Corréard and Savigny's later account.

Injured midshipman Jean-Daniel Coudein was at one end of the raft, trying to shelter a terrified twelve-year-old boy named Leon. The soldiers grabbed both and threw them into the waves. Heroically, Coudein managed to keep hold of Leon and clamber back on the raft.

At some point in the long night, the fighting once again subsided. Extreme exertion—mixed with fear, shock, injuries, hunger, dehydration and the disorienting darkness—had a strange effect. Many were literally losing their grip on reality, and finding themselves at the mercy of powerful hallucinations.

Corréard thought he was off travelling across the beautiful Italian plains. Others asked where their hammocks were, or thought they were back on the *Medusa*. One man reassured whoever would listen that he was busy writing a letter to the governor. Some could see ships or cities that weren't there. Savigny felt himself to be having a delightful time in a country filled with lush plantations.

Some shook off these delusions quickly. For the others, disaster awaited—'Their death was certain. Some became furious; others threw themselves into the sea,' according to Savigny and Corréard.

As dawn broke, many of the survivors felt the night's brutal events had themselves been a terrible hallucination, but daylight exposed the extent of the violence. Between sixty and sixty-five men had died during the night: about fifteen had committed suicide, the rest had been murdered.

As the survivors surveyed the carnage, many weeping, they

realised all of the water and most of the wine had been lost overboard. They were left with one cask of wine for more than sixty people. The raft was still drifting south in the open ocean, no nearer the coast. Sharks were circling, attracted by the blood from the dead and injured. An unsuccessful attempt was made to catch a shark using a bent bayonet as a hook.

It was July 7, and the survivors had been on the raft for more than forty-eight hours. Starvation led the men to start gnawing at whatever looked faintly edible: 'Some eat linen. Others pieces of leather from the hats, on which there was a little grease.' Corréard and Savigny reported one desperate man tried, unsuccessfully, to eat his own faeces.

The next step was inevitable. They 'fell upon the dead bodies with which the raft was covered, and cut off pieces, which some instantly devoured'. Many found the prospect of chunks of raw human flesh too disgusting, so it was decided to cut off and dry out strips to render them more palatable.

The third night on the raft began; the darkness frightened the survivors but at least the weather was calm. Sleep was almost impossible, most were standing in a huddle, knee-deep in water. If they did sleep, cruel dreams tormented them. The raft rang out with 'plaintive cries'.

By morning, ten more people were found to have died. The survivors threw the bodies into the sea, saving one for food. In the late afternoon, they had a rare moment of luck. A shoal of flying fish swam into the latticework of the wallowing raft and became trapped. The men were able to catch about two hundred small fish. After eating the roe raw, they mixed seawater, human flesh and fish in a barrel and somehow built a small fire underneath to make a stew, which greatly strengthened them. Violence flared again on the fourth night. A group of Spanish, Italian and African soldiers who were not part of the original mutiny devised a plan to drown the officers. They planned to seize a small bag of valuables which was hanging on the reconstructed mast, and somehow escape to the coast.

The plot was betrayed by a loyal soldier, so the officers and their supporters were ready when the attack started: 'A terrible combat again ensued, and both sides fought with desperate fury. Soon the fatal raft was covered with dead bodies and flowing with blood.'

In the fray, the washerwoman was again thrown into the sea, and again rescued. When the fighting petered out, calm returned. By the following day, only thirty people were still alive—and ten could no longer stand or walk. Days of immersion in saltwater, on top of their wounds, were causing the skin to peel from their legs and feet. Still there was no sign of the coast.

On their seventh day on the raft, two soldiers were caught siphoning wine out of the last remaining barrel. They were executed on the spot. Twelve-year-old Leon also died. Beloved by everyone, he had shown great courage and the adults had tried in vain to keep him alive.

Looking at those still alive, the stronger men—principally officers—decided there were insufficient supplies to sustain everyone. There were corpses to eat, but the lack of fluids was becoming critical.

*We were now only twenty-seven remaining; of this number but fifteen seemed likely to survive some days: all the rest, covered with large wounds, had almost entirely lost their reason; yet they had a share in the distribution of provisions, and might, before their deaths, consume thirty or forty bottles of wine, which were of inestimable value to us. We deliberated thus: to put the sick on half allowance would have been killing them by inches. So after a debate...it was resolved to throw them into the sea.*

Among those thrown overboard to drown was the raft's only female passenger and her husband. The washerwoman had given twenty years of service to the French army, and the only way Corréard and Savigny could justify the dozen murders was to blame those who had abandoned the raft in the first place.

The grim task was left to three sailors and a soldier; the officers looked away. 'Every thing in a word, had hardened our hearts, and rendered them callous to all feeling except that of self preservation.' Afterwards, the remaining men threw all the weapons overboard, retaining only a sabre, probably to cut up flesh.

The raft continued to float slowly south under the searing sun. A lemon and some garlic cloves were found secreted in a little bag. Fights broke out over how to share the bounty. A butterfly landed, provoking another argument between those who considered it 'a messenger of heaven' and those who wanted to eat it.

The men urinated in small tin cups, allowing it to cool before drinking it. They were forced to keep a close eye on the cups, as they were frequently stolen and drunk by other men. Much like connoisseurs discussing fine wine, they talked of how some men's urine tasted better than others. To combat dehydration, they sucked on pewter pellets, and dipped their faces, hats and hands in the sea.

The group managed to build a small raised deck near the centre of the raft to lie on. Large waves still saturated them, but the deck afforded some protection.

On the tenth day, three men could take it no longer, and proposed they should all commit suicide. The argument became more heated and was about to turn violent when a distraction occurred. Several huge sharks, larger than the earlier ones, appeared and swam right around the raft, so close one officer was able to strike them with the sabre. 'The blows which he struck these monsters, made them replunge into the sea; but a few seconds after they reappeared upon the surface, and did not seem at all alarmed at our presence.' In all likelihood, these were great white sharks, which are common along the West African coast.

They stayed with the raft for days. At times, the semi-suicidal men would lie naked in the water at the edge of the raft, tempting the sharks. To the men's surprise no one was taken, although they were badly stung by jellyfish. No doubt the sharks had already been feeding on the long line of corpses that drifted in the wake of the raft.

To distract themselves from their 'inexpressible anguish', the remaining fifteen men talked of past military campaigns. They still had some wine left, but the surgeon noted that even a tiny amount caused the men to fight because they became drunk so rapidly.

Increasingly they were revolted by their diet of human flesh, a *memento mori* reminding them of their own doom. They wondered who would be eaten next.

On the cloudless morning of July 17, an officer spotted a sail on the horizon. The men became frantic with joy, waving whatever was at hand. 'For above half an hour we were suspended between hope and fear.' But the ship disappeared, throwing the men into a despondency so profound that they envied the dead whose suffering was over.

With hope crushed, the men lamented their loved ones. Savigny doubtless thought of his girlfriend back in France, whose ribbon, now bloodstained and tattered, he still kept tucked in his pocket. The men lay on the platform, sheltered from the burning sun by a rough tent, awaiting death. Some decided to scratch their names and details of the shipwreck on a piece of wood, in the hope that it would reach their families somehow.

Two hours later, a cry rang out. 'Saved! See the brig close upon us.' It was the *Argus*, one of the ships from their fleet, bearing straight for them. Even those who couldn't walk crawled onto the platform with tears of joy pouring down their faces.

A small boat ferried the fifteen survivors to the brig. All were hovering near death, with Corréard the worst. On board, they were treated with great compassion and given strong broth and wine, their many wounds were dressed. Two days later they were docked in Saint-Louis, Senegal, to be greeted by the very man who had cast them adrift, Lieutenant Reynaud. They were immediately taken to hospital, where they met survivors from the other boats.

The captain of the *Argus* later reported the ropes that secured the raft's mast had been covered with strips of flesh drying in the sun. The raft was littered with human scraps.

Rumours of cannibalism rippled out through the town, to the great shame of the survivors. Corréard, distraught, had to be restrained from committing suicide.

It came as no surprise that the twenty-eight passengers aboard Captain Chaumareys' well-provisioned barge had been the first ones to be rescued. Governor Schmaltz's barge had also reached safety in just four days. All thirty-nine people on it had disembarked in good health.

The more crowded, less seaworthy boats had been wrecked at various spots along the coast and the passengers and crews had trekked south hundreds of kilometres through the Sahara. Lives had been lost.

The Picard family had travelled 280 kilometres by foot and donkey, to arrive in Saint-Louis desperately sick on July 13. They had been lost, starved, dehydrated and badly treated by the local 'Moors' (who manhandled them, ripped buttons from their clothing and spat at them) but miraculously all had survived, even the baby.

The colony of Senegal was in transition between English and French rule. The retiring English governor and residents were very kind to the survivors. To Governor Schmaltz, however, they were political dynamite—particularly the ones raising awkward questions about how the *Medusa* had been abandoned. The Picards were identified as troublemakers, and Schmaltz refused to help them.

Captain Chaumareys eventually faced trial in France. Despite the breathtaking incompetence and dereliction of duty he had shown, he escaped with a relative slap on the wrist. For abandoning his ship without the official log and while others were still on board, Chaumareys might have received a death sentence. Instead, he served three years in a comfortable jail. Of the fifteen raft survivors, five died from their injuries within the next few months. Griffon du Bellay, who drank saltwater continuously on the raft and who twice tried to kill himself, survived and eventually returned to France. Corréard remained in hospital for months. The scars from his prolonged immersion in saltwater caused him great problems for years.

While Corréard was in hospital, Governor Schmaltz repeatedly tried to force him to sign a report whitewashing the entire incident. Corréard refused, his anger growing with every day. Four months later he made his way back to France using three hundred francs given to him by a generous English major in Saint-Louis. Returning on the same ship was Captain Chaumareys, who was convinced the whole disaster was the fault of 'Jacobins'. Arriving on French soil, Corréard was readmitted to hospital. After this second discharge, he walked 120 kilometres, then took a coach to Paris, using money donated by another wellwisher.

Unemployed, spurned by the authorities and uncompensated, Corréard met an artist named Théodore Géricault. The young artist was just getting over a tempestuous affair with his aunt and the removal of their illegitimate son. In his gloomy state of mind, Géricault became morbidly obsessed with the *Medusa* incident, and decided to make it the subject of his next painting. He was meticulous in his research, interviewing survivors and obtaining limbs and heads from a hospital to add realism to his depiction of the raft.

Corréard posed for the work: the lieutenant can be seen to the right of the mast, angrily pointing to the sky. (Géricault also used his fellow artist Eugène Delacroix as the model for a corpse in the centre of the painting.) This painting is now regarded as one of the seminal works of French Romanticism and continues to anchor Géricault's reputation as an artistic genius.

Corréard and Savigny wrote an account of the *Medusa* tragedy which was a bestseller across Europe. Corréard became a political activist and the owner of a subversive bookshop. Savigny returned to France and married the young woman whose keepsake had helped keep him sane during those thirteen days on the raft. He moved to the rural town of Soubise, where he eventually became mayor.

A disturbing postscript occurred two months after the *Medusa* had run aground. The wreck, rumoured to contain a fortune of 90,000 francs, was discovered by the *Argus* still above water, but there was no trace of the money. Of the seventeen men who had been abandoned there, just three were still alive. These last survivors had regressed to a feral, rat-like existence. Hiding in three separate dominions deep in the ship, they emerged only at night—heavily armed—to forage for smudges of tallow or crumbs of salt pork. Their isolation and hostility towards each other had become all-consuming: 'When they met, they ran upon each other brandishing their knives.'

# FEAR

*He forgot his wounds, his hunger and his thirst,
and became fear; hopeless fear on flying feet.*

RALPH, *LORD OF THE FLIES*

**WHILE THE ROBBERS** Cave research was, in theory at least, 'controlled experimentation', most of the case studies in this book were precipitated by a single, terrifying, unintended catastrophe—a mine collapse, a ship ploughing into rocks or a plane crash. As a set-up for an unintentional experiment into humans at the mercy of the Lord of the Flies principle, a crash is a perfect start. And the first, overwhelming response to an unfolding disaster is fear: the irresistible biological reaction to immediate danger.

To understand the anatomy of real-life disasters, we have to consider how that initial fear, and the way those involved handle it in the first minutes and hours, are crucial to what occurs in the ensuing days, weeks and months.

In almost all the survival scenarios featured in this book, things get off to a terrible start, with people dying, injured, terrified and traumatised. Fear would have surged through the streets of the besieged city of Numantia in 134 BC just as obviously as it swept through the collapsed tunnels of the San José Mine in Chile more than two thousand years later.

A plane crashing or a ship capsizing are two of the most frightening experiences imaginable and victims may have just seconds to make critical decisions. Imagine for a minute that you were on the deck of the *Titanic* at 1am after the last lifeboats had sailed away. Consider the complexity of the decisions you are faced with. Should you jump into dark, freezing water, or stay on the deck and risk being pulled down with the ship? If you opt for jumping, should you put on warm clothes and risk drowning under their weight, or dress lightly and freeze? Once in the water, should you swim away from the ship and become invisible on the dark surface of the open ocean? Or stay near the ship and risk being hit by falling debris, sucked under or drowned by a panicking fellow survivor trying to climb on top of you?

Complex cause-and-effect decisions like these are primarily made in the frontal cortex of the brain. Unfortunately for us, the fear response also triggers the amygdala deep within the brain. Perceiving danger, the tiny, almond-shaped amygdala, part of the limbic system, activates a chain reaction of physiological changes and empties a cocktail of powerful hormones into our bloodstream. While this fear response evolved to help us survive attacks by animals (and other humans), it can have many detrimental side effects within the brain. Critical thinking skills can seize up, our senses can start supplying faulty information and our perception of reality can shift dramatically.

In other words, just when we need our conscious brain to be in peak condition and making snap decisions for us, it's been hijacked by the amygdala and may be completely beyond our conscious control. Bill McMahon, who escaped from high in the World Trade Center, summed it up neatly: 'Your brain—at least mine—just shut down…One thing you don't ever want to do is have to think in a disaster.'

Archibald Gracie, who survived the sinking of the *Titanic*, gave a vivid account of the effect of terror:

> *Fear has a visible effect on one. It palsies one's thoughts and actions. One becomes thereby short of breath; the heart actually beats quicker and as one loses one's head one grows desperate and is gone.*

Curiously, these primitive, automatic fear reactions may be far from our conscious mind, but we can see their footprints firmly in our language: think of *scared stiff* or *scared witless*; your *hair stands on end*, your *skin crawls* and your *blood runs cold*.

This was once over-simplistically described as 'fight or flight'; now modern neuroscience has expanded it to a more accurate *freezing, fleeing, fainting or fighting*.

The first response evolved as a reaction to a dangerous predator some distance away. *Freezing* the entire body into a state of 'attentive immobility' is a way to escape detection and remain safe. During this frozen state the brain is still hyper-aware and the body, primed by stress hormones (cortisol and adrenaline), is tensed ready for flight if the situation changes. Nevertheless, at a time when action may be desperately needed, the result is frequently the opposite.

Historical accounts of shipwrecks often record people being 'petrified' or 'stupefied'—rendered mute and unable to give or obey commands or even to move a muscle, standing like statues.

After the loss of the whaler *Essex* in the Pacific in 1820, sunk by two blows from an enraged whale, the crew scrambled desperately into a small boat as the ship sank. 'Not a word was spoken for several minutes by any of us, all appeared to be bound in a spell of stupid consternation.'

At the Robbers Cave campsite, during the night raid on the Eagles' cabin, the victims displayed typical characteristics of 'attentive immobility'. The boys had been fast asleep when a horde of screaming, painted attackers poured into their cabin, knocking things over and racing about in the dark. The staff were surreptitiously photographing the raid through the window so the camera flashes added to the chaos. No wonder most of the boys 'sat on their bed as though stunned', according to Sherif. In this case, the Eagles *were* being attacked, and freezing saved them from a beating: the Rattlers had stationed some boys outside the door to pounce on anyone fleeing.

One boy, codenamed Craig, remained paralysed in his bed 'playing possum' even after the raid had finished. This inaction earned him the label of 'yellow', and further eroded his status within the Eagles.

In a state of nature immobility serves its purpose only if the prey remains undetected. Once spotted by a predator, the prey must *flee* as fast as possible.

If danger is unavoidable and imminent, the hyperaware brain should automatically snap the body out of its frozen state. An uncontrollable urge to run can seize the mind and body. Without any rational instructions from the overwhelmed frontal cortex, people tend to run blindly, often yelling and screaming. At times the instinct to escape can be so powerful that it actually *causes* deaths, which is what happens in nightclub or theatre fires. The stampedes during the annual Hajj in Mecca have claimed thousands of lives in recent decades; the 1990 stampede alone resulted in over fourteen hundred deaths in the Al-Ma'aisim tunnel.

At this point the despair on victims' faces is so severe that there are frequent descriptions in survivor accounts of people being unrecognisable due to their distorted features and their white, yellow or green skin tones.

Other effects of extreme fear can include tachypsychia, a sense that time has slowed down, or tunnel vision, which can severely restrict the field of view, sometimes right down to a keyhole size. Hearing can fail completely, or become selective or strangely muted. On the other hand, some senses can actually be sharpened: an American police officer involved in a shootout reported being able to read the print on the shell casings fired by his fellow officers 'slowly floating' through the air in front of him.

Under the severest levels of stress, the brain can dissociate from reality, leaving the person feeling they are watching a play or movie.

Less frequently reported, but nevertheless common, is a sudden loss of bowel control; up to twenty per cent of American soldiers in World War II reported involuntary defecation when under fire. Again, an excellent survival reaction in an animal attack where the stench acts as a deterrent; not so useful in the aisle of a burning plane.

Obviously the biological urge to *fight* an aggressor is useless in a crash scenario but that doesn't mean it won't be triggered. As disasters unfold, a minority of individuals fail to control this impulse and become violent in the midst of the chaos, attacking indiscriminately with their fists or weapons.

At the other end of the response spectrum, some individuals experience 'tonic immobility' (if not actual *fainting*). This is a last chance, pan-mammalian response; all previous strategies dictated by the amygdala have failed as prey is overwhelmed by predator.

The urge to flee or fight vanishes, to be replaced by a floppy passivity in which the subject is conscious, unresponsive and free from fear and pain.

This condition, somewhere between freezing and playing dead, was carefully described by Dr David Livingstone after he was attacked by a lion in Africa in 1843. In the lion's jaws, in the midst of being mauled, he later recalled:

> *He shook me as a terrier dog does a rat. The shock produced a stupor similar to that which seems to be felt by a mouse after the first shake of the cat. It caused a sort of dreaminess, in which there was no sense of pain nor feeling of terror, though (I was) quite conscious of all that was happening. It was like what patients partly under the influence of chloroform describe...This singular condition was not the result of any mental process. The shake annihilated fear and allowed no sense of horror.*

Luckily for Livingstone, the instinctive response worked perfectly. The lion, thinking his prey already dead, dropped Livingstone and attacked another man nearby, allowing

Livingstone to get away. (Being a missionary and a Scot, Livingstone gave the Lord credit for his narrow escape, and his tartan jacket credit for warding off infection in the substantial wound.)

Tonic immobility is often experienced by rape victims, who typically berate themselves after the event for not fighting back, unaware that this is a hard-wired, automatic response that we have no conscious control over.

Freezing, fleeing, fighting or fainting: a disaster victim may experience all or none of these four reactions in varying order within the space of a few minutes or slowly over hours. The brain's responses are designed to enable an *individual* to survive an attack by a predator. When that individual is part of a group, the effects can become much more complicated, and potentially disastrous.

# PANIC

*They were all running, all crying out madly.*

LORD OF THE FLIES

**THE WORD *PANIC*,** like its cousin *pandemonium,* is derived from the god Pan, who the Greeks believed used spiteful tricks and magic to cause needless terror in people and herds of cattle, causing them to stampede.

At the Battle of Marathon, according to Greek myth, Pan had promised to help the Athenians defeat the Persians by afflicting their army with a disease. With the battle imminent, the disappointed Athenians secretly felt the prospect of a disease to be too slow-acting to be of much help. At the peak of the fighting, Pan unleashed his disease, panic, which quickly spread through the Persian ranks, leading to an Athenian victory. Later the grateful Athenians built a shrine in Pan's honour to repay their debt.

This legend illustrates a particularly dangerous facet of panic—it is the contagious face of fear.

Different emotions will exacerbate the surge of panic—terror, obviously, but also feelings of helplessness, and a fear of being trapped, even when it is unfounded.

Another human characteristic which contributes to an escalating group panic is our profound sense of empathy. Evolution has finetuned our social skills as a communal species and we are quick to sense and mirror the emotions of others (part of the reason we cry in a sad movie even though we know it's fiction).

Our biology contributes another ingredient to the witches' brew of group panic: sweat. Experiments conducted by neuroscientists at New York's Stony Brook University revealed that just smelling the sweat of terrified skydivers will trigger fear responses in another person's amygdala. Normal sweat will not produce this reaction. Researchers suspect that a human pheromone is responsible.

In a disaster scenario, people are also prone to a condition known as 'milling'. We drop what we are doing and gather together to exchange information, attempting to gain consensus on the degree of danger and the best course of action. In this situation the sight of others screaming in terror, or frozen and unresponsive, is extremely disturbing and likely to produce a similar response in the onlooker.

Since few situations are more terrifying than a battlefield, this poses a big problem for the military. S. L. A. Marshall, a combat historian from World War II, interviewed countless soldiers who had survived deadly encounters with the enemy and reached some startling conclusions. In his book *Men Against*

*Fire: The Problem of Battle Command*, he stated, 'Panic gathers volume like a snowball', and went on to claim that as many as seventy-five per cent of American soldiers in lethal fire fights either never fired their weapons, or were unable to sustain fire due to fear and panic. While these high figures are still the subject of some debate, his observations ring true.

'I have seen such panic in the faces of men during amphibious operations. The enemy confronted them and the sea was at their back…They sat there dumbly in the line of fire, their minds blanked out, their fingers too nerveless to hold a weapon.'

Among the causes of battlefield panic and flight, Marshall identified poor communication and men blindly copying the behaviour of others. He described a typical scenario from Normandy in 1944. A sergeant in charge of a squad was injured during a fire fight and decided to run back for first aid without informing his men. Not understanding what he was doing, his men broke the line and ran after him. Others nearby, seeing the fleeing men, panicked and followed suit, igniting a chain reaction down the line that caused its collapse.

Given what we know of fear and panic, it is easy to understand how fast the hysteria on the deck of a stricken ship or a nose-diving plane can escalate. Facing the real possibility of death, some individuals respond to the freeze, flee, faint or fight demands made by their amygdalas. Other bystanders, observing these reactions, mirror them—the result is widespread chaos.

On the sinking ship *Northfleet* in 1873, survivors recalled, 'in that direful struggle for life a wild panic rendered the mass of human beings on the deck almost inhuman and wholly uncontrollable.'

But consider this example.

In June 1770 Captain James Cook ran his ship through the uncharted waters of Australia's Great Barrier Reef and, in the middle of the night, struck a coral reef about twenty-five kilometres from the coast. For twenty-four hours the *Endeavour* was stuck on the razor-sharp coral. The crew worked their three pumps frantically to control the rising water level inside the ship. They knew that even if they managed to get the ship off the reef, it was likely the unplugged hole would rapidly overwhelm their pumps' capacity to clear the water out of the ship.

Among the ninety-one men on board was the botanist Sir Joseph Banks, who described this dire situation in his journal:

*She must sink and we well knew that our boats were not capable of carrying us all ashore, so that some, probably the most of us, must be drownd: a better fate maybe than those would have who should get ashore.*

Even if they could make landfall, they had already found Australia to be barren of food and they weren't sure how the indigenous population might react to their presence. At best, Banks considered, they would be stuck there until their deaths.

Even the unflappable Captain Cook held a similar view of their chances: 'This was an alarming and, I may say, terrible Circumstance and threatened immediate destruction to us.'

Extreme danger, darkness, the strong probability of death either immediate or lingering—the perfect recipe for panic.

Instead, conditions on the deck of the crippled *Endeavour* were quite different.

Banks recorded:

> *During the whole time of this distress I must say for the credit*
> *of our people that I believe every man exerted his utmost for*
> *the preservation of the ship, contrary to what I have universally*
> *heard to be the behaviour of sea men who have commonly as*
> *soon as a ship is in a desperate situation began to plunder and*
> *refuse all command.*

Indeed, Banks wrote, the men worked with 'surprizing chearfullness and alacrity: no grumbling or growling was to be heard'.

Cook also noted the absence of panic: 'In justice to the Ship's Company, I must say that no men ever behaved better... every man seem'd to have a just sence of the Danger we were in, and exerted himself to the very utmost.'

Ever the keen observer, Banks wryly noted one big change in the crew's behaviour: they all stopped swearing. Later writers attributed this to the crew attempting to make themselves presentable to their Maker, on the assumption that a meeting was imminent.

It is curious to find the words 'cheerful' and 'calm' appearing repeatedly in descriptions of groups in disastrous, life-threatening situations.

On the deck of the sinking *Titanic*, Lawrence Beesley saw 'no indication of panic or hysteria; no cries of fear, and no running to and fro'.

From a sinking ship off the coast of North Africa in 1815, Captain James Riley observed his crew: 'All were obedient to every order I gave, and seemed perfectly calm.'

From a crash-landed US Airways plane sinking in the freezing Hudson River in 2009, Captain Chesley Sullenberger described his passengers: 'I saw no one crying or sobbing. There was no shouting or screaming. People were relatively calm.'

So what causes these diametrically opposite reactions in the face of disaster? Why is it fear/panic or calm/cheerfulness?

# FAITH IN COMMAND

*Seems to me we ought to have a chief to decide things.*
RALPH, *LORD OF THE FLIES*

**IN THE INITIAL** stage of a crisis, when individuals are in the milling phase, most will look to others for clues on how to react. Most importantly, they will look to any apparent authority figures for information and appropriate responses.

In many cases, there is an existing structure of authority. On a ship or a plane, people will instinctively look to the captain or crew. If the authority figures want to forestall wholesale fear and panic, they have a brief window of opportunity to do so. The first step in this process is to appear calm and in control of the situation. On the *Endeavour* in 1770, Joseph Banks commented on the lack of panic:

*This was no doubt owing intirely to the cool and steady conduct of the officers, who during the whole time never gave an order which did not shew them to be perfectly composd and unmovd by the circumstances howsoever dreadfull they might appear.*

In the case of a long sea voyage, the crew are in a position to assess their leader's competence over a period of time. If a crew lacks confidence, that will be magnified when disaster strikes. Commanders such as James Cook and Ernest Shackleton were obeyed with unswerving loyalty. However, an incompetent leader is in a precarious position. Any orders he issues are likely to be ignored as the crew make individual decisions to ensure their own welfare. Result: chaos.

Just as panic can be sparked by imitation, it can be halted by the same force. As S. L. A. Marshall put it, referring to the battlefield, 'To the man who is in terror and verging on panic, no influence can be more steadying than that he sees some other man near him who is retaining self-control.'

When the English frigate *Alceste* wrecked in the Java Sea in 1817, panic was stemmed during the evacuation by the example of William Amherst, the leader of the expedition. John McLeod, the surgeon aboard the *Alceste*, recorded how Amherst 'Afforded to others an example of calm fortitude, and a cheerful readiness to share in every privation, which never fails on such occasions to have a powerful and beneficial effect, more especially when that example is found, where it ought to be, in the first rank.'

The *Alceste* wreck occurred the year after the loss of the *Medusa*. The contrasting behaviour of the crew was not lost on England's *Quarterly Review* later that year:

*In the one case, all the people were kept together in a perfect*

*state of discipline and subordination, and brought safely home*
*from the opposite side of the globe; in the other, every one*
*seems to have been left to shift for himself, and the greater*
*part perished.*

Accounts of other life-and-death episodes stress the vital importance of communication. In Marshall's words, 'the voice of the leader must cut through fear'. In 1944 Staff Sergeant Deine watched as paralysing fear gripped his platoon during a fire fight against the Japanese in the Marshall Islands. 'I asked myself why it was that we felt fear in each other and I realised it was because all of the leaders had quit talking.' He resumed his attack on the enemy spiderholes but this time shouted encouragingly to his men, 'Watch me! This is what you're supposed to do. Get at it. Keep working.' The sergeant's commands were perfect—short, uncomplicated and repetitive. The tide of panic was stemmed and the reinvigorated American soldiers won the battle. His conclusion was: 'Leaders must talk if they are to lead. Action is not enough.'

In a time of crisis, even when the message is dire, it is often enough for people to hear the calm voice of an authority figure. Never has this been more convincingly demonstrated than during British Airways Flight 009's catastrophic flight through a plume of volcanic ash over Indonesia in 1982. As the cabin filled with choking fumes and the passengers witnessed huge jets of flame shooting from the 747's engines, chief steward Graham Skinner explained it was 'Nothing to worry about, just a minor hiccup.'

Then all four of the engines stopped dead, leaving the plane with no power and falling towards the dark ocean. A seemingly calm Captain Eric Moody addressed the passengers: 'Ladies and gentlemen, this is your captain speaking. We have a small problem. All four engines have stopped. We are doing our damnedest to get it under control. I trust you are not in too much distress.'

Astonishingly, this was sufficient to suppress hysteria and panic from overwhelming the 248 passengers, who remained 'very tense and very quiet'. After dozens of attempts to restart the engines, the crew miraculously succeeded but not before the plane had dropped 7300 metres (24,000 feet). BA Flight 009 went on to land safely with no casualties.

Even if the authority figures are secretly terrified, they must *appear* calm. Aboard the crippled ship *Wager* in 1741, the mate, Mr Jones, managed to reanimate some of the paralysed men with short, simple commands: 'Come, lend a hand; here's a sheet and here's a brace; lay hold.' He later admitted that his confidence was all bluff: 'he thought there was not the least chance of a single man being saved.'

Unfortunately, leaders themselves are sometimes consumed by panic, and either become hysterical or freeze. Occasionally another person will then step forward and seize control, adopting the mantle of authority for the critical first few hours or even days. One such person was twenty-five-year-old Marcelo Pérez, who was a passenger on Uruguayan Air Force Flight 571 when it crashed in the Andes in 1972.

Pérez, captain of the Old Christians rugby team which was aboard the flight, was injured. Nevertheless when he crawled out of the wreckage, reported fellow passenger Nando Parrado, he 'immediately took control. His first action was to organise the uninjured boys and set them to work freeing the passengers who had been trapped under the heap of wrecked seats.' While working hard on the rescue, Pérez calculated the timeframe of a possible rescue and realised the group would have to survive the night on the mountain by themselves.

'Marcelo set to work. First he gathered a crew of healthy survivors and gave them the task of removing the dead and injured from the fuselage.' Next he directed them to clear the floor of the plane of debris, and as darkness fell organised for the injured to be carried back inside the plane. Finally he scavenged available materials to construct a wall at the end of the fuselage to protect the living from the lethally cold night air. Nando Parrado concluded:

> *His strong presence in the first few hours after the crash prevented what could have been total panic. The rescue operation he quickly organised saved the lives of many people who were pulled from the tangled seats, and without the sheltering wall he built that first night, we all would have frozen to death.*

The next day, Pérez tried to question Carlos Roque, the crew's mechanic and also a member of the Uruguayan Air Force, about the plane's flares, radio and batteries. Unfortunately Roque was traumatised and could do little but weep uncontrollably and rant. Next Pérez organised an inventory of their food supplies, gave the survivors their first meagre rations and rebuilt the crucial wall more carefully.

Pérez was everything the survivors could hope for in the first critical period. He rose above his panic to make rapid, methodical, intelligent decisions and didn't hesitate to delegate. Sadly, Pérez went on to develop psychological and emotional problems that crippled his ability to lead, and he died in an avalanche later in the group's seventy-two-day ordeal. However, his quick and decisive actions at the beginning saved the crash survivors from dying of exposure in the first few days.

There are two common problems concerning leadership during the initial phase following disaster. First, the designated leader can abandon his responsibility towards the group and use his authority to commandeer resources in order to save his own skin and escape as soon as possible. When this happens, those left behind are outraged and thrown into an authority vacuum.

A typical example was seen on the deck of the shattered barque *Neva* when she ploughed into rocks in Bass Strait in 1835. It was 5am, and Captain Benjamin Peck had in his care twenty-five male crew and his passengers—159 women and fifty-five children. As soon as it became apparent the ship was lost, the captain and surgeon rushed to launch a small boat in an attempt to save themselves. The boat was swamped when a large number of 'panicky women' tried to join them. Peck struggled back to the *Neva* and launched the longboat, this time taking most of the crew. By the time the survivors were rescued all fifty-five of the children and 153 women had perished.

Alternatively, the pre-existing leader may not be craven but simply incompetent. The best decisions for long-term survival are not always obvious. In the age of sail, most shipwrecks occurred in darkness. If a ship hits rocks on or close to shore, it may well remain there for days until the surf eventually pulverises it. (The hull of the *Medusa*, for example, remained above water for at least ten months.) The first impulse of the captain may be to get off the ship as fast as possible, often empty-handed. If the leader can suppress this urge and wait until daylight, there is a greater chance of saving more passengers, as well as items that may later prove pivotal to their survival.

If the survivors have the misfortune to find themselves in an uninhabited part of the globe, they face the daunting prospect of being trapped for weeks, months or years, so the right decisions at the outset are crucial.

As the period of isolation extends, and the situation of the survivors deteriorates, the strands of pre-existing authority almost inevitably unravel. When this occurs, a different form of leadership is required if the group is to survive.

# ALCOHOL

*Punished James Tunley with 12 lashes for*
*taking Rum out of the Cask.*

CAPT. JAMES COOK, 1769

**YOU MIGHT EXPECT** that anyone facing grave danger in a crisis would hope to be at their mental and physical peak. They might need to crawl through a burning corridor, swim to a life raft, or run from a gunman. The wrong choice could prove lethal.

So why is it that in so many historical accounts of disasters, people who should have been struggling to stay alive chose instead to make a beeline for the nearest supply of alcohol and get paralytically drunk? Making a conscious choice to consume a substance that slows reflexes and impairs vision, co-ordination, balance and judgment at a time of crisis seems almost beyond belief.

On board the crippled *Batavia*, wrecked off the west coast

of Australia in 1629, the crew broke into the officers' bottle room and commenced 'wanton drunken drinking'. In this state, one man decorated his hat with knives which he then hurled at anyone who disagreed with him. When an officer tried to break up the drinking party, a drunken gunner slashed him with a knife shouting, 'Out, rats and dogs, you have been masters here long enough.'

Three hundred and eighty-one years later, thirty-three Chilean miners were trapped in a copper mine deep under the Atacama Desert. When the outside world managed to contact them, one of their first requests was for alcohol to be sent down. The request was denied at first, for safety reasons.

Sometimes drinking binges by survivors have lasted for weeks. The crew of the crippled, leaking ship *Peggy*, adrift in the Atlantic for two months in 1765-66, spent almost their entire ordeal drunk, helping themselves freely to the cargo of brandy and wine. Captain Harrison abstained but was powerless to stop the excessive drinking, noting that his men's 'continued intoxication, however, seemed in some measure, to keep up their spirits, though it hastened the destruction of their health'. When they were rescued by a passing ship, the mate had been drunk for so long his stomach could no longer tolerate food. He died soon after, 'a martyr to his inebriety'.

The cause of this self-destructive behaviour lies once again in the brain's capricious assistant, the amygdala. Alcohol is anxiolytic in nature; it alters neurotransmission inside the amygdala, resulting in a short-term drop in fear and stress levels.

The fear-suppressing function of alcohol has been known for centuries. 'Dutch courage' has been used by militaries the world over as a cheap way to help soldiers overcome the terrors of war. According to John Keegan's book *The Face of Battle*, at the Battle of Agincourt in 1415, both the English and the French troops were 'less than sober, if not, indeed, fighting drunk'.

Unfortunately, when it comes to alcohol it is difficult to judge the correct dose. At Waterloo, a Belgian battery was so 'beastly drunk' during the fighting, they attacked their own side. Drunk and deranged sailors have been known to damage their own lifeboats.

Victims of a disaster who self-medicate with alcohol may find they are swapping fear-induced mental and physical handicaps for ethanol-induced ones.

Exhausted and starved survivors often comment that the negative effects of alcohol were greatly exacerbated by their physical condition. 'Alcohol, even in small quantities, has now a deleterious effect upon us,' wrote Dr Frederick Cook, stuck for over a year aboard an icebound ship in Antarctica. The doctor observed it was causing the crew's heart and kidneys to malfunction. Alcohol rushes straight through an empty stomach, where normally fifteen per cent of it would be broken down. Consequently, it is all metabolised into the bloodstream and absorbed much faster than usual.

In individuals suffering from dehydration, studies have shown that the blood alcohol concentration can be seventy-five per cent higher than in a normally hydrated subject. Unsurprisingly, in starving *and* thirsty survivors, the effects of even minimal amounts of alcohol can be disastrous. The hungry, thirsty men adrift on the *Medusa* raft drank wine which rapidly 'disordered their brains', causing them to become aggressive and suicidal. Being a diuretic, alcohol exacerbates dehydration, which creates more problems for kidney and liver function.

Another downside of alcohol consumption is its effect on survivors in a cold environment or, even worse, a cold, wet environment. Six of the female convicts who managed to get ashore after the wreck of the *Neva* were dead from exposure within twenty-four hours. The captain later claimed that several of the deaths had been hastened by an inordinate use of rum (unfortunately a cask had also washed in from the wreck).

A normal response to mild hypothermia is the constriction of blood flow to the peripheral parts of the body, to preserve core temperature, and the onset of shivering, which helps warm the body. Drinking alcohol has the opposite effect because it produces vasodilation (widening of the blood vessels), sending the blood back out to the extremities and skin. Furthermore it interferes with the body's ability to shiver—and may also suppress an individual's perception that they are freezing and need to do something about it. A 1984 study in Sweden found that in two-thirds of hypothermia fatalities, the victims had consumed alcohol, and had a mean blood alcohol concentration of 1.6 grams per litre—three times the legal driving limit.

At times, the potentially poisonous effects of alcohol on survivors are recognised by prudent leaders. In 1797, Captain Guy Hamilton of the *Sydney Cove* had the misfortune to be shipwrecked with a crew of fifty men and a cargo of 7000 gallons (31,800 litres) of alcohol on a small, desolate island in Bass Strait, north of Tasmania. The captain soon discovered 'the Crew made a very improper use of the Spirits and Wines'. His solution was to transport the entire cargo to an adjacent island in a longboat, and then dispatch the boat to the embryonic colony in Sydney for help.

So strong is the lure of alcohol to the desperate that when news of this veritable Shangri La—a rum-soaked island near Tasmania—became known in Sydney, a group of convicts set out in a stolen boat determined to sail the eight hundred kilometres to get their hands on it. In January 1798, the astonished explorer George Bass stumbled on seven European men stranded near Rum Island. They had been abandoned there by their convict co-conspirators after failing to locate the wreck of the *Sydney Cove* and its bounty of rum. Incredibly, the thirsty convicts had arrived five weeks before the explorer after whom the strait is named.

# FAIRNESS

**IT IS ALMOST** impossible to overstate the evil effect that fighting over resources can have on a group of stranded, desperate people. To survive as a group, people must reach consensus on the division of food, liquid, shelter and labour. Unfortunately some leaders feel they have a natural right to a larger share than the rest of the group.

Captain James Cook was a rare exception and he had strong feelings on the subject: 'Whatever refreshments we got that would bear a Division, I caused to be equally divided amongst the whole Company, generally by weight.' Regardless of rank, every crewman, including himself, was given an equal share of the supplies. He recommended that other commanders do the same. Furthermore, while stranded on the coast of

Queensland, he insisted the small amount of fresh fish the men caught be given to the sick crewmen rather than the officers.

William Bligh, who had trained under Cook aboard the *Resolution*, followed the example of his former captain on his 5800 kilometre open-boat trip following the mutiny on the *Bounty*. Bligh personally divided up food and drink, using a scale he fashioned from two coconut shells with a pistol-ball as the counterweight. The supplies amounted to just five days of normal rations, plus a few scavenged items. At one point he was forced to divide a noddy tern (about the size of a small pigeon) between eighteen men. First he gave the blood to the three weakest men, then distributed the tiny portions of the bird, using a slow and complex system involving two other crew to ensure perfect impartiality. Their supplies managed to sustain the men for their epic forty-eight-day voyage.

More typical were the leaders who assumed they had a right to more provisions than everyone else. Following the grounding of the *Medusa*, the unequal division of food and water cost scores of lives. On the sturdy barge carrying Governor Schmaltz, his entourage and some strong sailors to man the oars, each person was given: over half a kilogram of food (in the form of hardtack or ship's biscuit) and two bottles of liquid (wine and water). The superior seaworthiness of the barge meant they were at sea for just four days, and all thirty-nine people survived in good condition.

On the smaller craft carrying the Picard family and others, forty-two people had a total of three small glasses of water each and less than half a sea biscuit. It was eight days before they reached safety, all in a dire physical state.

On the raft, which was no more seaworthy than any other

piece of flotsam on the open sea, the 147 passengers had to make do with just seventy-five grams of sea biscuit each. They had only six casks of wine and two of water between them to last the thirteen days until they were rescued. By that time, 132 had died.

In 1914, quarrels over the division of food almost destroyed the group from the *Karluk,* which had become icebound in the Arctic. After the ship had been fatally crushed in pack ice, Captain Robert Bartlett spent twenty-four hours evacuating and unpacking the ship, before her inevitable destruction: 'Putting Chopin's Funeral March on the Victrola, I started the machine and when the water came running along the deck and poured down the hatches…I stepped off.' The small, exhausted group watched as the mangled ship disappeared into sea, the last sombre strains of Chopin accompanying her into thirty-eight fathoms of water.

Left behind on the frozen East Siberian Sea were fourteen crew, five scientists, five Alaskan Inuit and the ship's only stowaway—a black cat. After extensive preparations which included setting up forward caches and sewing a reindeer skin sleeping bag for the cat, they set out to walk and sled 120 kilometres across the ice to the nearest land, the uninhabited Wrangel Island. Four of the Inuit were a single family with two daughters, eight-year-old Helen and three-year-old 'Mugpi'. The terrain was appalling, with huge ridges of rafted ice pushed up to as high as thirty metres. At one point it took four days to travel less than five kilometres.

Adding to the group's many troubles, the ice was under enormous pressure and would crack without warning, revealing the sea beneath. One night a metre-wide crack opened in the centre of the Inuit igloo, directly under where Mugpi was sleeping. Her mother saved the girl's life by shoving her little sleeping bag to the other side of the crack just as it started opening.

Despite the awful conditions, Bartlett recorded, 'Keruk carried her baby, Mugpi, on her back all the way to Wrangel Island; the older girl covered the entire distance on foot.' The conditions had already killed eight of the men. On reaching the island, Bartlett and the Inuk hunter Kataktovick continued trekking towards the Siberian mainland to get help for the rest of the group.

Stranded on Wrangel Island north of Siberia for six freezing months, the remaining eleven men and the Inuit family of four split into three widely separated camps in an attempt to quell the fighting.

Each group was allotted a fair share of the supplies (primarily pemmican—a mix of beef, raisins, sugar and suet pressed into a block—and any game they could catch), but one camp consistently ate their ration too quickly and went hungry. This led to begging and lies about the amount of game that had been caught. The result was a total loss of trust. As soon as one group became aware they were being cheated, there was a sharp increase in 'violent arguments' and a festering hatred developed between the factions.

When Robert Williamson, the second engineer, started to spread lies that the sixty-year-old carpenter John Hadley was trying to steal seal meat and shirk work, the rest of the men decided to kill Hadley. Luckily, he was away on a long hunting trip at the time. Nevertheless, the half-starved men decided to march out, find and kill him. Typical of this form of mob violence, the designated leader had assigned the murder to a low-ranking crewman. The posse set out but was forced to turn back after snow blindness severely affected two of the men. Returning the following day, Hadley was able to clear his name and persuade the others that the accusations were lies. Over the following months, fights over rations became so bitter one crewman shot another through the eye, probably over lies about how many seagulls they had caught.

Heightened aggression over unfairness would come as no surprise to neuroscientists who have studied the brain's response to the 'ultimatum game'. In this experiment, two people are given a sum of money, say a hundred dollars. One of them must decide how to split it, and the other must accept or reject the split. However, if he or she rejects it, both get nothing.

A fifty–fifty division is always accepted, but an eighty–twenty split is rejected half the time. In other words, many people would rather have nothing than an unfair share. Not only that, the principal motivation for their rejection is the desire to punish the person who is attempting to rip them off. This punishment is accompanied by 'an instant aggressive emotional response': fMRI scans show that unfairness triggers activity in the amygdala. Once again, it is the primitive brain that is calling the shots. Pharmacological suppression of the amygdala significantly increases the number of people who will accept an unfair share.

Our problem with accepting an unfair distribution undoubtedly dates back to the hundreds of thousands of years we spent living in tribes. Any individual who accepted a lesser share of, say, a mammoth carcass, was entrenching his or her lower status in the tribe. This, in turn, would increase the chance of the same unfairness occurring the next time the tribe divided up food. Evolution dictates that unfair distribution of resources has become a rapid neural shortcut to an aggressive reaction.

Some people caught up in life-or-death situations have gone outside the authorised distribution system to get a 'fairer' amount of food or some other important resource. Theft was a huge problem for almost every group analysed in this book. Not surprisingly, the most frequently stolen item was food, followed by alcohol and other liquids. Other items stolen were more curious: sailors had a definite tendency to steal clothes—not practical clothes, but the expensive, elaborate clothes, along with the jewels and money, of wealthy passengers.

Summary execution of individuals caught stealing food was a normal and accepted punishment in survivor groups. Usually justice was swift and brutal—if they were lucky, the thieves were abandoned to die. Others were drowned, stabbed or whipped to death. If they were shot, it was often in the face—reflecting the deep personal hatred evoked by this 'most heinous crime'.

Yet, in a surprising number of survivor accounts, the authors admit to stealing. Usually it is brushed off as a casual, minor event (even when it has occurred repeatedly), without any hint of guilt or remorse. The admission is usually couched in terms such as 'I didn't want to but I just couldn't resist the temptation' or, in the words of a hungry Jane Poynter inside the artificial micro-community of Biosphere 2 in 1993, 'sometimes my hand just found itself in the bowl'.

When anarchy descends, the sense of fairness tends to give way to 'every man for himself', even in people who have demonstrated an ingrained morality. In 1816, French engineer Charles Brédif from the *Medusa* washed up onto a beach at the deserted edge of the Sahara. He and the other survivors faced a long, dry trek to safety. They had little more than the clothes they stood up in and a few precious barrels of water.

Brédif, who had just saved another man from drowning, witnessed a commotion on the burning fringe of sand.

> *The sailors had saved the barrel of water; and as soon as we were on shore, they fought for the drinking of it. I rushed in among them, and made my way to him who had got the barrel at his mouth. I snatched it from him and contrived to swallow two mouthfuls, the barrel was afterwards taken from me...but for them I could not have lived more than a few hours.*

Half an hour later Brédif spotted the Picard family struggling to get in through the surf after their boat had overturned. He stripped off his clothes and shoes and plunged in to save them. Back at the beach, he soon discovered that one of his fellow shipmates had stolen his clothes and, more importantly, his shoes. This drove Brédif into a fit of angry despair.

Dehydration appears to drive survivors in groups to steal even faster than starvation. 'It was the painful sensation of thirst that we most dreaded,' said Archibald Robbins, able seaman from the *Commerce*, shipwrecked off Morocco in the early nineteenth century. Desperate men would quickly resort to drinking their own urine, often saving it in bottles to cool off before they drank it. The liquid was a valuable resource, inviting theft. Even the scrupulously fair captain of the *Commerce*, James Riley, became so racked by intolerable thirst while trudging through the desert that he stole urine from his cook's bottle. Men often commented that others' urine tasted worse than their own. This was the case with Captain Riley, who complained that the cook's urine just tasted of salt and 'it seemed, if possible, to increase my burning thirst'. Later Riley and his nine remaining men would be forced to drink pig's blood and camel urine, which they caught in their hands as it gushed from the animal. Riley noted it was bitter but not salty.

Control over the division of resources confers great power within the group, and may allow one faction or individual to seize overall control. Following the *Batavia* shipwreck in the Abrolhos Islands off Western Australia, groups were segregated onto different islands. Dozens of murders ensued, but the presence of permanent water on one island enabled that faction to eventually seize the balance of power.

If the food and water supplies are being divided fairly, it follows that labour should be equally divided. This has rarely proved the case. More strenuous work is often delegated to the 'inferior' members of the pecking order. Persistent laziness by certain individuals is another major cause of tension in survivor groups.

When Sir John Franklin led his first expedition to the Arctic Circle in 1819–22, the English explorers expected their local companions, either indigenous Yellow Knife people or French Canadian fur trappers known as *voyageurs,* to do the vast majority of the physical labour and hunting. The officers would work only if it was an unavoidable necessity. Assuming a natural superiority, the explorers' attitude to the locals was paternalistic at best, heartless at worst. If any of the hunters happened to be joined by family members, Franklin would complain they were using up their resources. The journals of the officers, Franklin, surveyor George Back and surgeon Sir John Richardson, are peppered with comments such as:

> During the day one of the women made a hole through the ice, and caught a fine pike, which she gave to us; the Indians would not partake of it, from the idea…that we should not have enough for ourselves: 'We are accustomed to starvation,' said they, 'but you are not.'

The explorers complained about the rough trekking over jagged rocks concealed by ice and snow, then casually mentioned that the women walking alongside were 'heavily laden with furs, and one with a child on her back'. The officers carried only their personal belongings. At another point, when George Back needed to establish if a lake was sufficiently frozen for them to cross, he sent a man (either a Yellow Knife or a *voyageur*) out to see if he would fall through the ice. So much for the White Man's Burden.

Even though he relied on natives to provide much of the food, Franklin objected when they had the temerity to eat the group's cached supplies. When the winter became worse and the deer had migrated, Franklin encouraged his Yellow Knife companions to go out and fish rather than eat the stores. He complained, without a trace of irony, 'they felt little inclined to do so, and gave scope to their natural love of ease'.

A fair system for an equal division of labour within a group is almost impossible to implement; the cook, for example, might have non-taxing labour next to the warmth of a fire or under a shelter, while a hunter might have to hike for miles in search of game at sub-zero temperatures. Group leaders frequently feel that, by dint of their superiority and the mental burden of decision-making and responsibility, they should be exempt from the grunt work of digging for water or finding firewood.

Occasionally a group will hit upon a system for a near-perfect division of labour. The fairest method is to divide all labour into roughly equal tasks and then implement a revolving roster, giving each man or woman, regardless of rank, an equal share of the work. Not surprisingly, the few groups that have adopted this system tend to be the ones with the greatest levels of harmony.

# PROBLEMS IN PATAGONIA:
## The Wreck of the *Wager*

**LOCATION:** Wager Island, coast of Patagonia, South America
**NATIONALITY:** English
**DATE:** 1741
**FATALITY RATE:** 74%
**DURATION:** 8.5 months

In 1740, a fleet of eight ships under the command of Commodore George Anson set sail from Portsmouth in England in an audacious but ill-conceived plan to harass the Spanish fleet in the Pacific. One of the English ships was the *Wager* (599 tons, twenty-eight guns), soon to be under the command of Captain David Cheap, after the first captain died.

The *Wager* was sailing off the western coast of Chile in 1741 when disaster struck. At 4am on May 14, in the grip of a violent storm, the ship crashed into rocks off a small island known to this day as Wager Island. The ship, stranded on the rocks, was slowly being pulverised by the storm. The infirm confined below deck soon drowned.

On deck there was pandemonium. Captain Cheap had dislocated his shoulder and was unable to take effective command. Seventeen-year-old midshipman John Byron (later the grandfather of the poet Lord Byron) looked around in astonishment as some of the crew, 'petrified and bereaved of all sense, like inanimate logs, were bandied to and fro by the jerks and rolls of the ship, without exerting any effort to help themselves'. Others fell to their knees and prayed, or ran about in blind panic. One sailor, insane with fear, armed himself with a cutlass and slashed at anyone who came near, until someone knocked him out.

As some of the officers struggled to launch a lifeboat, a large contingent of the sailors began looting, heading straight for the casks of wine and brandy. The looters then armed themselves, and started dressing up in stolen clothes: 'they plunder'd chests and cabins for money and other things of value, cloathed themselves in the richest apparel they could find, and imagined themselves Lords Paramount.' Byron noted how ridiculous the sailors looked with layers of lace finery piled on top of 'their greasy trousers and dirty checked shirts'.

Eventually some of the men became so drunk they fell overboard. Others drowned in the flooded areas inside the ship 'and lay floating about the decks for some days after'.

Fighting soon broke out among the looters and one man was strangled. Towards dawn, the crew began to evacuate the ship, but the contingent of looters refused to leave. Later they tried to kill a man who had rowed out to help them.

On Wager Island conditions were appalling: the freezing storm continued and there was little shelter. On the first night, three men died of exposure. The captain, the surgeon and several officers sheltered in an empty Indian hut. The rest of the men huddled under trees.

The following day, the looters had a change of heart and demanded immediate evacuation from the wreck. When help was not forthcoming, they fired a cannon at the captain's hut, narrowly missing it.

When the storm abated slightly, some of the men on Wager Island were ordered to row out to the wreck. Many refused, declaring 'everybody was at liberty to shift for themselves [to act independently]'. Midshipman Alexander Campbell, aged just seventeen, tried beating the men into obedience. The looters were fetched from the wreck, disarmed and stripped of their lace garments. The boatswain, who had stayed on the ship, had not only failed to assert any authority over the looters, he had been 'a ringleader in their riot'. When he came ashore he was knocked unconscious by the furious captain.

The food stores and arms were placed in tents, but this proved futile. The food tent was robbed almost every night and the men sneaked out to the wreck to fetch more arms for themselves.

It was eleven days before the captain began to release rations to the hungry men, who were scavenging on the shore for shellfish and 'wild celery'. There was certainly game in the area—wild dogs, fish, seals and birds—but no hunting parties were organised, despite the abundance of weapons.

The captain made only a feeble attempt to explore the surrounding area. There was no real effort to build accommodation to protect the men from the 'almost incessant tempests'. The wreck had provided timber and tools and they had a carpenter and carpenter's mate, yet it was months before the men began to build adequate shelter.

Meanwhile, rather than providing guidance and leadership, Captain Cheap was preoccupied with maintaining control and 'the enforcement of his authority; of which, indeed, he was jealous to the last degree', commented Byron. The captain was fearful of full-blown mutiny, but did little to reassert his authority other than committing sporadic acts of violence against unruly individuals. Many of the men felt that, because the ship was wrecked, the captain's command was at an end. In Campbell's words, 'the ship being in effect entirely lost, we were involved in a state of anarchy and confusion'. The social cohesion of the group of 140 survivors began to unravel rapidly.

The first sign of this, aside from the fighting and insubordination, was the group physically moving apart. John Byron later described how the discontent 'shewed itself by a separation of settlement and habitation' as the men separated.

One faction of ten men quickly deserted, stealing a substantial amount of provisions. They struck out in an unsuccessful attempt to leave the island and reach the mainland, but after several days it was found they had set up camp five kilometres away. They had been planning to blow the captain up before they moved on, and Byron claimed that a cask of gunpowder and powder trail to his tent were already in place before the plot was uncovered.

Another two men were planning to murder Midshipman Campbell, and he was forced to take precautions. The pair had resented being ordered about after the shipwreck.

Grievances about past issues on the ship bubbled to the surface. When a man's body was found stabbed and mutilated, nobody bothered to bury the corpse.

The men might have been reassured by a firm plan of action, but none was forthcoming. The best that Captain Cheap could come up with was to repair the small boats and lengthen the longboat they had saved from the wreck.

Just off the beach the wreck was slowly giving up its cargo to the tide; casks of meat and wine washed in. Sailors scavenging along the shore for shellfish were horrified to discover decomposing corpses washing up alongside the supplies. When vultures flocked to the beach to feast on the bodies, the hungry men killed and ate any birds they could catch. At times the waves would pound the bodies against the rocks, tearing them to shreds. Crew members were reported to be surreptitiously eating any raw pieces they could scavenge on the beach. Byron reported the cabin boy found an entire human liver and had to be restrained from wolfing it down.

On June 6, three weeks after the shipwreck, tensions boiled over. Mr Cozens, a midshipman popular with the men, got into a drunken shouting match with the captain, calling him 'a rogue and a fool'. The captain responded by striking Cozens and confining him to a tent. A few days later, an inebriated Cozens got into a fistfight with the captain's main ally, the surgeon, followed by a fight with the purser. The purser screamed, 'Captain Cheap! Here is Cozens come to kill us!' and shot at Cozens, just missing his head.

Cheap, assuming this was the mutiny he so feared, rushed out and shot Cozens point blank in the face. To make matters worse, the captain then publicly tried to stop the midshipman being treated by the surgeon (although he did receive some attention eventually).

Estimates differ slightly, but Cozens took around a week

to die. It was a slow and agonising death. Some of the men whispered that the captain would be kinder to shoot him again and finish him off, than 'suffer him to languish in a cold wet place in pain and misery'.

Cozens' death was a tipping point for many, principally a strong group of eighteen 'stout' men, led by the gunner John Bulkeley and the carpenter John Cummins. This faction lived in the same tent, and was known for drinking and fighting. For all his faults, Bulkeley at least recognised 'there was a necessity for action, and a great deal of it too'.

Bulkeley formulated a plan that the three boats should head south for the Straits of Magellan, then sail up the eastern coast of Argentina. He and many others felt this was their best chance to reach civilisation. At first, Captain Cheap appeared to agree, then insisted they sail north and attempt to capture a Spanish ship or rejoin the rest of the fleet.

Meanwhile, the health of the men was deteriorating. By the end of June, about forty men had died from famine and exposure. They were living on a tiny ration of flour and salted meat and whatever they could forage, primarily limpets and seaweed.

A group of Patagonian Indians who had briefly visited the group returned with their families and set up camp. Indigenous to the area, they had no trouble finding food, principally fish and nutritious 'sea eggs' (sea urchins), for which the women would dive. They generously provided food to the starving men, but the crew of the *Wager* drove them away by trying to 'have to do with their wives'.

Morale slumped even further after this. A group of men took a stray dog that Byron had tamed and ate it. Three weeks later Byron, in the absolute desperation of the starving, found the dog's rotten paws and skin and ate them.

As malnutrition and apathy set in, nothing was being done. Work on the boat stopped as factional fighting and theft escalated. Two men who had been caught stealing flour were sentenced to six hundred lashes each (one hundred lashes was considered potentially lethal) and to have their rations halved. The other men protested that the punishment was too lenient, so it was amended to four hundred lashes with no more rations, meaning the men would die of starvation.

The only provisions in plentiful supply were wine and brandy. At one point Captain Cheap had the supply buried, but the men quickly demanded it be exhumed, further insisting that their ration of brandy be increased to a pint a day. Sentries were placed around the provision tent, but it was soon discovered that the purser had been plying the guards with brandy in order to facilitate wholesale theft by one particular faction. Rumours of plots swirled through the camp. Bulkeley learned that the quartermaster was plotting to kill him, and Bulkeley himself hatched a plan to maroon the purser.

There were more demands for marooning as a punishment. Bulkeley considered it a penalty 'next to death' in its severity.

By August, as deaths from starvation increased, some of the men began to go blind and others deserted to the mainland. For the rest, 'there is a sort of a party rage amoungst the people' as the 'go-south' faction continued to grow in strength. Still the captain refused to give consent. To add to their worries they were hit by four earthquakes.

In August, nine men were caught with stolen supplies, five deserted and four were abandoned on the mainland of Patagonia. After sixteen weeks, the whole group was in turmoil: 'scarce any work done this week past; everything is at a stand[still]; we have among us no command, order or disciple.' The idle men demanded more and more wine, drinking to pass the time: 'The People very much disorder'd in Liqour,' complained Bulkeley, 'and very quarrelsome.'

Bored witless, some of the men took to shooting wildly around the camp to pass the time. This activity, combined with the increased alcohol ration, led to the carpenter Cummins, the most important member of the group, almost being killed when a shot narrowly missed his head. This was the third time Cummins had been shot at.

Bulkeley and his 'cabal' made one last, unsuccessful, effort to persuade the captain to leave with them. Fearing the worst, everyone in the camp armed themselves and the boats were zealously guarded.

Matters reached a head on October 9. Bulkeley's men surprised the captain in bed, tied him up and announced their intention to take the boats south. Only the captain, the surgeon and Lieutenant Hamilton decided to remain behind, as well as the eight deserters still ensconced in their nearby camp.

Four days later, the other eighty-one men abandoned the island and sailed south. One of the boats was wrecked almost immediately in the rough seas. Even on the first day some, including Byron, were having second thoughts. The penalty for mutiny was hanging, and the navy could be ruthlessly persistent about hunting down offenders.

On pretence of getting more sailcloth, Byron and eight men took one of the boats and sailed back to the island, where they were joyously greeted by the captain.

Bulkeley's expedition—now comprising seventy-two malnourished, weary men in two boats ill-suited to the open ocean, and scarcely twelve days' rations—struggled onwards.

To maintain control, Bulkeley had written a mini-constitution, forbidding the men from:

1. Stealing food.
2. Causing the boats to separate more than the reach of a musket-shot.
3. Making death threats or using violence against other crew members.
4. Unfairly dividing any food they might find.

The penalty for any of these offences was 'to be put onshore and left behind'. To maintain his authority, Bulkeley wrote out many different declarations and lists and forced the men to sign (his journal contains multiple versions). No doubt he hoped his 'solidarity in numbers' attitude would save him from a possible charge of mutiny.

For three weeks they slowly headed south, in atrocious weather, foraging onshore when possible. The rations were down to 110 grams of flour per day. To make matters worse the smell of their own saturated, mouldy clothing was making the men nauseated.

On November 6, disaster struck when the cutter sank, drowning one man. There were too many men for the remaining longboat. Eleven men were chosen and abandoned onshore with a few meagre provisions. Bulkeley claimed they 'insisted on being put ashore' but, given that meant almost certain death, this seems unlikely. It is significant that these men were not members of Bulkeley's cabal, and the majority hadn't signed the numerous declarations. The remaining men were so close to 'mutiny and destruction' that Bulkeley and Cummins threatened to leave them, forcing the 'thoughtless wretches' to submit.

As the men approached death from starvation, an outrageous trade in the tiny flour ration began, with men paying one guinea for a ration of flour (145 times the going price back in England). There was no escaping the next step: 'This afternoon died George Bateman, a Boy, aged sixteen Years: This poor creature starved, perished and died a skeleton.'

Three days later, a twelve-year-old boy died. Bulkeley described the boy's harrowing last hours, lying in the bottom of the boat and desperately begging his guardian shipmate to return his money in order to buy some flour. The man refused, aware that soon the money would be his to keep.

'Hunger is void of all Compassion; every person was so intent on the Preservation of his own Life, that he was regardless of another's,' Bulkeley noted, trying to explain how the entire crew could turn a deaf ear to the boy's pleas.

Occasionally the men could scavenge something to eat, such as a two-week-old seal skin, but it was never enough. The others would know when a death was imminent, as the doomed man would become delirious and start joking and laughing in the hours before his death.

On January 12, after two weeks at sea and with the men on their last legs and out of water, the longboat pulled in near the coast. Fourteen of the men volunteered to swim ashore and fill up casks of water. One died of exhaustion a few metres short of the beach, but the others found water and game. Several men towed the casks back to the boat. To the horror of the eight men still on the shore, the longboat sailed off, leaving them behind.

On the beach, the men collapsed in despair at the sight, or as Bulkeley described it later, 'fell on their knees, and made signals wishing us well'. One of the eight was Isaac Morris, who described the betrayal as 'the greatest act of cruelty'. The only things the men had were a few guns, some 'necessities' and the rotting clothes they stood in. They quickly concluded they had been encouraged to swim ashore as part of a callous plan by Bulkeley's faction to abandon them.

Already near death, the men found a trench on the beach, where they spent the next month. Against all expectations they survived, sleeping under the stars and emerging to find food during the day. Slowly, they recovered their strength and took stock of their situation. They had been abandoned and betrayed by their companions, but this had an unexpected benefit: Morris's group were now united, bonded by their hatred of the others.

The new band of eight survivors took on an entirely different dynamic.

Gone was the vicious mentality of individual self-preservation at all costs; they co-operated efficiently as a group to find food and, eventually, shelter. Tasks were divided up 'in order to avoid disputes', and rotated to ensure the division of labour was fair. There was little discord; in its place there was 'the strictest harmony and good-nature between us'. The men discussed their plans and acted upon a consensus.

This group proved very resourceful. Finding several litters of wild dog puppies, the men raised them to hunt. The trained dog pack eventually caught wild pigs, armadillos and even a deer for the men to eat. Two captured piglets were also raised for later use. When the men set out anywhere they were followed by a tame retinue of sixteen dogs and two pigs. Not only was this safer, it meant they had a fresh food source that didn't need to be carried to sustain them when they eventually attempted to walk north.

Conditions weren't easy. There were wild animals, including cougars, and the land was sparse and dry. Firewood had to be collected from a small forest miles from their camp. Twice the men attempted to walk north to Buenos Aires, but were forced to return to their camp, defeated by the hostile environment. The men were greatly hampered by their inability to carry water. They had tried using seal bladders, but discovered they rotted after a few days. On the second attempt, the men argued about whether to return to camp or press on. In the end, all eight went back together.

Eight months after they had been abandoned by Bulkeley, and with winter behind them, the men noticed an alarming increase in dangerous animals around their camp. They were twice attacked by a cougar. Planning to leave once more and walk the 480 kilometres to Buenos Aires, they decided to collect a month's food supplies.

One afternoon, four of them returned from seal hunting to find some of the dogs running about the camp and the hut destroyed. Near the remains of the hut they found the bodies of two of the men, dead from knife wounds: 'One had his throat cut and one was stabbed.' The other two had disappeared. Isaac Morris knew the four had all fallen victim to an attack by an unknown group, Spanish or Indian, because the group didn't possess a knife.

The remaining men were shattered. 'This was the most afflicting stroke of any we received since our residence in this unhappy country. I won't pretend to describe the horrors we felt,' Morris wrote. Terrified, they resolved to leave quickly, lest the attackers return.

The four survivors walked further than previously, but reached an impassable swamp and turned back. At their camp, the men were attacked and taken prisoner by a hostile band of Patagonian Indians.

They were later sold as slaves to the Spanish and spent several years toiling on a Spanish warship where, to their astonishment, they were reunited with Alexander Campbell, who had stayed with Captain Cheap. Three of the men, including Isaac Morris, survived this ordeal, and eventually made their way back to England in July 1746, five years after the *Wager* was wrecked.

Meanwhile, Bulkeley and the thirty men left on the longboat *Speedwell* had struggled on. Another man drowned trying to swim to shore, and several more—including the eighty-two-year-old cook—died of starvation. A week after abandoning Morris's group, Bulkeley managed to get ashore himself and had the good fortune to run into some Portuguese-speaking locals. These men sold them some bread at the exorbitant price of four guineas, twenty times its value, but it enabled the crew to continue their journey north.

A week later, with no food left at all, the boat limped into Rio Grande in southern Brazil. Boats from the town came to their aid. The gravely ill were hospitalised, the starving fed and housed: the *Speedwell*'s three-month ordeal was over. Of the eighty-one who had initially boarded the longboat, thirty disembarked after the staggering 4500 kilometre trip.

Bulkeley made no attempt to send help for Morris's men, abandoned just two weeks before. In a letter he sent to the Royal Navy explaining his circumstances, he made no mention of them. With the threat of a mutiny charge hanging over them, Bulkeley and Cummins must have had a nervous trip home as it was.

On January 1 1743 they were among the first survivors of the *Wager* to arrive back in England. At the end of his journal Bulkeley summed up his position with alarming honesty: 'Since the loss of the Ship, our cheifest [*sic*] Concern was for the Preservation of our Lives and Liberties; to accomplish which, we acted according to the Dictates of Nature.'

Despite having abandoned nineteen men, including eight who had risked their lives for the common good, Bulkeley escaped censure and was actually promoted.

The day Bulkeley set foot in England, Captain Cheap's party were still far from safe. Back at Wager Island, Cheap's group of twenty men struggled on for two months after the *Speedwell*'s departure without much change. They argued, scavenged, ate seaweed fried in candle tallow and continued to be plagued by theft. Two men caught stealing food were tied to a tree and severely whipped. One was then dumped on a barren island to die of exposure, the other managed to escape and vanished.

Captain Cheap's procrastination ended only when the men insisted they depart for the north. Setting out in two ill-suited boats, a yawl and a barge, the group left the island on December 15.

Storms and high seas hampered their progress. By

Christmas, they had survived an earthquake and landslide while ashore, and starvation had reduced them to eating their shoes. Byron estimated they had been soaked to the skin for a month.

One night in early January, the yawl sank in wild seas and the quartermaster drowned. The other boat was forced to move away from the breakers to avoid a similar fate. Half the group were now trapped onshore, killing and eating seals. Somebody managed to throw a seal's liver to the starving men on the cutter. They hastily devoured it, causing them to suffer an 'excessive sickness, which affected us so much, that our skin peeled off from head to foot'.

There were now too many men for the remaining boat. Four men were chosen to be left behind. According to Byron, they were all so exhausted and full of despair that they didn't seem to care if they lived or died.

The rest made painfully slow progress in the worst seas they had yet seen. Finally, they gave up and sailed back to Wager Island, stopping to search for the four men they had stranded. Nothing was found but a gun and ammunition. The men had vanished.

The two-month-long attempt had been an abject failure; they had lost five men and the yawl, and were in a much worse physical and mental state. To make matters worse, they were plagued by irrational fears, exacerbated by a lack of hope.

After another death from starvation, whispers started among the men that their only option was to kill and eat one of their companions. They were spared this 'horrible proceeding' when a cask of preserved meat from the *Wager* was found. But the thefts and fighting continued. One man stole a warm coat and deserted. Captain Cheap and Lieutenant Hamilton fought bitterly over some beef fat, as the unequal division of food caused increasing anger.

Luckily for the starving men, a Spanish-speaking Indian and his servant appeared at their camp. He offered to guide them north to a settlement in exchange for their boat. Taking some seal meat to sustain them, they headed north again, accompanied by two canoes.

This trip involved a great deal of rowing. Two men died of starvation in the boat, one pleading pathetically for food while the captain hoarded his considerable supply of seal meat. Cheap even slept with his head on his bag of rotting seal flesh, something which, Byron recorded acidly, did little for his appearance, smell or reputation. The others complained that his inclination towards 'self-preservation' at all costs was inhumane, and said he 'deserved to be deserted by the rest for his savage behaviour'.

When they put ashore to search for food, six of the men sneaked back and stole the boat with all the supplies. Byron, left on the shore with the captain and three others, was shocked by the treachery. But the remaining five men continued on in canoes and finally reached a small Indian village. The captain was treated well but made no attempt to get food or shelter for the others.

By March they were on the move again. The surgeon, a close friend of the captain, died of starvation and exhaustion. Byron stumbled on, walking in bare feet and a ragged pair of trousers. The men were tormented by lice; Captain Cheap was so bad he resembled 'an anthill, with thousands of those insects crawling over it.'

Pacific Ocean

ARGENTINA

Valparaiso  Mendoza                    Buenos        Rio Grande
        Santiago                       Aires

CHILE

Chiloé
Island

Wager
Island

N

0        500 km

▬•▬•▬•▬•▬  The path of the *Wager*
-------------  Isaac Morris's group after they were abandoned
───────────  Captain Cheap and John Byron's party
•••••••••••••  Bulkeley's faction
▭▭▭▭▭▭▭▭  Alexander Campbell, after leaving Cheap's group at Santiago

As the long march north continued, Byron felt that his
own death was approaching. The four survivors no longer even
bothered to talk to each other. When, after four months, the
group reached Castro, a small town on the coast of Chile, they

had travelled 590 kilometres. There they were met with care, compassion and adequate food, and began to recover.

Unfortunately, their next stop was a flea-ridden Spanish jail, followed by two years' residence in Chile as they negotiated their return to England. Alexander Campbell decided to remain behind, rather than set foot on a ship with Captain Cheap, whom he now despised. (Campbell's hatred of his captain was further exacerbated by Cheap's refusal to give Campbell a fair share of six hundred dollars donated to them in Chile.) Instead, Campbell chose to cross the Andes on a mule to reach Buenos Aires, over a thousand kilometres away.

Five long years after the wreck of the *Wager*, Byron, the captain and Lieutenant Hamilton arrived back in England. Byron, who had been presumed dead, was joyously greeted by his sister and went on to a sterling career in the Royal Navy. Captain Cheap survived the disgrace of a court martial, received a promotion but died soon after.

While none of the narratives written by the various survivors directly blames the captain for the disaster, it was obvious where much of the responsibility lay. The threads of his authority began to unravel the second the *Wager* struck the harsh coastline of Patagonia. A deplorable lack of leadership, an inability to make and keep realistic plans, and a vigorous devotion to his own well-being at the cost of his men condemned Captain Cheap from between the lines of all four narratives.

Of the three main groups that survived the ordeal, it was Morris's party that fared best. True, factors beyond their control resulted in the deaths of half the group. But only one-fifth of the captain's group survived and Bulkeley lost more than half of his group, despite having the best boats and the most supplies.

So what was it about Morris's band that made it function so differently? Superficially they were in the worst position: stabbed in the back by their fellow crew members; abandoned, lost, no boat, no food, no water containers, no shelter, no officers.

Two factors stand out. They seemed united in their bitterness at having been left for dead by the others, and they vowed never to inflict the same crime on any member of their own band. The eight men had one other characteristic in common: they had already risked their lives in order to help the survival of the group as a whole. This streak of altruism and generosity led them to share resources and labour, and value the group over the individual. It seems likely that if they hadn't been attacked, they would probably all have survived.

# FRAGMENTATION

*You go away, Ralph. You keep to your end.*
*This is my end and my tribe. You leave me alone.*

JACK, *LORD OF THE FLIES*

**THERE IS MUCH** evidence that humans as a species are adapted to living in groups. Our nearest relatives on the evolutionary tree, the primates, live in moderately sized groups; the average size of a chimpanzee community is thirty-six members, gorillas around nine members, baboons about thirty members. Orangutans alone among the great apes live a semi-solitary life, probably due to the combination of their dietary requirements and forest environment, which cannot support large numbers feeding together.

Fossil evidence shows our ancestors lived and travelled in small groups. We have highly developed language skills which facilitate our complex social organisation. Solitary humans are less happy, less safe, have more trouble finding food, and have less chance to reproduce or safely raise offspring. In many societies, ostracism is considered one of the cruellest punishments, as is extended solitary confinement within the penal system.

An experiment conducted in 2003 by Naomi Eisenberger and colleagues demonstrated the degree to which our brains are hardwired to hate social exclusion. Subjects were included in a trivial game of virtual catch—'Cyberball'—then intentionally excluded from playing by the other two participants. fMRI scans of the rejected players' brains revealed activity in the dorsal anterior cingulate cortex, normally associated with physical pain. In other words, social exclusion and rejection from a group, even over something as insignificant as a few rounds of pretend catch, can be just as painful as physical injury. Incredibly, taking a painkiller such as Tylenol can ease the severity of social rejection.

People need other people, and evolution has selected and rewarded our gregarious traits. However, large groups—particularly random conglomerations of travellers thrown together in extreme circumstances—tend to be socially unstable, and destined to split into subgroups of like-minded individuals. This happens even when they are confined to a small area, such as a mine. In a random group of people thrown together, birds of a feather really do flock together and people with similarities—age, race, culture, religion, socio-economic status or experience—will cluster.

Once a subgroup is established, its members have a tendency to conformity, and an intolerance of deviation. They will adopt communal attitudes and prejudices that help to reinforce their sense of belonging to a particular faction, with a shared identity. This can extend to shared values and shared language,

**Pitched battle**: the *Batavia* survivors fight it out on Batavia's Graveyard, off Western Australia, 1629. Illustration from Francisco Pelsaert's *Unlucky Voyage of the Batavia*, published in 1647.

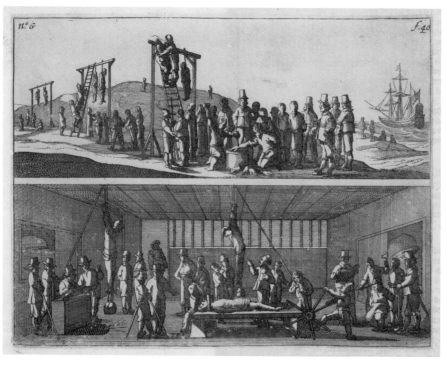

**Dutch justice**: the torture and execution of the *Batavia* mutineers on Seal Island, 1629, also from Pelsaert's book.

Théodore Géricault's famous painting of the raft of the *Medusa*, 1819. The painting depicts only the platform of the huge raft. (Corréard is in the group by the mast, gesturing towards the horizon.)

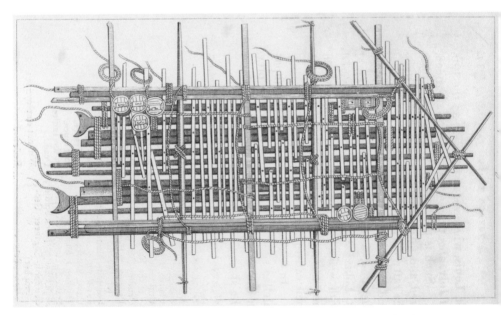

The frontispiece of Alexandre Corréard and Henri Savigny's 1818 book, showing the lattice-work structure of the huge *Medusa* raft.

Captain Thomas Musgrave of the *Grafton*.        François Raynal, mate of the *Grafton*.

"THE TRAJECT WAS NOT ACCOMPLISHED WITHOUT DIFFICULTY AND DANGER."

**A few good men:** Thomas Musgrave rescuing François Raynal from the *Grafton* wreck on Auckland Island in 1864. Etching by Alphonse de Neuville from Raynal's book *Wrecked on a Reef*.

**Frozen hell**: the view from the upturned boat on Elephant Island where Ernest Shackleton's malnourished men survived five weeks in 1916 with no loss of life. Photo: Frank Hurley.

*Residence of John Adams, Pitcairns Island.*

**Death in paradise**: the *Bounty* mutineers slaughtered each other in this idyllic setting on Pitcairn Isla The etching shows Adamstown, named after John Adams, the last man standing.

slang, in-jokes and shared anecdotes, and a location that they may feel belongs to them. (Even under normal conditions, there is a tendency for members of a clique to sit at the same seats around the same table.) As this homogenisation increases, the internal factional bonds will become tighter. Any new members will rapidly change to fit in with the factional norms, a process psychologists refer to as 'behavioural assimilation'.

In the Robbers Cave experiment, all the Rattlers demonstrated shared values—they had 'our' creek, flag, nicknames, insults and even behaviour. The Rattlers adopted a norm of toughness, swore enthusiastically, and disapproved of crying even when a boy was hurt. When one boy, Swift, failed to meet the communal expectation of toughness, the other Rattlers ignored him as punishment.

Even though all the boys in the experiment were from similar backgrounds, the Eagles valued very different traits. They were strongly against swearing and homesickness, but were tolerant of crying. They all swam in the nude at their creek, something which none of the Rattlers did.

William Golding, who had spent more than a decade teaching boys when he wrote *Lord of the Flies*, was well acquainted with the process of group fragmentation. In the novel, the boys' first meeting on the beach is interrupted by Jack and the choir, who march in wearing identical black costumes. This immediately differentiates them from the other boys. Indeed, Golding often refers to the choir as a single individual. In the novel, a chance remark from Jack 'brought sniggers from the choir, who perched like black birds on the criss-cross trunks and examined Ralph with interest. Piggy asked no names. He was intimidated by this uniformed superiority.'

Later at the meeting, Ralph magnanimously declares that the choir belongs to Jack, to be whatever he wants them to be. Ominously, Jack identifies the choir as hunters.

Golding understood this process for a very good reason. As he was writing his manuscript he was conducting research on his students by deliberately provoking friction between them and watching the results. On an excursion to the ruins of a hill fort known as Figsbury Ring, conveniently located about six kilometres from the school, Golding encouraged his boys to split into two groups and fight each other, in the guise of attacking and defending the fort. It is a large site with concentric rows of ditches and embankments, and would have been perfect for brawling. The more liberty Golding allowed them, the worse it became. He later hinted that this 'experimental science' reached the point where it became life-threatening, but wisely failed to supply any further details.

Once subgroups have formed, people show an inevitable bias towards members of their own clique. This is part of the social glue that holds the members together. Not only do they want to like each other, they want to *be* like each other. They seek to avoid internal conflict by going along with the group's shared values and views.

This compulsion to conform was famously demonstrated in the 1950s by American psychologist Solomon Asch in an elegant experiment involving small groups of students. The participants were seated together and asked simple questions with obvious answers—such as the length of a certain line. Only one person in each group, however, was a genuine test subject: unknown to him, the other students had been secretly instructed on how to answer. As each question was asked the conspirators would give their prepared answers and the real test subject answered last. If even two of the group gave the wrong answer, the subject became more likely to opt for the incorrect answer too. If all of the others gave the wrong answer it was extremely unlikely that the subject would disagree and give the correct answer.

Original footage of these experiments is available online and it makes fascinating viewing. The compulsion to conform to the majority decision overrides the subject's individual perception, even when it is obvious they think the answer is wrong.

Being part of a clique offers a lot of benefits: protection, information, companionship, sharing tasks and provisions; comfort when it is needed. Most of us are willing to quash a few individual traits to enjoy the membership of a faction, be it a political party, a reading group or a soccer team. We have probably all laughed at a joke we didn't get, or stifled a socially unpopular sentiment out of a desire to get along. Being an entrenched member of a faction also confers a sense of strength and security that individuals on their own simply can't achieve.

Unfortunately for everyone, in order for a group to be a group and achieve a coherent identity, it must somehow distinguish itself from other groups. *We like these things, and we do this! But we don't like those things, and we'd never do that.*

In *Lord of the Flies*, the choir had their distinctive uniforms and, under Jack's command, they transformed into hunters. They were responsible for looking after the fire and manning a lookout. They valued aggression and strength, and felt no duty to protect the 'littluns'. They were armed with spears, wore face paint and had their own chant. They shared collective triumph for killing pigs, and collective failure for letting the signal fire go out. Later they developed a group norm of hating Piggy, and then Ralph.

Holding a passport to belong usually comes with a tendency to rank one's own group as superior to others. Muzafer Sherif found the Rattlers and the Eagles both considered themselves superior: all were likely to attribute positive personality traits to members of their own group and negative ones to members of the out-group. Even before the Eagles and Rattlers had met, both sides referred to each other derogatorily as 'those guys' and 'they'—such as when a Rattler said: 'They better not be in our swimming hole.' Just hearing the distant voices of the Rattlers was enough to prompt one of the Eagles to refer to them as 'nigger campers'.

In nearly all of the situations we have considered, when the community is thrown into crisis it quickly fragments into groups of like-minded individuals. Some of these groups are stable, others less so. Among the stranded crew of the *Wager*, John Bulkeley's faction was the largest and most feared. John Byron, who was not a member, described them thus:

> *This cabal was chiefly held in a large tent, which the people belonging to it had taken some pains to make snug and convenient, and lined with bales of broad cloth driven from the wreck. Eighteen of the stoutest fellows of the ship's company had possession of this tent, from whence were dispatched committees to the Captain, with the resolutions they had taken with regard to their departure; but oftener for liquor.*

These men had a group norm of heavy drinking, rough

behaviour, insubordination and making demands. When writing of the cabal, Byron (like Golding) tended to describe them as identical parts of one whole. He typified their behaviour as full of 'riotous applications, menaces, and disturbance'.

Their cohesion gave them a collective power that gradually increased, frightening the others and disrupting the authority structure. Henry Cozens, whom the captain shot in the face and killed, was a member of this cabal. By executing one member of the faction, the captain incurred the wrath of the rest. 'This was looked on as an Act of Inhumanity in the Captain and contributed very much to his losing the Affections of the People,' Bulkeley wrote. As the cabal's power increased, its ranks grew. Eventually they mutinied and struck out on their own. But the stresses and problems hadn't gone away. The men were still isolated, hungry, lost and in danger. So this core faction then continued to fragment, carving off into splinter groups. Two subsets of the faction were simply abandoned and left to die along the coast of South America.

Survivors will often attempt to stem the fragmentation by forcing the men to sign documents or oaths stipulating that they will act together. Bulkeley was particularly fond of this tactic, with at least five proclamations and oaths signed. Ultimately, it had little effect. Presumably being forced by collective pressure into signing something is not the same as a voluntary binding commitment. (Ironically Bulkeley's second oath stated 'the People [are] separating into Parties, which must consequently end in the Destruction of the whole Body'. Unfortunately, he seemed incapable of seeing the truth in his own words.)

Isolated survivors are often aware of the dangers of fragmentation. Samuel Avalos, who was one of the thirty-three

Chilean miners trapped 700 metres below the Atacama Desert following the mine collapse of 2010, said: 'If warring groups had formed, the strong against the weak, the majority against the minority, then anything could have happened—it was coming.'

Despite this knowledge, the men split into three clans based on where they slept—the *105* (high status individuals, sleeping in the driest, best ventilated area), the *Refugio* (next in the pecking order, in an uncomfortable but safe spot) and the *Rampa* (left to sleep in an area running with water). These divisions were established on day two of their ordeal. Two weeks later, some of the weaker men felt they were being identified as 'candidates'—to be eaten by the others if they died.

But on day seventeen came the news that a rescue mission was on its way. Along with food, water, sedatives, a phone connection, cigarettes, mp3 players and a TV, this helped the miners to suppress factional conflicts for their remaining fifty-two days underground.

When more problems arise within a fragmented community, the next step is to single out and blame a faction. *It's not us, it's them!*

A fascinating example of this scapegoating occurred inside the besieged city of Numantia in Northern Spain in 134 BC. Outside the formidable walls of the city stood one of Rome's greatest tacticians, Scipio Aemilianus Africanus the Younger, with his army of sixty thousand Roman troops equipped with catapults and ballistae. Inside the walls sat the Celtiberian inhabitants of Numantia, snug and confident, with plentiful supplies and a natural water source.

The Celtiberians had a fearsome reputation as the finest

mercenaries in the known world. They were skilled horsemen, well armed, and even the Romans admitted they fought with valour, honour and tenacity. Back in Rome, when it became known the army would be facing them in battle, the young men desperately avoided enlistment, using excuses that were, according to the historian Polybius, 'disgraceful to allege, unseemly to examine, and impossible to check'.

The Romans and the Numantians had unresolved issues. Two decades earlier, an attack on the city failed miserably when the Roman elephants stampeded after one animal was hit by a well-aimed Numantian rock. The result was a wholesale friendly-fire rout. Scipio did not want to face the Numantians again on the battlefield. His tactic was to seal the city up tight and wait. Unwittingly, he was about to conduct an eight-month experiment into social collapse on an epic scale.

A fortified wall nine kilometres long was quickly erected, encircling the city. The only way out for the Numantians was the River Durius, which flowed past the city. With typical Roman ingenuity, engineers strung long tree trunks embedded with sharp blades and spear heads across the river, where the current would spin them, creating an impassable slicing machine.

Appian of Alexandria recorded, 'Thus was accomplished what Scipio especially desired, namely, that nobody could have any dealings with them, nobody could come in, and they could have no knowledge of what was going on outside.'

The Numantians had prepared for warfare and a siege; they had expected to be able to open their gates and attack the Romans if they wished. The Romans had removed that choice, and replaced it with involuntary imprisonment. Initially things were not too bad inside the city, but within a few months food supplies were running low, and the warp and weft of society began to unravel.

With conditions worsening, the leaders secretly sought help from the nearby town of Lutia. A few Numantians escaped the city in the dead of night and convinced Lutia to commit four hundred soldiers. Scipio got wind of the plan, and had the four hundred men's hands amputated. The Numantians were on their own.

With Scipio still refusing to fight and the food gone, the Numantians' next plan was to send a delegation of six men to discuss terms with the Romans. They chose their best and brightest: after all, their city's fate depended on the negotiating abilities of the delegates. The chief delegate, Avarus, pleaded with Scipio to allow the city to be surrendered 'on fair terms', saying the Numantians did not deserve an ignominious fate. But the Romans knew that conditions inside the city were verging on disastrous, so Scipio demanded '*deditio*'—unconditional surrender, demanding that the warriors give up their weapons.

When the delegation returned to the city with the terrible news, the townspeople held them responsible for the failed negotiations. To make matters worse, the paranoid Numantians suspected that Avarus and the other envoys had betrayed them and cut a secret deal with Scipio, to their own benefit. All six were accused of being traitors and executed—an example of fragmentation and scapegoating at its most damaging.

A natural leader like Ernest Shackleton will recognise and deal with the dangers of fragmentation. Frank Worsley, from the *Endurance* expedition to the Antarctic, explained:

*Little cliques and factions grew up, but Shackleton's tact and diplomacy soon destroyed that spirit. He would redistribute the occupants of the tents on some pretext far removed from the real one, and would remind each man that strength lay in unity.*

But for almost all stranded and stressed communities, social fragmentation is an inevitable and destructive development with far-reaching consequences that frequently push the entire group into a fresh set of problems.

# CARING FOR THE WEAK
# AND INJURED

*The littlun Percival had early crawled into a shelter and stayed*
*there for two days, talking, singing, and crying, till they thought*
*him batty and were faintly amused.*

*LORD OF THE FLIES*

**ONE EARLY INDICATION** of the moral character of any group is how
it chooses to treat the weak, sick and injured.

In late 1863, the *Grafton* sailed from Sydney to the
sub-Antarctic's Great Southern Ocean with a crew of five
under Captain Thomas Musgrave. In January of the following
year, in the grip of a storm, the ship ran aground on the rocky
shore of the Auckland Islands which, even today, are uninhabited, freezing and seldom visited.

One of Musgrave's men, a French adventurer named
François Raynal, had been extremely sick for weeks before the
ship got into trouble. At their last port of call, Campbell Island,
Musgrave had quietly dug a grave for Raynal in anticipation
of his imminent death. When the shipwreck occurred, Raynal

was weak, bedridden and feverish. He survived only because the captain lashed the Frenchman to his back and carried him along a rope they had strung from the stricken *Grafton* to the shore. 'Though I was of no more use than the shattered wreck they were on the point of quitting, my companions would not abandon me,' Raynal later wrote.

It was a heroic rescue: Musgrave almost drowned when the weight of the two men on the rope dragged them down into the waves. The captain risked his life to save a man who all the crew expected would die from illness within the next few days. Raynal later wrote that he was astonished he survived. Once on shore, the Frenchman remained weak and frail for more than a month, but the other men continued to look after him.

Five months later another ship foundered, on the same island. The *Invercauld,* out of Aberdeen, ploughed into rocks at the north end. One of the *Invercauld*'s sailors was also unwell when the ship was wrecked. Tom Page, a young Londoner, had been sick for only a few days, but was afforded no help when it came time to abandon ship, despite his pleas of 'for God's sake. Don't leave me.' Page died on the ship, presumed drowned. This dereliction of care and compassion set the tone for the future behaviour of the *Invercauld* survivors, which we will look at more closely later.

Often in dysfunctional survivor groups, a division quickly appears between the healthy and strong, and the weak and sick. Anyone who displays an illness, injury or loss of strength can find themselves with a target on their back, particularly when the group starts doing the survivor maths calculations. Survivor maths reasoning works like this: if there is a set number of people consuming limited provisions, and it is likely that some will die in a few days anyway, why should the group waste precious food or water on the dying? Sometimes this means abandoning them, but at other times the calculation is much more ruthless.

Such was the situation aboard the dinghy of the *Mignonette*, in the infamous case of the cabin boy, Richard Parker. The *Mignonette* was sailing from England to Sydney in 1884, when the flimsy yacht suddenly sank after being hit by a large wave. Richard Parker found himself on a dinghy with three other men, floating over a thousand kilometres from the nearest land. After two weeks adrift, the captain, Tom Dudley, raised the issue of drawing lots and killing the loser. At first, the others refused, saying they should all die together. But the captain tried desperately to persuade them: 'So let it be, but it is hard for four to die, when perhaps one might save the rest.'

After several more days, Parker became (according to the others) sick and possibly comatose, at which point he became the loser of survivor maths. He is said to have muttered, 'What, me?' as Dudley drove a penknife into his jugular. In his legal depositions, Dudley would initially claim Parker was unconscious, but somewhat later in his eight different versions of the truth, he admitted that Parker had spoken. (By bizarre coincidence, forty-six years *earlier*, Edgar Allan Poe had written a novel in which a cabin boy called Richard Parker was eaten by his three fellow crewmen, adrift after a shipwreck.)

Survivors who have disposed of the weak or the sick often get caught out later mixing up their justifications. On the one hand, they love to claim that the near-dead victim was in a coma and thus would have felt no pain, or even been aware of their abandonment or murder. But problems emerge because there is also a tendency to claim that the victim had taken part in the lottery, approved of the communal decision and willingly agreed to sacrifice their life for the common good. Of course, in order to give consent, the victim must be conscious, so the survivors get snared in their own contradictory versions of the truth, and in the long run, no one believes either story.

Singling out the sick and weak is useful to a survivor group in two ways. First, it can provide a seemingly legitimate rationale for abandonment or murder. Second, sick and weak people are much easier to dump or dispatch.

The Lord of the Flies principle is ruthless: if the strong are battling to survive, why should they waste care and resources on the weak? After all, one man dead would mean more food and water for the rest.

This simplistic equation masks a more complex reality. Within a group the individual members are not all of equal value to the survival of the whole. For the weeks that it took François Raynal to recover, he was a liability to the others. However, following his recovery, he became the most valuable member of the *Grafton* group. He helped maintain morale and iron out festering interpersonal issues.

Raynal was also an extraordinary problem-solver and contributed a vital set of skills to the group—from designing their hut to making tools and shoes. We will return to his many achievements at a later point in the book.

For now, it is enough to note that if Raynal had been left to die in the wreck of the *Grafton*, the others would almost certainly not have survived their nineteen-month ordeal.

The psychological care of the weak and injured can prove to be just as vital as their physical care. Many of the initial twenty-eight survivors of Flight 571 in the Andes were still in their teens and early twenties. Stranded at more than 3500 metres, in deep snow and with no resources other than what the plane had been carrying, they were in one of the worst situations possible. Starving, freezing and physically unable to leave the vicinity of the plane's fuselage, they watched many friends die in the crash itself, or afterwards from injuries. They were forced to remain among the frozen corpses; later they sustained the crushing blow of hearing on the plane's radio that the search parties had given up looking for survivors.

One of the group, the only uninjured woman, was thirty-four-year-old Liliana Methol. When despair or fear tormented the young men, they would turn to Liliana for comfort and advice. Eduardo Strauch called her 'the motherly figure for everybody', and Nando Parrado wrote that they all drew solace from her 'warmth and kindness'. Right up until her death in an avalanche she provided spiritual and emotional guidance, and her loss affected the survivors worse than any other death.

Neglect of the sick, injured or helpless has another and more sinister effect. It sets in process a moral decay and erodes the foundations of acceptable behaviour within the group. The first step might be failing to help a seriously ill individual, but once the precedent has been set, there seems to be no going back. Next thing, someone with an injured leg has been left behind to die of exposure, starvation or thirst (as occurred after the *Invercauld* and *Wager* wrecks). From there it is a logical progression for the strong to abandon the weak, or to kill the sick in order to 'shorten their suffering'. When such murders are recounted later, they are often characterised by the perpetrators as acts of charity. Finally the restraints of civilised behaviour are cast off altogether and we can see sick people, the disabled and children being killed on the basis that they are 'useless mouths'—as happened during the *Batavia* insanity.

# 'POLAR DISEASE'

*Why do you hate me?*

RALPH, *LORD OF THE FLIES*

**INDIVIDUALS FIGHTING FOR** survival under appalling conditions face a further threat that will be perfectly familiar to anybody who has ever worked in an office or institution. Confined with the same people day after day, survivors tend to get on each other's nerves. Sometimes the only thing worse than being alone is *not* being alone. People in survival scenarios are often terrified at the prospect of being left utterly alone. But the alternative—being cooped up with people they can't stand—is almost as bad.

This condition, sometimes called 'polar disease' or 'expedition cholera' is particularly prevalent in cold environments, where people are frequently confined to small enclosed spaces for months on end. Outside lie vast stretches of unrelenting white, snow or ice, but inside are the sights, sounds and smells of their companions, day in and day out. The same faces, the same stinking ragged clothing, the same snoring, the same complaints. It is often enough to drive people demented.

Over time, personalities grate on each other, tolerance becomes frayed and familiarity can go far beyond contempt and well into hatred. Stranded in the Antarctic ice on board the *Belgica* in 1898, the ship's doctor Frederick Cook elaborated:

> *When men are compelled to see one another's faces, encounter the few good and the many bad traits of character for weeks, months and years, without any other influence to direct the mind, they are apt to remember only the rough edges which rub up against their own bumps of misconduct.*

William McKinlay, trapped inside the Arctic Circle on the *Karluk*, described the amplifying effects of interpersonal friction in a closed community: 'our situation multiplied every weakness, every quirk of personality, every flaw in character, a thousandfold.'

The Nobel Prize–winning zoologist Konrad Lorenz experienced this condition firsthand when locked up in a Soviet prisoner-of-war camp.

> *In such a situation, as I know from personal experience, all aggression and intra-specific fight behaviour undergo an extreme lowering of their threshold values...one reacts to the smallest mannerisms of one's best friends—such as the way in which they clear their throats or sneeze—in a way that would normally be adequate only if one had been hit by a drunkard.*

Lorenz concluded in his groundbreaking work *On Aggression* that an isolated group would turn on itself, as it had no outlet

to disperse aggression externally. Knowledge of this 'tortur-
ing phenomenon' might prevent it escalating to murder,
but it couldn't remove the problem. Lorenz recommended
removing oneself from the vicinity of the group and smashing
something loudly to deflate the aggressive urge.

(Dr Desmond Lugg, the former head of polar medicine
for the Australian Antarctic Division, has devised a 'Rule of
10' for coping with living within a closed polar community.
Essentially his rule dictates that one's initial response to inter-
personal interaction in a polar setting will be ten times stronger
than is appropriate.)

Stranded from 1881 at Fort Conger, inside the Arctic
Circle, expedition commander Adolphus Greely found himself
sharing a small room with three other men. This foursome
constituted the tip of the power echelon within the group
of twenty-five: the leader, the two officers and the expedition doctor. At the beginning of the exploratory expedition
Greely was full of praise for his medic, Dr Octave Pavy, and
second-in-command, Lieutenant Frederick Kislingbury. Before
long, positive comments about the two men disappeared from
Greely's journal as the friendships began to sour. Little, irritat-
ing habits began to grate.

Greely found much fault with the inability of Kislingbury
and the doctor to show up at breakfast punctually. After repri-
manding them several times over the issue, a war of wills
developed, as petty as it was damaging. Greely insisted the men
be seated at the breakfast table at 7.30am sharp. The doctor, he
recorded, managed to be seated on time only twice a week on
average, being five minutes late on the other five days. Greely
found Kislingbury's behaviour particularly infuriating: the

lieutenant got up on time, but then slowly dressed and brushed out his whiskers. Eventually he sat down '10 to 15 minutes late—just late enough to annoy me but not late enough for me to make trouble about it'. Then, to add to Greely's indignation, Kislingbury would be seated at the table for a mere two minutes, then stand up and wind the clock and change the calendar. Greely fumed that the lieutenant did this almost every day. One hundred and thirty years on, it is still very easy to feel the pent-up fury over these inconsequential issues hissing out of Greely's pen. Not only was it driving him crazy, but after a while he began to suspect the men were deliberately goading him.

It is intriguing to note that the only roommate with whom Greely remained on good terms was the other officer, Lieutenant Lockwood. Every morning, Lockwood had to be woken several times and always arrived at the breakfast table about twenty minutes late. Not only did Greely not complain about this, he excused Lockwood's tardiness with the sympathetic explanation that he wasn't sleeping well (a problem that plagued all the men). In all likelihood, it was not the lack of punctuality that was driving Greely mad, but the individuals themselves.

As the months went by, Greely's references to the doctor and Kislingbury became increasingly negative. Kislingbury was 'insubordinate', 'a spoiled school-boy' with 'low tastes'. Sadly, Greely's techniques to improve morale probably didn't help. One of his favourite ideas for cheering the men up was daily lectures, presented by himself. 'Talked for nearly two hours today on the State of Maine, touching on its climate, its vegetables and mineral products, its river systems, mountain ranges,

principal cities, its most important resources and manufactures.'
His plan was to cover all the states.

Kislingbury resorted to taking long hikes alone for up
to seven hours through the perpetual darkness of the Arctic
winter, no doubt putting himself in considerable danger.

Dr Pavy was soon being described by Greely as 'an arrant
mischief-maker' and a 'tricky, double-faced man, unfit for
Arctic work', a liar and a thief. Greely became convinced the
two men were plotting to turn the others against his command
and foment mutiny, his deepest fear. He went so far as to have
Pavy arrested.

In June 1884, when Pavy died of starvation (hastened,
Greely wrote tartly, by self-administered doses of ergot, which
has LSD-like properties), Greely managed to record only a few
words of praise about the dead doctor, before he lapsed into his
usual mode:

> His medical skill was great and contributed much to the
> general welfare of the party last winter. His defects and short-
> comings have been lightly touched on in my diary. It should be
> added that his uncertain and changeable moods, and the habits
> arising from his previous Bohemian life, unfitted him for duty
> where his actions were subject to restrictions and limitations
> from others.

Dr Pavy's body was dumped into an ice crack the following day.

Kislingbury had died of starvation a week before the
doctor, and his corpse suffered a worse fate. Perhaps Greely
didn't recognise the bitter irony that after all his complaints
about his second-in-command not being punctually seated at

the table, Kislingbury ended up *on* the table—eaten by the small handful of survivors.

Outside the polar environment, what tends to happen after the inter-personal tensions become unbearable is that the group will split up. People will take whatever possessions they have left and march off to set up a new camp.

Golding illustrates this perfectly in *Lord of the Flies* when Jack's tribe of hunters decamp, after a fight, to the opposite end of the island and start fortifying their new position. The two groups are never reconciled.

Typically, in real life, disgruntled factions move out of visual range. They literally can't stand the sight of each other and, at times, it will be a considerable distance. In 1740 a break-away group from the *Wager* shipwreck moved five kilometres away, and Byron moved off by himself with just a dog for company. The factional camps of the *Karluk*'s survivors on Wrangel Island were roughly fifty kilometres apart.

Even after most of a group has died, 'polar disease' can still affect those who remain. After three months shipwrecked on the Auckland Islands, only three of the nineteen original survivors of the *Invercauld* were still alive. Nevertheless, they still fought bitterly. Finally it became too much to bear. Seaman Robert Holding recalled:

> *It culminated in disruption. At last they decided to make a hut for themselves no more than sixty yards away but that was far enough to keep us apart...It was a disgraceful state of affairs in our position, but it shows how easily people can be divided under such circumstances.*

At times the separation takes another form. In 1973, NASA

got an uncomfortable taste of this on its Skylab 4 mission. The crew had been arguing with mission control over their workload. After the team on the ground refused to budge, the crew switched off communications for twenty-four hours. (The Chilean miners trapped in the Atacama in 2010 also employed this tactic, threatening to stage a hunger strike against the authorities, who they considered were treating them like children and censoring letters from their families.)

The tendency for individuals to get on each other's nerves is of great concern to NASA and other international space agencies, for obvious reasons. Extensive study of polar and space missions has shown that 'crews characterised by such a clique structure exhibit higher levels of tension-anxiety, depression, and anger-hostility...than crews whose members identified more with the whole group'.

When it is simply not possible to put physical space between the factions, desperate people will use other means to blot out individuals they can't stand. In 1991, four men and four women were sealed inside Biosphere 2 in Arizona. They voluntarily entered into the project on good terms with each other, expecting to be part of 'a utopian group living in harmony'.

The party rapidly descended into petty fighting and power struggles, fracturing into two groups. Sealed as they were inside a huge glass enclosure, avoiding the people they had grown to hate was impossible. Instead, they erected psychological barriers.

Jane Poynter recorded that she would shrink back when forced to pass people she loathed in the corridors and made absolutely no eye contact with two members of the group for the final fourteen months she was there. By the time the two years were up, 'we despised each other'. Given that there was no danger, the participants could leave if they wanted, and they all had regular communication with their loved ones, this was an extreme level of hostility.

# STARVATION

*Oh God! I'm hungry.*

RALPH, *LORD OF THE FLIES*

**THE BODY OF** an average seventy-kilogram human male includes 41.5 kilograms of water, 12.5 kilograms of fat, 12.5 kilograms of protein, one kilogram of calcium and an assortment of tiny amounts of other minerals. When the food supply is cut off or greatly reduced, the body goes through some drastic changes.

Surprisingly, the body usually contains only a very small amount of stored carbohydrates, enough energy for around twelve hours. After that, all cellular energy must come from metabolised supplies of stored fat and protein. In the first week of starvation, the body freely helps itself to fat and protein equally, but soon it adapts and limits the amount of protein being used. The fat deposits will continue to be used up until they are essentially gone.

In the second phase of starvation (week two onwards), protein metabolism is drastically reduced to preserve the critical supply, but by about the sixth week the body shifts into the final phase and the proteins are under siege again. Once the supply of protein drops to around half the normal amount, death follows quickly.

All other factors being benign, a thin person can last around seven to eight weeks without food; a fat individual may last a few weeks longer.

Symptoms of starvation include raging hunger, weakness, susceptibility to cold, irritability, declining mental skills, hallucinations, constipation or diarrhoea, muscle pains, convulsions, organ damage, heart failure and coma. Opportunistic respiratory and gastrointestinal infections may add to the misery.

Victims, such as David Brainard of the Greely expedition to the Arctic, speak eloquently of the suffering;

> *Food! Food!—is the constant cry of the hungry, the continual topic of conversation among us! This gnawing hunger has driven from our minds all other thoughts and feelings; and, like animals, we have little left except the instinct for eating.*

Frequently this instinct to eat has driven starving survivors to consume things that were better left alone. The *Wager* crew made a soup of old ship's biscuit crumbs and a seagull. John Byron recorded the unpleasant results: 'we had no sooner thrown this down than we were seized with the most painful sickness at our stomachs, violent reachings [*sic*], swoonings and other symptoms of being poisoned.'

Byron was right: they had found the crumbs in a bag that had previously contained tobacco, and inadvertently consumed seagull, crumb and nicotine soup. They were lucky to survive.

If food stores are drastically low, the daily rations can be interesting to say the least. Greely's men had their ration cut to a diabolical mixture of preserved meat, seal blubber, lard, dried fruits and dog biscuits. This concoction, the men's only daily meal of 99 grams per person, was mixed into slurry and then warmed a little, as they didn't have enough fuel to cook it.

An even worse brew was eaten by the *Belgica* expedition to Antarctica in 1899. The crew attempted to make hot chocolate. 'It contained, besides chocolate, milk and sugar, much butter, penguin oil, blood and pieces of fishy meat, some "bonne femme" soup (made from penguin meat) and reindeer fur.' Even the starving men described the taste as 'scandalous!'

When the supplies run out, people frequently throw caution to the wind and eat rotting food, sometimes the scraps from previous meals they have consumed weeks earlier. In 1881, George Melville, recently escaped from the icebound American ship *Jeannette*, was trekking across Northern Siberia. Most of his fellow crew had already died when the famished survivors found the skeletal remains of an old caribou carcass. Hacking scraps of frozen, raw meat off, Melville attempted to eat them.

> So long as it remained frozen the meat did not exhibit the vile extent of its putridity; but directly I had taken it into my mouth it melted like butter and at the same time gave off such a disgusting odor that I hastily relinquished my hold upon it.

Still determined, Melville took some more of the meat, complete with frozen maggots and cut it into tiny pieces which he swallowed one at a time like pills. His triumph was short-lived: 'In a little while my stomach heated up the decomposed mess, an intolerable gas arose and retched me, and again I abandoned my breakfast.'

The myopic perseverance of the starving drove him on to a third attempt, 'and swallowing the sickening bits as before, my stomach retained them out of pure exhaustion'.

Sir John Franklin became famous in the 1820s as 'the man who ate his boots', but the annals of survivor groups are full of similarly unappetising meals—from *tripe de roche* (lichen scraped off rocks) to the fresh blood of almost any animal (turtle, dog or camel) the starving people can get their hands on. Here are some other examples:

- A whole, raw flying fish that had just been regurgitated by a seabird. (Survivor in an inflatable from the yacht *Auralyn*, 1973).
- Bird entrails and sea flea soup, with slimy dog biscuits 'thoroughly rotten and covered with green mould'. (The Greely expedition, 1884, Arctic Circle.)
- A baby wallaby: 'living, raw, dying—fur, skin, bones, skull and all.' (Ernest Giles, 1874, Gibson Desert, Australia.)
- The raw contents of a musk-ox's stomach, followed by its raw intestines. (John Franklin, 1821, northwest Canada.)
- Fish and human body parts soup. (*Medusa* raft, 1816, off the coast of Africa, Atlantic Ocean.)
- Whole rats boiled in seawater. (Jean de Léry's ship, 1585, the equator.)
- The ship's cat, including its tongue, eyes and brain. (The *Peggy*, 1765-6, Atlantic Ocean.)
- Fish cut out of the stomach of a leopard seal and fried in

leopard seal blubber. (Ernest Shackleton's party, 1916, adrift on an ice floe off Antarctica.)

The livers of large mammals are often the first thing starving people eat, frequently raw and straight from the carcass. John Byron and his *Wager* companions shared a fresh, raw seal's liver and almost died.

Some survivors have been suspicious of livers, but usually not suspicious enough. In 1911, the Danish Arctic explorer Ejnar Mikkelsen and his engineer Iver Iversen became trapped for more than two years in East Greenland after becoming separated from the rest of their party. When their rations were gone, they were forced to kill one of their huskies. Suspecting the liver might be poisonous, they took the precaution of boiling it with a piece of silver, which Mikkelsen believed would discolour in the presence of poison. It didn't, so they ate the boiled liver. 'Shortly after we had eaten it, we fell into a heavy doze and only awoke twenty-four hours later, and then with splitting headaches.'

The men swore that if forced to kill their remaining dog they would discard the liver, but when the time came Iversen found himself incapable of following through. Mikkelsen reproached Iversen, and got his own boot onto the dubious organ, intending to kick it into the sea, but starvation stayed his foot.

After a protracted debate the men decided that, since the last liver had only made them very sick, but hadn't proved fatal, they would go ahead. Again they were unconscious for twenty-four hours and awoke with atrocious headaches. But worse was to come. Within days their bodies were aching, their skin was peeling off and large, raw sores had developed. The skin on the soles of their feet came away, making walking agony; the sores would break open whenever they moved. The pair took weeks to recover, cursing their greed and stupidity.

The trouble with livers is that they store vast quantities of vitamins. The human liver, for example, can hold a ten-month store of vitamin A. Depending on the species, a seal's liver may contain 14,000 IU (International Units) *per gram*. Our recommended daily intake of vitamin A is just 3000 IU, so even a little piece of seal's liver can cause toxicity, a condition known as acute hypervitaminosis A.

Arctic carnivore livers are the worst, with polar bears and huskies particularly dangerous. The polar bear's can contain up to 30,000 IU per gram, so even a mouthful can be lethal to humans. As humans are omnivorous, our own livers can also be poisonous.

When starvation becomes more advanced, desperate survivors will start eating anything that resembles an organic product. Leather-eating is common among victims of starvation: hide buttons, belts, even the sweatbands inside hats. The sailors from the drifting ship *Peggy* ate all the leather parts of their ship's pump. Next would come fabrics—the men on the *Medusa* raft tried eating cotton and silk. Tallow candles were quickly consumed.

Jean de Léry, becalmed on board the *St Le Jacques* on a trip back from South America in 1585, faithfully recorded the desperation as the food ran out. His ship had been hit by a bad squall, which the crew had failed to notice due to a protracted punch-up between the mate and the pilot. Several days later, with the ship crippled, the captain and crew took off in the longboat, leaving the passengers with the threat that they would slice off the arms of anyone who tried to swim after them.

Over the next few weeks, the hungry passengers ate all the provisions, then the exotic pets on the boat (parrots and monkeys), followed by the fittings and straps from their luggage. De Léry roasted and ate two Brazilian shields made of tapir hide that he was carrying back as souvenirs. Next, the passengers ate the horn panels in the ship's lanterns (the horn was used in place of glass). These gone, they took to hunting down the rats, 'with so many kinds of rat-traps invented by each of us' that a trade in rat bodies sprang up. One man ate four roasted rat's feet and declared 'he had never tasted partridge wings more savoury'.

'When the bodies are weakened and nature is failing,' wrote De Léry, 'the senses are alienated and the wits dispersed; all this makes one ferocious and engenders a wrath which can truly be called a kind of madness.'

Just how mad they became was demonstrated when several of the passengers tried eating hunks of brazilwood from the hold.

Throughout history, desperately hungry people have resorted to 'food substitutes' to fill their stomachs when they have run out of rodents, insects and grass. During Chairman Mao's catastrophic Great Leap Forward, which began in 1958, famine drove many starving Chinese to eat *guanyin tu,* a fine white clay. While a small amount might ease hunger pains, it was indigestible and too much would solidify in the bowel, causing a slow, painful death.

Acute hunger also causes profound changes in behaviour. As Nando Parrado said of the Andes, 'Primal instincts had asserted themselves.' Even in this high-functioning group, bonded by compassion, Parrado admitted at times they were all driven to steal food from each other.

The other terrible side effect of starvation is the effect it has on people's treatment of others. For any group driven to abandon centuries of social conditioning, starvation can open up a path deep, deep into the woods.

# STUPIDITY AND INERTIA

*'I ought to be chief,' said Jack with simple arrogance, 'because I'm*
*chapter chorister and head boy. I can sing C sharp.'*

LORD OF THE FLIES

**THE SUCCESS OR** failure of any isolated group can teeter on the
fulcrum of the decisions they make. Poor choices can erode the
well-being of the survivors and provide fertile ground for the
seeds of resentment and eventually hatred. For a textbook study
of mental ossification, lack of foresight and plain pig-headed
stupidity, it is hard to go past the castaways from the *Invercauld*,
wrecked on the Auckland Islands group in 1864.

Four hundred kilometres south of New Zealand, these
sub-Antarctic islands are in the path of fierce ocean currents
and seem to prove the old nautical adage, 'Below the 40th
parallel south there is no law. Below the 50th, there is no
God.' Credit, in that case, for the design and positioning of
the Auckland Islands must go to the devil, which seems

appropriate given that they have been perfectly masterminded to cause shipwrecks.

Frequently shrouded in fog, sleet or rain, the uninhabited islands also cause magnetic compasses to become completely unreliable in their vicinity. Sheer, towering cliffs enclose much of the coast. Waterfalls spilling off the cliffs have been seen to flow upwards like smoke under the pressure of incessant winds that buffet the islands. As if this wasn't enough of an invitation to disaster, one of the principal charts in use during the nineteenth century, the British Imray chart, had the islands incorrectly marked fifty-six kilometres to the south of their true position. Even though the island group is just forty-five kilometres long, it was responsible for nine shipwrecks between 1864 and 1907.

The *Invercauld* of Aberdeen was a state of the art 888-ton square rigger on her maiden voyage when the crew caught sight of a rocky coastline dead ahead. For several hours the twenty-five men fought to keep the ship off the rocks but eventually, around midnight on May 10, she was wrecked on the north-west coast of the main island.

Despite his decades of experience at sea, the captain, George Dalgarno, lost control well before the ship struck. He and the two officers ran about the deck in a state of 'delirium', shouting impossible and contradictory orders. No concerted effort was made to launch the lifeboat, nor was there a formal command to abandon ship. As it became a case of every man for himself, the able-bodied fled the ship, but six others (including two teenagers and the sick crew member, Tom Page) drowned.

The following morning, the freezing survivors found themselves stranded on a narrow strip of stony beach in a small cove surrounded by cliffs and rocky slopes. The only fresh water lay in brackish puddles among the rocks. Although the ship had been in grave danger of wrecking for several hours, no supplies had been thrown overboard in preparation and the only useful things the nineteen men brought to shore were two boxes of damp matches that happened to be in the pockets of the Spanish cook and the steward. It wasn't much, but at this point only the matches stood between the men and death from hypothermia. Most of the men had no warm coats, and many had lost their shoes.

The men managed to light a fire to ward off the cold. The cook attempted to dry his matches by spreading them out near the fire but, to the disgust of the others, managed to set the entire box on fire. The mate took the other box and accidentally set it on fire too. A young English sailor, Robert Holding, made a frantic grab for the burning box and saved some of the remaining matches, which he hid in his pocket.

On their first day in the cove the captain and officers failed to show any leadership, make any decisions or establish any order. A fatal pattern was set for the duration of the ordeal: at best, the group was a collection of individuals acting in their own immediate self-interest.

The day of the wreck, the men found two pounds of pork and biscuits washed up. A few roots were found growing on the cliff face, but apart from this the cove was devoid of resources. The men could also see 'the most tragic sight'—the naked body of a man hanging upside down by his ankle in the smashed remnants of the *Invercauld*. Another body washed up on the shore. Under these grim circumstances there was an urgent need for decisions, particularly as the men's only chance of survival was to get out of the tiny bay. Unfortunately the day was passed largely in silence, with no plans being discussed. That night they ate *half* of their entire food supply.

The following day, they ate the rest. Four men then decided to see if they could climb out of the cove while Holding and the others remained there, listening to the captain's dog barking forlornly in an adjacent bay.

The exploration party didn't return until the next day. They told the main group they had reached the top and seen animal tracks—but also that one man, John Tait, had fallen on the rocks, and was presumed dead. Holding decided to leave immediately and climb out by himself. He soon reached the top and saw two sheltered harbours just a few kilometres away. When night fell he was forced to sleep on the open ground in the pouring rain.

Holding returned to the cove in the morning to persuade the others to leave, but a fatal inertia had set in and the men insisted on waiting another day before attempting the climb. Meanwhile, everyone was becoming weaker from lack of food. Tait had also turned up, badly injured from his fall.

On May 16, after *five days* in the cove, the men climbed out. One agreed to stay and look after Tait but soon abandoned this task, leaving his injured shipmate to die alone on the shore-line. At the top, three men caught a piglet and immediately ate its raw liver. The rest of the hungry group lit a fire to cook the tiny carcass.

The plan was for two men to explore the smaller of the two harbours, a narrow inlet only four hundred metres away, while the others went to the larger harbour. However, they proved incapable of carrying out even this simple proposal. Although it was critical to find shelter from the incessant rain (on average in the Auckland Islands it rains twenty-seven out of every thirty days) and freezing wind, the plan quickly disintegrated. Five men, including the cook, decided to go pig-hunting. The two men who were assigned to explore the narrow inlet failed to go there and lied about it.

(When Holding finally explored the inlet two weeks later he found a sheltered beach with a creek, plenty of large shellfish, seals basking on the sand and abundant firewood. If the two men had done as ordered, the entire party would have been saved. Even worse, because they reported the bay was devoid of food, the site was ignored.)

The main party slowly walked towards the larger harbour but made little progress. Meanwhile, the pig-hunting party returned empty-handed, minus the cook, whom they had lost. The entire group sat down out in the open and refused to go on. Holding lit a fire with his precious matches and the men huddled around the flames. They heard the cook shouting nearby and, although they could see he was only a few hundred metres away, no one went to help him.

The day afterwards—almost a week after the wreck—the weather finally improved. Holding, who was the only person to show any initiative, sent two men out to search for the cook, but they failed to find him. The group struggled on but gave up after a very short distance and built a rough shelter of branches to sleep under. They also found edible roots (*Stilbocarpa polaris*, the Macquarie Island cabbage) and fresh water from a creek.

The following day passed in almost total silence, with the group moving a short distance. The men sent two seventeen-year-old apprentices to fetch water, using their boots as buckets.

By nightfall, one of the boys had failed to return, even though the puddles of water were less than fifty metres away. By now it had begun to snow and the men struggled to stay warm as the fire kept going out. The group had travelled only about five kilometres from the wreck site and still hadn't reached the harbour. Morning saw the men refusing to move at all.

Holding knew their survival was 'hanging in the balance'. Disgusted at the group's inertia, he and the German boatswain decided to return to the shipwreck cove to look for anything washed in from the wreck. En route, they soon found the corpses of the cook and Tait, both lying where they had been abandoned. Down at the rocky cove, they located some rotten meat which they cooked and ate, though it was so putrid it fell off the roasting stick. Predictably they became sick.

To their surprise they were joined by four others the next day. Under a rock, they scavenged the decomposing body of a pig. Despite its state, the six men ate it. After another hungry week in shipwreck cove, the boatswain proposed drawing lots and killing the loser for the other five to eat. Holding refused but quickly realised this had put his own life in jeopardy. He declared he would leave the cove the next day and invited the boatswain to join him. Holding and the boatswain were the two strongest men, and had come to regard each other with mistrust. Holding suspected 'dread treachery' was afoot, and stayed awake all night, terrified if he fell asleep it would be tantamount to an automatic short straw.

At first light, it became obvious Holding's fear was not idle paranoia. He fled the cove, half expecting an attack from behind 'as a blow on the head unawares would have given them a great advantage'.

The main problem with murdering members of one's group for food is that as soon as the idea becomes public knowledge, any shred of trust between the group members is extinguished. After the first murder, everyone wonders who will be next. After all, to starving men, one corpse is as good as another.

This dynamic of fear was at work in the cove. As the two strongest, Holding and the boatswain should have co-operated. Instead, their strength became a liability as each came to see the other as the only man who could physically overpower him. Furthermore, as Holding described, falling asleep under such circumstances was a terrifying prospect. Stress and the lack of sleep had a devastating effect on the already weakened men.

The fate of the five who stayed in the cove remains a mystery. They were never seen or heard of again. Given their intentions and hunger, it is safe to assume their demise was swift and savage.

At the top of the cove, a relieved Holding travelled quickly down to the narrow inlet, the one two men had claimed was barren, where he found plenty of food. He lit a fire, cooked and ate some shellfish, dried his clothes and hiked back to where he had left the captain's party. All this took Holding less than a day. He found the others exactly where he had left them over a week before, still doing nothing. The spot was 'very uncomfortable', according to first mate Andrew Smith, 'owing to its exposed position, while there were only a few bushes to shelter us from the heavy showers of hail and rain that were continuously falling, and the wind was still blowing very hard'.

This group, paralysed by apathy, hunger and cold, comprised all the senior authority figures from the *Invercauld*: the captain, both mates, the carpenter, and the steward.

Holding managed to persuade a group of five to walk to the relatively dry and sheltered large harbour that was a mere five hundred metres away. There they found plenty of shellfish, roots, fish, seabirds and dry firewood. Even more importantly, they were at last out of the incessant wind.

Over the next two days most of the men made it to the harbour—minus two men who remained on the hillside and presumably died of starvation and exposure. No one from the harbour went to check on them or take them food.

It was now June 5, just over a month since the crew had left Melbourne together. Writing later about the events, first mate Andrew Smith stated he didn't know the names of the two dead men. This admission highlights yet another problem that caused this group to function so poorly: they didn't get to know each other at all. Such a lack of bonding and communication would have had a devastating effect on morale. 'It is probable that had we been better acquainted with each other things might have been somewhat different,' wrote Holding.

Then fate threw the survivors a life-line. The men at the harbour made a momentous discovery—an old settlement with the remains of several large houses, complete with a partial roof and a fireplace. The remnants of the settlement of Hardwicke, abandoned twelve years earlier, offered the *Invercauld* survivors their first decent shelter since the shipwreck. Moreover, it stood by a freshwater creek and would be visible from the sea, in the unlikely event of a ship passing.

Scavenging through the area, the men found an adze, an axe head, a spade, several yards of wire, some sheet metal which they could use for cooking, a substantial number of large wooden planks, and six large tins. For men with nothing but a few matches, this hoard was potentially life-saving. When a stray cat approached, the mate threw a brick at it, frightening it off. Their final discovery was the remnants of a vegetable garden, containing viable potatoes, cabbages and turnip seeds. But the men, whose hopes were pinned on rescue, not self-reliance, waited nine months before planting the seeds.

Near the settlement they managed to kill a seal. For once everyone had plenty to eat, and a sheltered spot in which to sleep: Holding wrote that the men were 'more comfortable than at any previous time since we were wrecked'. There were ten survivors now: six men had drowned, and another nine had died or been killed on the island.

According to Holding, the men now regarded him as their unofficial leader. But from now on it was feast or famine—mainly famine. The men caught the occasional seal and, to avoid infestation by flies, tried hanging the uneaten meat in trees—only to find it crawling with maggots soon afterwards. They made no attempt to cure the meat (despite a ready supply of salt from the seawater), or to smoke it or even just bury it in the cold, wet beach sand—a process that would have preserved it for several weeks. Instead the meat rotted.

Holding showed energy and initiative, but was prone to wanderlust, his own form of stupidity. Even when he was comfortable and safe, he couldn't remain in the same place for long. Soon he abandoned the others at Hardwicke to explore further north round the harbour. In his absence, apathy again seized hold of the other men, who spent much of the time huddled miserably around the fire.

Starvation wore down their strength. One afternoon the ship's steward, who was sitting next to the fire with the others,

refused to move over for the captain and 'the poor fellow...
was found to be dead'. By the time Holding returned, the two
young apprentices had also died. The scene was squalid and
demoralising. The second mate lay beside the fire, which had
by now burned deep into the peat, wearing the clothes he had
stripped from the apprentices.

Holding soon persuaded the strongest three (first mate
Smith and two sailors, Harvey and Fritz) to leave their sanctu-
ary and accompany him north. This time Holding selfishly
took everything useful with him, 'as I did not intend to go
back there to live'.

Just two kilometres away, Holding's group killed a large
seal and butchered it on the spot. Fritz was given the liver, skin
and head to carry, but he soon fell behind. When the others
turned back he was seen 'kneeling down on a rock with the
skin and liver, devouring it like a dog'. The men now had at
least fifty kilograms of perishable seal meat, but rather than
returning to Hardwicke, they went further away to Holding's
new camp.

On the second night at camp, Fritz got into a fight with
Harvey, who threw him out of their primitive stick shelter
face first, because he was being a 'nuisance'. In the morning
Fritz was found frozen and dead where he had landed. The
remaining three dragged his body to one side and covered
it with branches. Several days later, Harvey was sent back to
Hardwicke to fetch the others.

Harvey died not long after he reached Hardwicke. The
captain went foraging with the carpenter but returned alone.
The dying carpenter was found by Holding the next morning
wedged in a crevice. When Holding arrived back at Hardwicke,

he admitted, 'We were losing our members at a rapid rate.'

That evening, the second mate Mahoney threatened to knife Holding, who defended himself with a brick. The next day, Holding and Smith went back to the new camp. They left the second mate (who had an injured leg) with the captain, on the understanding that they would follow when Mahoney recovered.

Captain Dalgarno arrived at the camp some time later, explaining that Mahoney would join them when his infected leg was better. Weeks later, Holding returned to Hardwicke to find Mahoney's decomposing body lying next to the fire exactly where the captain had abandoned him to starve. Holding left the corpse unburied.

Three months after the shipwreck, only three men remained alive. An increasingly hostile relationship was brewing between Holding, Smith and Dalgarno, and even small incidents provoked fights. Their food supply was tolerable—the occasional seal, birds and limpets, as well as fish from traps that Holding had built—but they still made no attempt to preserve the excess.

First mate Smith and the captain outranked Holding and continued to order him about. British naval law at that time stated that following a shipwreck the captain retained authority over his crew. (This law was a direct result of the aftermath of the *Wager* shipwreck.) From their point of view, Holding had no right to disobey orders—it was insubordination.

Holding saw things differently. At twenty-three, he was younger, fitter and more resourceful, and felt they should acknowledge his natural ability to find food and superior bush skills. While he normally shared food, Holding also admitted to surreptitiously eating what he found at times, noting that 'self-preservation had become a vital matter'. Holding considered his superior officers lazy and parasitical, trading on their rank to get more food and do less work. Tellingly, many younger, fitter men had died while Dalgarno, at forty-one, and Smith, aged thirty-six, were still alive.

There were several more unspecified incidents at the camp, culminating in a 'disruption', almost certainly a physical fight, after which Dalgarno and Smith moved away from Holding to set up their own camp. The two parties avoided each other for weeks.

Holding also grappled with another difficult issue that plagues survivor groups. He feared being on his own—'I had always in mind the dread of being alone on the island'—yet he quickly became exasperated by the others' behaviour. It was definitely a case of 'can't live with you, can't live without you' writ large.

In his isolation, Holding gazed out at a tiny island five hundred metres offshore (now known as Rose Island) and decided to move there. He needed to build a one-man boat from seal skins and branches and eventually had to ask Dalgarno and Smith for help.

It is difficult to fathom how the men considered this a good plan; the island had almost no shelter, resources or firewood. Crossing the treacherous stretch of rough water to the island would be very dangerous, and they had no idea if there was even fresh water. Nevertheless, in early November Holding carefully paddled his flimsy coracle over, nearly drowning in the process. He discovered the island populated by starving rabbits and little else. However, he returned and persuaded

Smith and Dalgarno to move there. The coracle was too small, so they used boards from Hardwicke to make a primitive 2.5 metre boat.

The construction took months, but just after they were finished, Dalgarno and Smith tied their precious boat to a piece of seaweed and it was swept away by the rising tide. Understandably, Holding was furious. They were forced to construct *another* boat, using more timber from Hardwicke.

Eventually, the men relocated to Rose Island, accidentally leaving several essential tools behind. Returning to retrieve them, Dalgarno and Smith nearly drowned. To make matters worse, Rose Island's rabbits proved impossible to catch.

It was in this inauspicious location the men finally built a substantial hut, again from Hardwicke timber, to shelter them from the vicious weather. They also planted their precious seeds, on an island inhabited by 'thousands of rabbits'. Needless to say, the men never harvested any vegetables. Luckily, it was summer, and they were able to scavenge baby birds, eggs and, very occasionally, a seal. But a long winter was closing in and they still hadn't preserved any meat. Smith added to their woes by accidentally setting fire to the hut.

All along, the men's only rescue plan was to signal a passing ship, but they had done nothing to prepare for this. They even cut up a long pole from Hardwicke that would have made an excellent flagpole.

On the afternoon of May 22, as Holding was considering yet another move, he heard the captain shouting in the distance. He ran down, assuming the hut was on fire again, only to find Dalgarno had seen a ship thirty minutes earlier. Dalgarno's only reaction to this miracle was to run about hysterically shouting,

'*A SHIP A SHIP A SHIP A SHIP*'.

The vessel disappeared behind an island. The men waited 'a long time' until the ship reappeared a few kilometres away, then decided to try to signal it. All they had was a blue shirt to wave. At sea level, it would have been virtually invisible to a ship, so Holding raced uphill to wave it. At this point, Smith and Dalgarno started to build a signal fire. The men were in luck: the ship wasn't just passing, but putting into the harbour to repair a leak. The *Invercauld*'s last three survivors were saved.

Smith later wrote that with winter approaching, and with no food stored, 'I am sure that we would have all died in a short time.'

Given the litany of mistakes made by the *Invercauld* survivors, it is difficult to nominate the worst example of their stupidity, but failing to use the bounty of resources and shelter at Hardwicke must be a contender. Within a month of landing on the island, the survivors found enough pre-cut planks and tools there to construct two boats and the hut.

Then there's the group's failure to move from its initial positions, which were so open to the elements that there were four fatalities from exposure. (Survivors of the *Dundonald*, another ship wrecked in the Aucklands, escaped the lethal weather by digging small individual burrows in which they lived for seven months. They also kept their first fire burning for the entire time.)

And after the *Invercauld* survivors finally reached the safe haven of Hardwicke, rather than remain there, they wasted enormous resources and energy on constantly relocating.

The group was plagued by inaction, poor problem-solving, and a shocking inability to foresee impending difficulties. Their inertia and stupidity contributed to an eighty-four per cent death rate among the men who survived the initial wreck. The three who were eventually rescued owed their salvation mainly to dumb luck.

Excessive confidence can also lead to fatal errors. Sir John Franklin's final expedition of 1845-8 bristled with expertise and experience. Franklin had extensive polar and naval experience, had survived the Battle of Trafalgar, been Lieutenant-Governor of Van Diemen's Land (Tasmania), explored the coast of Australia with his relative Matthew Flinders, and earned a knighthood to boot. Now, nearing sixty, he expected this expedition to the Northwest Passage to be another feather in his cap and honour for Queen and Country.

When his two ships departed England in May 1845, they were engorged with provisions—including half a tonne of mustard, one tonne of tea, three tonnes of tobacco, 4286 kilograms of chocolate and ninety kilograms of pepper. 'The Admiralty have, in every respect, provided most liberally for the comforts of the officers and the men,' a newspaper reported. Each ship had its own organ and thousands of books for the men's entertainment. The officers had ornate writing desks, a lavish supply of fine wines, and of course their own monogrammed silver cutlery. Before long the entire bloated expedition of 129 men vanished. The mystery became the obsession of the age.

In 1859, fourteen years after the expedition sailed off into oblivion, a search party stumbled upon a bizarre and disturbing find in the subzero wilds of King William Island in Northern Canada: an eight-metre open boat, sitting on top of a heavy sled. Inside the boat were two skeletons. One set of bones, those of a young, slight man, lay in a 'much disturbed' state. The other, a 'large, strongly-made, middle-aged man' dressed in layers of clothes, lay with a strange pile of belongings at his feet. Apparently, he had spent his final hours in the company of two loaded guns, five gold watches, tea leaves, chocolate and twenty-six pieces of monogrammed silver cutlery. Both skulls were missing.

Francis McClintock, who examined the site, estimated the combined weight of the empty boat and sled at over 630 kilograms. The contents were a further 450 kilograms of what McClintock called 'a mere accumulation of dead weight'. It had been dragged over rough terrain seventy kilometres from the place where the *Terror* and *Erebus* had become trapped in ice, and abandoned. However, given that the boat was now facing towards the shipwreck site, McClintock felt it had been in the process of being dragged *back* to the frozen ships when the last men died.

Inside the snow-dusted boat lay an eclectic collection of junk, including a copy of Oliver Goldsmith's *The Vicar of Wakefield*, a silver pencil case, tobacco, a stick of red sealing wax, embroidered gentleman's slippers, a sponge, scented soap, towels, a collection of brushes and combs, and some silk handkerchiefs.

Embedded in the ice near the site lay the bones of between six and fourteen men, in a confusion of shattered bones that made no sense.

Evidently, Franklin and his officers had made some seriously stupid mistakes—most notably supersizing and overburdening the expedition with inappropriate, useless status symbols better suited to a weekend pheasant shoot on a country estate than a long haul through the unexplored Arctic Circle. A smaller, lighter expedition would have been more mobile, more flexible and faster.

The detritus of the expedition has slowly continued to reveal itself. To date more than a thousand items have been found scattered over an immense area, shedding more light on the bad decisions. They hadn't bothered to take Arctic essentials that would have been considerably more useful than embroidered slippers. The stranded men were forced to cobble together snow goggles (essential to prevent snow blindness) from scraps. The expedition's guns were more suited to grouse shooting than hunting large game. The men's clothes were made from wool and flannel, not fur.

Exacerbating this stupidity was an inability to adapt to changing circumstances. After their two ships became icebound, and facing a dangerously long overland trek, the survivors should have dumped every belonging not essential to their survival. Instead, they dragged and carried silverware, clothes brushes, medals, beaded purses and so on across the frozen wastes, dying slowly in a long, staggering line of men dropping in their tracks. There were no survivors.

The Franklin expedition failed to observe and exploit the environment to their benefit, a skill that can be crucial. For the desperate, the creative application of a casual observation can save lives. The crew of the *Belgica*, stranded in Antarctic pack ice in 1898, noticed something intriguing about penguin carcasses. Penguin meat had become vital to their survival, and the men noticed that, while they could drag no more than two dead penguins on a sled, it was a simple matter to haul *six* bodies without a sled. Evidently, the penguins had evolved feathers that were incredibly frictionless over snow: 'The lesson which we have learned from this experience is that sledges, if possible, should be shod with a strip of penguin skin with feathers attached.'

They duly modified their sled the following day. This was just one of several innovations that helped the crew survive their long imprisonment in the ice with just one fatality.

While almost every disaster has a degree of stupidity at its core, it is how the survivors behave and respond that often separates the living from the dead.

# CASTAWAYS IN THE SUB-ANTARCTIC

**LOCATION:** Auckland Islands
**NATIONALITY:** Multinational crew
**DATE:** 1864
**FATALITY RATE:** 0%
**DURATION:** 600 days

While the other case studies we have considered can easily be categorised as abject failures, this example shows that a group can sidestep the Lord of the Flies principle even in the harshest of circumstances.

Five months before the *Invercauld* wrecked, a fatal combination of a savage storm and a broken anchor chain put the *Grafton* on the rocks of Auckland Island.

The *Grafton* was small but sturdy: a schooner with a crew of five men, under the command of Captain Thomas Musgrave, an English migrant to Australia with fifteen years' sailing experience. Musgrave and François Raynal had undertaken the trip as a business venture: they were prospecting for seals.

The hired help were three sailors, with varying degrees of experience. The twenty-eight-year-old Norwegian Alick Maclaren was a strong, quiet, experienced seaman. The Portuguese-born cook Henry (Harry) Forgès, who was twenty-three, had been at sea since he was thirteen (although Raynal said Forgès had spent years in a leper colony in Samoa from where he had only recently escaped, cured but badly scarred). The final member was the nineteen-year-old English cabin boy, George Harris. All three were hired in Sydney, from where the *Grafton* sailed in November 1863.

The *Grafton* wrecked at exactly midnight on January 3 in Carnley Harbour, twenty-seven kilometres south of where the *Invercauld* was later to come to grief. The five men didn't abandon ship immediately, but waited until morning to make for the shore. The south end of the island was especially forbidding and their newly purchased ship had been destroyed. 'The vessel leaves her bones here,' wrote Musgrave in his journal, 'and God only knows whether we are all to leave our bones here also.' All the men wept at their plight.

They managed to save a dinghy and a few tools from the ship, as well as some provisions, including tobacco belonging to Musgrave and Raynal. This was immediately shared among the five men. They had a small, damp box of matches, and managed to light a fire. Once it was lit, the five men took turns to stay awake, to ensure the precious flame didn't go out. Even so, sleeping on the wet, stony ground, with just a sail for shelter, soon put the others on the sick list along with Raynal.

Despite being ill, the men searched for a cave to use as a shelter, but found nothing. Their misery was made worse by hordes of flies, which spread maggots through their clothes.

Musgrave knew that, without better shelter, they would die of exposure. The men decided to build a cabin and scoured the area for the best position. It took three days just to clear the site of the densely twisted undergrowth. At first, Raynal was too sick to help, but he contributed by carefully tending the fire, cooking, mending clothes and designing the cabin.

Using his considerable intelligence and his experience working on the Australian goldfields, Raynal came up with an optimal design—a cabin measuring seven metres by five, with an internal fireplace. Great care was needed with the fireplace: in an extremely windy environment sitting on top of solid peat, the cabin could very easily burn down if they got the design wrong. Raynal realised that to contain the sparks, they needed cement for the chimney and hearth.

As soon as he was well enough, he slow-roasted some shells in a strong fire to produce calcium oxide, or lime. This was mixed with the finest gravel he could find to make a basic mortar. Raynal carefully applied it to the hearth and chimney, despite the lime burning the skin off his hands. Finally the chimney was lined with copper sheets stripped from the *Grafton*'s wreck. It worked perfectly.

Erecting the large cabin took a sustained effort. The men salvaged what they could from the wreck and toiled even in atrocious weather, including two weeks of near-continuous, heavy rain. Musgrave worked as hard as the others, and made sure all the provisions were shared equally.

When they struck problems with the construction, such as the incessant wind blowing through cracks in the walls and causing the chimney to flame dangerously, they crafted effective, innovative solutions—sewing the island's tussock

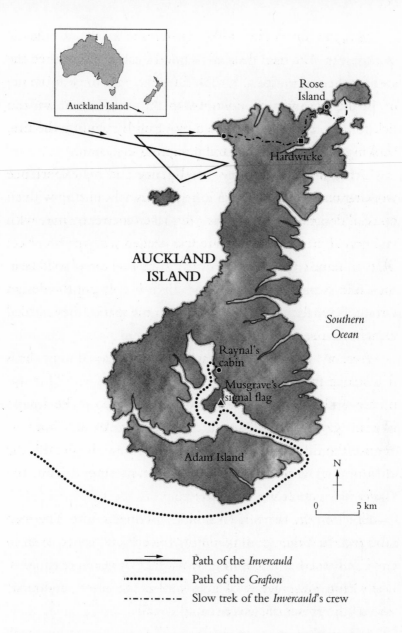

Path of the *Invercauld*
Path of the *Grafton*
Slow trek of the *Invercauld*'s crew

grass into arm-sized bundles and thatching the walls with overlapping layers. Everyone's hands were severely cut by the razor-sharp tussock grass. But the resulting barrier, which took five thousand separate bundles to construct, was thirty centimetres thick and insulated the cabin so it became 'very warm and comfortable'.

Breaks in construction work were put to good use, exploring and hunting for food. Two weeks after the shipwreck, Captain Musgrave took a prudent step: 'This morning we went down the harbour in the boat and planted a flagstaff, with a large canvas flag on it, where it may be seen from the sea, and we tied a bottle to it, with a note inside it directing anyone who may see it where to find us.'

It took nearly eight weeks to finish the cabin and once the roof was on, things improved slightly. If the rain was too severe, the men would stay indoors and make furniture— tables, beds, benches and shelves from items scavenged from the wreck. Musgrave and Raynal understood it was important to avoid 'shameful and senseless lethargy'.

Nevertheless, despair and ill-health still dogged the men, particularly Musgrave. He felt depressed, guilty and anxious about his family back in Sydney and his crew trapped in the Aucklands. Death was a real and ever-present possibility. The cliffs, rough terrain and treacherous weather made fatal accidents or hypothermia likely; the incessant noise from the wind and the huge waves pounding the cliffs compounded the stress. Raynal was convinced 'if we had not been supported by the continual work on which we kept ourselves employed, and which left us little leisure to think of our misfortunes' they would have succumbed to madness.

Musgrave also knew 'we have to be very frugal with our own little stock', so the men hunted seals and birds for food and salted or smoked excess meat. They had a gun, but quickly learned the best way to kill a seal was a blow between the eyes. Some potatoes had been saved from the wreck, but were planted rather than eaten. Unfortunately they failed to grow in the peaty soil.

Both Musgrave and Raynal kept records of the events and conditions on the island, using seal's blood when the ink ran out. The men agreed that if they all died, the last survivor should place the journals at the door of the cabin.

Weather permitting, the men continued to explore the huge harbour that surrounded them, charting and recording the depth as they went. On an island they discovered traces of an old campsite. Like seasoned detectives, the captain and his mate examined it meticulously, deducing that two tents full of people had camped there for about a week, processing seal oil. This cheered the group greatly; if sealers visited periodically, they had a chance of being rescued.

Raynal and Musgrave studied their environment with great care, and their keen observations helped them find resources as they were needed. One day, foraging for food, they discovered four chicks of a small green parrot; rather than eat them, they decided to raise them as pets.

The men studied the seals' behaviour, learning to recognise individual animals. They became particularly fond of the dominant bull-seal, whom they nicknamed Royal Tom.

By studying the seals, they became more efficient hunters, but Captain Musgrave urged them to be humane. One of the few times Musgrave became angry occurred when he discovered the men teasing Royal Tom.

The clouds of flies played havoc with their attempts to preserve meat. Unlike Captain Dalgarno's crew, the *Grafton* castaways figured out that if the meat was hung *high* enough, the maggots wouldn't infest it. The five men formed an interesting symbiotic relationship with the tiny songbirds that surrounded their cabin—they would shoot at the falcons that attacked the birds, and let the birds pick flies off their clothing and skin. The birds would repay these favours by singing, and more importantly, by sounding loud warning calls when the falcons got too close to the meat hanging in the trees.

When the men found the harsh vegetation was destroying their clothes, they devised a way of curing seal skins:

> *This is by stretching them and fledging them clean, and rubbing them well with strong lye (made from ashes) two or three times a day, until they are perfectly dry; then scour them well with sandstone, take them down, roll them up tight and beat them on something solid with a smooth piece of wood until they are quite soft.*

This complicated method, achieved through persistent trial and error over several months, eventually gave them warm clothes and blankets of seal fur. Next Raynal set his sights on new shoes. He extracted tannin from native ironwood chips, then set about tanning the leather properly. He made pitch (mixing tar from the wreck with seal oil) and strong thread (by weaving long hairs from a sea lion's mane with unravelled sailcloth threads). Raynal's first pair of shoes took a week to produce, but the result was useless. He adapted and redesigned until finally he was satisfied. The shoes wouldn't pass muster in the fashionable salons of Paris, Raynal admitted, but they were a solid defence against the damp and cold. He made five pairs.

Sometimes their ingenious plans failed, but faced with

a lack of success, they simply tried something else. When Musgrave discovered his signal flag had blown down in a gale, he put up a large white signal board in its place. (It was still standing thirty years later.) Apathy and helpless resignation to their fate were simply not part of this group's culture.

As winter closed in, the cold, sleet and snow kept them indoors more often. They fended off cabin fever teaching each other languages, mathematics, reading aloud from the Bible and fussing over the pet parrots, which were learning to talk. Musgrave made a solitaire board, while Raynal carved a chess set with his trusty pocket-knife. 'My pocket-knife!' he wrote later. 'May I not be allowed a few words respecting it? It is a debt of gratitude which I am anxious to discharge.'

Raynal also made a pack of cards, but rather than helping ease the boredom it resulted in an unpleasant discovery— 'Musgrave, in spite of his eminent and excellent qualities, was a bad player…when he lost, he lost his temper also.' Raynal knew that it was vital to keep discord at a minimum, so after a game which had caused Musgrave and himself to 'exchange some unpleasant words', Raynal threw the entire pack into the fire.

The provisions from the wreck were now a distant memory, except for a few biscuit crumbs 'which are regularly placed on the table, but only to look at.' A curious ritual probably only understood by the victims of long-term starvation.

Their six-month anniversary on the island came. Although they didn't know it, the men were no longer alone: the *Invercauld* survivors were wandering the northern end of the island. (Weeks later, combing the shoreline for seals, they discovered scattered parts of a recently wrecked ship. Curiously, this almost certainly wasn't from the *Invercauld* but another, unknown ship. The men searched for survivors but found no one. It was a harsh reminder that, should a ship arrive, there was no guarantee it could navigate in safely to rescue them.)

Musgrave's depression was becoming worse: he recorded in his journal that only mental images of his family waiting in Sydney were keeping suicidal thoughts at bay. Raynal watched his friend with great concern.

Seals were becoming scarce, so the hungry men relied on occasional fish, roots, mussels and their preserved seal meat. As the winter wore on, the exhaustion that accompanies a starvation diet debilitated them all. The weather was unimaginably foul. Musgrave kept detailed accounts in his journal, such as this entry from August 7: 'During the whole of last week the weather has been very bad; it has been blowing a very heavy gale...with either hail, rain or snow continually falling.' One night, the island was shaken by an earthquake, the men were terrified but the cabin stood firm.

Spring progressed, and still no ship appeared. Musgrave declared he would take the dinghy and set out for New Zealand, but the others dissuaded him, realising it was a suicide attempt cloaked in desperation.

The weather improved, but only by the Auckland Islands' very poor standard, with strong winds, rain and the temperature sporadically dropping to freezing. Christmas Day brought deep despondency, and the realisation that after one year, no one was coming to rescue them. Raynal made an outrageous suggestion: that they construct a small, ocean-going boat from the bones of the *Grafton*. Even for Raynal, it was insanely ambitious.

*To build a boat we must provide ourselves with a sufficient store of tools...but to fabricate new tools, a forge was necessary. It was then with the erection of a forge—that is to say, of a furnace, an anvil and a pair of bellows—that I must in the first place busy myself.*

Faced with a wall of scepticism and incredulity, Raynal decided action was the optimal tool of persuasion and commenced the herculean enterprise by himself. He waded out to the wreck and started pulling out nails and strips of copper.

Armed with his precious pocket-knife, a few basic tools, the scrap metal, some seal leather and a few old planks, Raynal built a functioning two-chambered forge bellows in a week. If he was missing a vital part, he improvised: the hinges and valves in the bellows were made from seal skin. Musgrave was soon infected with the spark of hope, although he considered success would be a miracle, given that New Zealand was four hundred kilometres away through the treacherous Southern Ocean.

Before long, the whole crew joined in. The sheer volume of work was overwhelming—so they abandoned their previous rotating schedule and settled on two men, George and Harry, taking over all hunting and domestic chores, while Musgrave, Raynal and Alick (who was the strongest) worked on the boat building.

Because they were building from scratch, every aspect was painfully complex. The forge, for example, needed huge amounts of charcoal for fuel. Alick had to cut enough wood to make a pile three metres deep, then cover the mass with a layer of turf before igniting it. The wet, peaty soil under the pile made a controlled burn almost impossible, and the first attempt burned too hot and produced nothing but ash. For the next attempt, the stoic Alick was forced to monitor the makeshift kiln continuously over a twenty-four-hour period.

Once the forge was operational, Raynal made a pair of pincers using a block of iron salvaged from the ballast as an anvil. He went on to produce two small pincers, three punches, three hammers, a nail mould, a cold chisel, an axe, several hatchets, a saw, a pair of tongs and sundry other tools.

Then, after at least three months of preparation, the men hit two insurmountable barriers. Much of the wood taken from the wreck was too old and inflexible to use, and the island's rata trees were too twisted to provide workable timber. The other problem was that they desperately needed a large drill bit, an auger. Musgrave recorded, 'His ingenuity and dexterity at the forge has indeed passed my expectations, but making augers has proved a hopeless failure.' Try as he might, Raynal couldn't manufacture a large spiral cutting edge.

Musgrave took the news that they had failed 'like a shot to my heart'. But acknowledging they had no other choice except death, Musgrave and Raynal agreed they must adapt the plan to rebuild the dinghy.

At three metres long, and 'very old and shaky', the little boat was totally useless for a long sea voyage. Essentially, they would build another boat over the core of the dinghy. The men all committed themselves to the new plan and work commenced the next day.

They made masts, a new keel, sails, bolts, and seven hundred large nails (each of which had to be sharpened by hand to a very sharp point to avoid splitting their precious timber). They hauled the dinghy out, lengthened it, raised the sides considerably, and fitted the mast. Work started each day at 6am and finished at 11pm. Morale was good, but the hectic schedule was taking a toll. Musgrave's hair was falling out and boils covered his hands. All the men were tormented by swarms of sandflies, which bit their exposed skin and crawled into their clothing to continue feasting.

Two months into the work on the dinghy, fate played a cruel trick. The long-awaited ship arrived at the north end of Auckland Island, and rescued the three remaining survivors of the *Invercauld*. Musgrave had deduced from glimpses of distant smoke and domesticated dogs that perhaps there were other survivors at the unreachable north end of the island. Captain Dalgarno had no such inspiration, and the rescue ship promptly sailed off to Peru.

Meanwhile, thirty kilometres to the south, three weeks of heavy snow were a reminder that winter was nigh. This was followed by a bad bout of dysentery, which struck all of the exhausted *Grafton* survivors hard. 'Grim starvation which all along has been gnawing at our bowels' added to their misery. A small consolation was the taming of a cat which lived under the cabin, attracted by the warmth.

One of the last additions to the dinghy was a deck with three man-sized hatchways. To prevent waves spilling down these holes, Raynal nailed on three tubes of sailcloth; 'Into these openings we could insert our legs, and completely shelter them, while seated on the edges, we pulled the sail-cloth right up under our arms.' Secure straps also went across the men's shoulders, to prevent them from being washed overboard. The end result was a five-metre boat–kayak hybrid, with a mast and a lug sail.

In late June the little boat was finally finished and christened *Rescue* in honour of her task. They gave her a test run to the other side of the Carnley Harbour, but she handled so badly Musgrave was seriously concerned and the others were frightened she might capsize. It was obvious that *Rescue* couldn't carry all the group. They had always vowed to stay together, but Musgrave was faced with the heart-wrenching task of choosing who should risk their lives at sea, and who should remain behind, possibly trapped on the island for the rest of their lives.

The cook, deeply worried about the seaworthiness of the 'nutshell', was an obvious candidate to stay behind. Musgrave chose George to remain with the cook, as the pair were the closest in age and had always got on well. All that was left was to stow some food and water on board and wait for suitable weather.

On the nineteenth of July, conditions seemed perfect: clear with a south-westerly wind. The men gathered at the shore, profoundly upset.

> *The hour of departure had arrived: we were on the point of separating from two of our companions—from George and Harry—who for nineteen months had shared, day after day, our struggles and our sufferings, with whom we had lived as brothers.*

At 11am, the boat sailed out of Carnley Harbour. Four hours later they passed the top of the island and continued north. *Rescue* leaked but Raynal had taken the precaution of installing a small pump. As darkness approached, the weather deteriorated and the swell picked up. The little boat was tossed between huge waves, making the men seasick. Night brought 'showers of biting hail and snow, to increase the horrors of our situation'.

The following day the bad weather continued, but the seasickness abated. The men tried eating some roast seal, but it had gone bad so they threw it overboard. The second night a huge wave crashed directly over the boat, 'and rolled it to and fro like a cork...we thought our last moment had come'. The sailcloth tubes saved their lives.

As the storm raged over the following days, the men worked the pump continuously. They drank a little water and desperately scanned the horizon for land.

*We were in a deplorable condition, soaked by the sea-water, which had penetrated our clothes, and whose corrosive action made itself painfully felt, frozen with the cold, overcome by fatigue—for we had not closed our eyes a single moment—and above all, exhausted by want of food.*

On the morning of the fifth day they sighted land—but good luck once again cut a wide berth around the *Grafton* survivors. The wind failed and none of them had the strength to row. To their dismay *Rescue* started drifting back out to sea. Musgrave was convinced they were fated to die in sight of the land. In the evening they managed to sail a light breeze back towards the coast, but couldn't make landfall in the darkness.

Somehow they survived the long night and the next morning sailed into a large bay, but found it deserted. They sailed on up the coast, although manoeuvring was almost impossible: 'our hands were swollen and scarred by the double effect of the cold and the salt water'. Musgrave and Raynal both felt death was approaching. Finally, as they rounded a headland, a scene of civilisation's normality met their eyes: neat houses, trim gardens, a man walking his dog, children playing and a group of Maori women mending nets.

They had reached Stewart Island. Alick passed out and Musgrave and Raynal were speechless and had to be carried ashore. But none of that mattered; 'an immense joy, a profound gratitude' filled their hearts.

They were taken to the home of the dog walker, Captain Tom Cross. They shed their 'miserable rags', defrosted in hot baths and were clothed and fed (fish, pork, potatoes and fresh hot bread). After just a few mouthfuls the three men fell into a 'profound and irresistible sleep'.

When they woke over twenty-four hours later, they were astonished to find themselves back on a ship. It was the *Flying Scud*, Captain Cross's fishing boat, and he was taking them to the nearest big town, Invercargill on the southern tip of New Zealand's mainland, to get help.

The ship was towing *Rescue*, but as they rushed into the harbour near Invercargill on a falling tide, her cable snapped. Before the disbelieving eyes of Raynal, Alick and Musgrave, the product of their superhuman labours was dashed to splinters on the rocks. *Rescue* had been in New Zealand waters less than two days. Raynal couldn't hold back his tears.

Personal pain aside, Musgrave was extremely anxious that a rescue mission be despatched immediately, but found himself snarled in red tape.

The New Zealand Government was officially sympathetic

but refused to help, so private donations helped hire a ship (the *Flying Scud*), but a vexing question of insurance for the trip had to be ironed out. Eventually, Musgrave, who wanted to return to Sydney as soon as was humanly possible, was persuaded to accompany the rescue mission in person. Raynal was astonished his friend, still weak and sick, was prepared to return to Auckland Island: 'proof of a courage and a devotion of which few men would have been capable.'

Thanks to a faulty compass and the weather, it was twenty-five days before they reached Carnley Harbour. Gales and dangerous conditions made the passage a terrible trial, even for the *Scud*—a large ocean-going fishing boat, and not a converted dinghy. At first, George and Harry couldn't be found and Musgrave feared he had arrived too late but eventually the emaciated pair were tracked down. Harry passed out on seeing them, and George, in tears, couldn't stop saying, 'How are ye? How are ye?'

In the five weeks since parting, the two men had been reduced to eating mice to survive. Their relationship, which had been strong for nineteen months within the group of five, had collapsed. Immediately after *Rescue*'s departure, the area had been battered by a frightful storm, and George and Harry were convinced the boat must have sunk. Depressed and overwrought, they fell to arguing. The fighting had become so intense that the two men were on the point of separating when Musgrave arrived.

Back on board the *Scud*, the men spent five days combing the coast for the other shipwrecked survivors Musgrave suspected were there. His conscience and compassion gnawed at him; 'The thought that some poor wretch should be left upon it to suffer what *we* suffered pursues me incessantly.' They discovered Hardwicke but the *Invercauld* survivors were long gone.

On September 5, they braced themselves for the trip back. Some of the worst weather Musgrave had ever seen battered the ship, but after several days they limped into Invercargill, to be greeted on the dock by Raynal, Alick and most of the local population. (News of their ordeal had spread far and wide—the press had dubbed them 'The Auckland Island Crusoes'.) Raynal and Alick had been waiting on the dock every day for weeks, terrified that the *Scud* had not survived the rescue mission.

> *Never, never shall I forget the mighty joy which we felt on meeting, all five in safety and good health, in this hospitable land. We threw ourselves in our excitement into each other's arms. We could utter but one word: 'Saved! Saved!'*

Once the celebrations had subsided, the companions, having been to hell and back, went their separate ways. Captain Musgrave was reunited with his family in Sydney, but quickly took up a lucrative paid offer from the Australian Government to scour the Auckland Islands for any shipwreck survivors (which he initially offered to do for free). Raynal later reported that George had joined the New Zealand gold rush, Harry had gone to work on an Australian sheep station, and Alick, undeterred by his awful experiences, had returned to his career at sea. Raynal and Musgrave were eventually reunited in Melbourne before the Frenchman headed up to Sydney to raise funds by hitting the lecture circuit. The Australian Government also paid him for the meteorological records he had kept on the Auckland Islands. Eventually he was able to head back to France.

After a twenty-year absence, Raynal was overjoyed to find his parents still alive and well. Although permanently weakened by the ordeal, he went on to write a book of his experiences, which became a bestseller and is still in print today. Something of a celebrity in France, Raynal was awarded various academic and literary accolades and awards. Astronomers listened to his advice on the placement of an observatory in the Southern Oceans. He was given the respect and public recognition he deserved.

Thomas Musgrave's wife Catherine was still waiting patiently, but Musgrave's fears during his absence had not been without reason: his young son Walter had died. The captain of the ill-fated *Grafton* wrote a well-received book about their survival, but he never enjoyed the limelight like Raynal.

It is difficult not to compare the fate of the *Grafton* and the *Invercauld*. The *Invercauld*'s crew spent twelve months on the island, with a fatality rate of eighty-four per cent. The *Grafton*'s crew survived nineteen months, with no fatalities. The *Invercauld* castaways were rescued by another ship. The *Grafton*'s crew saved themselves.

Back in the Southern Ocean, ships continued to be attracted to the rocks of Auckland Islands like flies to a corpse. After several more shipwrecks and scores of deaths, public outrage compelled the New Zealand Government in 1868 to install several castaway depot boxes across the islands. To stop light-fingered sealers pilfering the contents, a timeless warning was written on the lid of the box:

> *The Curse of the widow and the fatherless*
> *light upon the man who breaks open this*
> *box whilst he has a ship at his back.*

# THE SHIFTING SANDS
# OF AUTHORITY

*He isn't a prefect and we don't know anything about him. He just
gives orders and expects people to obey for nothing.*

JACK, *LORD OF THE FLIES*

**DISPUTES OVER WHO** is in charge will tear the very fabric of a
survivor group. If the pre-crisis leader survives, the group
initially remains obedient. On a ship, plane or military expedition, disobeying orders can be a breach of the law. Mutiny was
and is a very serious crime, particularly in the armed forces.
Up until 1998 in Britain, it could still attract the death penalty
(along with its sister in anarchy, treason).

Consequently, for a while, the power status quo tends
to hold in survivor groups. Most people will be compliant
from force of habit, but inevitably resentment starts to build,
frequently over the delegation of chores.

Stranded in the high Arctic wastelands on Ellesmere Island
in October 1881, Commander Adolphus Greely (a cavalry

officer and veteran of the American Civil War) asked for a volunteer to wash the four officers' clothes. Bearing in mind they were 1700 kilometres above the Arctic Circle and that the temperatures were dropping to minus twenty-five degrees Celsius, Greely should not have been surprised that no one put their hand up. He took this lack of enthusiasm as an assault on his authority and ordered an enlisted man called Connell to do the work. When Connell protested, dissent spread through the entire group, causing the commander to overreact. Sergeant David Brainard recorded the alarming situation in his journal:

*A long talk was given to the crowd of angry and excited men by Lieut. Greely, who said that he was not a man to be trifled with and in case of necessity he would not stop at the loss of human lives to restore order.*

Greely typified the leader who becomes obsessed with maintaining his control at all costs. Later in his journal he wrote of a particularly 'acrid' discussion with Dr Pavy.

*I ordered him four times to drop the matter, and finally told him were he not the doctor I would kill him. As a consequence Private Bender attempted to defend the doctor, and, despite repeated orders would not be quiet. A mutiny seemed imminent and I would have killed him could I have got Long's gun...I fear for the future.*

Greely later defended his desire to shoot both Dr Pavy and Bender by stating, 'threats and force to insure obedience are fully justifiable.'

The more the leaders become exclusively focused on control, rather than exerting themselves on behalf of the group, the more the rest will rebel. It can become a self-perpetuating downward spiral into anarchy, such as occurred in Patagonia, where the *Wager*'s crew finally marooned the mutiny-obsessed Captain Cheap.

At times, the entire group may unite against the leader in a bloodless coup and simply inform him his rule is at an end.

The American sloop *Peggy*, returning from the West Indies in 1765 with a hold full of merchandise, was crippled after losing her sails in two weeks of violent storms in the mid-Atlantic. The ship drifted for several weeks until the men had eaten all the provisions, some pigeons and the ship's cat. With starvation looming, they resorted to a more drastic solution: selecting and eating someone on the ship. When Captain Harrison objected, the crew informed him that 'it was indifferent to them whether I acquiesced or not...they would oblige me to take my chance as well as another man, since the general misfortune had levelled all distinctions of persons'.

In modern parlance this process within group dynamics is called 'status levelling'. More skilful leaders will recognise that circumstances have changed and adapt, rather than sticking to inflexible authoritarianism. Ernest Shackleton instinctively understood that 'a man must shape himself to a new mark directly the old one goes to ground'.

As conditions became increasingly dire for Shackleton's party, he would call meetings, invite discussion and input from the men and explain his decisions. Rather than stridently demanding loyalty, Shackleton asked his men for their trust. It was a strategy that paid off.

Captain Riley of the *Commerce*, shipwrecked off the

Western Sahara in 1815, also understood when the ground had shifted. Immediately after the loss of his ship, he divided his own money, a thousand Spanish dollars, among his ten crew 'in the hope of its being useful to them in procuring a release from this country in case we should be separated'.

On the Auckland Islands, after just five weeks trapped on the island, Captain Musgrave detected an undercurrent:

*Up to the present time the men have worked well, and conducted themselves in a very obedient and respectful manner towards me, but I find there is somewhat of a spirit of obstinacy and independence creeping in amongst them.*

At times when he gave them a task to do, they didn't object but he detected in their demeanour a clear message: 'Why don't you do it yourself?' No martinet, Musgrave admitted that he could no longer simply *expect* them to be obedient.

François Raynal was aware of the dangers: 'If habits of bitterness and animosity were once established amongst us, the consequences could not but be most disastrous: we stood so much in need of each other!'

After careful consideration, the pragmatic Raynal came up with a characteristically brilliant solution. The group should choose 'not a master or superior, but a "head" or "chief of family".' Raynal also proposed a mini-constitution which instructed the leader to:

1. Be firm but fair in keeping order.
2. Work to avoid disharmony and controversy within the group.
3. Adjudicate quarrels and hand out punishments.
   Punishment for offenders would initially be a just

reprimand, followed by temporary or permanent
ostracism for recidivists.

4. Assign daily chores fairly for all including himself.
5. For major decisions take a vote, with a majority
verdict to decide the outcome.

The men added a caveat which Raynal worded as follows:

*The community reserves to itself the right of deposing the chief
of the family, and electing another, if at any time he shall
abuse his authority, or employ it for personal and manifestly
selfish purposes.*

With these constitutional guidelines written down on the
blank pages of a Bible the men had saved from the wreck, they
set about electing 'the president of our little republic'. Raynal
proposed Captain Musgrave for the position, and was met
with unanimous assent. The only benefit Musgrave obtained
as leader was that he was excused from the cooking roster.

In essence, by voluntarily surrendering authority, Musgrave
regained a practical and unopposed form of power and control,
a perfect solution to a tricky problem. From that point on, the
men knew they could vote Captain Musgrave out at any point
they chose. Indirectly it granted them considerable power over
their own fate. The grumblings stopped and the men were
content to accept his authority and follow his orders without
question. With the new regime in place, the group could
devote all their energy to finding solutions to the daunting
hardships that faced them, with the fabric of their community
intact. They were also able to sidestep the insidious issue of
fragmentation.

# COMPASSION

*What about the littluns?...Someone's got to look after them.*

RALPH, *LORD OF THE FLIES*

**IF WE HAD** to search for one magic ingredient to create a high-functioning successful group, compassion would be a strong contender. Certainly compassion is notably absent in the worst cases, and for the best, compassion is as important a resource as food and shelter.

Among the horrible carnage of the *Medusa* shipwreck, one man stands out: the second lieutenant Jean-Baptiste Espiaux. The lieutenant had already proved his bravery in 1808, fighting the British at the siege of Cadiz. Wounded and captured, he had dived off a British ship to return to the fighting. Described by Charlotte Picard as 'brave and generous', Espiaux was put in charge of the leaky and unstable longboat. When he realised that dozens of people had been left on board the *Medusa* by the other boats, Espiaux ordered his longboat back to the wreck. 'It is he who, notwithstanding the various dangers with which he was surrounded, following only the impulse of his courage, succeeded in saving them.'

Somehow Espiaux managed to cram forty-seven more people onto the longboat, bring the total to ninety. It was now grossly overcrowded, uncontrollable, and taking on water. Espiaux gingerly made his way to Governor Schmaltz's comparatively empty barge and requested to transfer some men. The governor, 'busied in the care of his own dear self', refused. So did all the other boats.

Minutes later, when the towline was cut and the raft abandoned, Espiaux tried to persuade the men on his boat to attempt to pull the raft. His men refused, knowing this would probably prove fatal to the oarless longboat. Facing a mutiny, Espiaux was forced to make for the coast.

After their first 'long and dreadful night' at sea, sixty-three of the passengers aboard the longboat decided to take their chances walking across the desert and demand Espiaux put them ashore. This left twenty-seven people in the longboat, which continued sailing south. Hours later they saw some of the other boats struggling through the heavy seas. Espiaux sailed over and offered to take some more men on board his (now less crowded) longboat. The other boats feared it was a trap and fled:

> *This distrust came from their thinking, that, by a stratagem, we had concealed all our people under the benches, to rush upon them when they should be near enough, and so great was their distrust that they resolved to fly [from] us like enemies.*

As we have seen, selfish behaviour had become the norm for the *Medusa* survivors from the second they set foot on the rope ladder off the doomed ship. There was no trust, it was every man for himself. Unfortunately the captain and the governor had led by poor example, with the others following. Yet Espiaux stuck to his principles, offering to help others when there was no hope of reciprocity.

Not long after, the sea became much rougher. The tiny yawl, with fifteen men on board, began to sink. Espiaux sailed over and rescued all of them.

After another night at sea, Espiaux spotted a battered boat from the *Medusa* and sailed over to check the occupants were all right. When he heard they had lost their only cask of wine in the storm, Espiaux took the astonishing step of giving them two bottles from the longboat's tiny supply of liquid: this tided them over until they made landfall and may well have saved the twenty-five men from death by dehydration. By now Espiaux had single-handedly saved eighty-seven people: twenty-five on this latest boat, fifteen from the yawl and the forty-seven abandoned on the *Medusa*.

Such outright altruism is shockingly rare in communal survival situations, but it does occur. Captain Musgrave risked his life to save Raynal from the wreck of the *Grafton*. Nineteen months later, just five days after he reached safety in New Zealand, Musgrave desperately wanted to return to his family in Sydney. He was exhausted, covered in boils and his feet were in such bad shape he could barely walk. Musgrave nevertheless agreed to return to the Aucklands to rescue the two remaining crew.

Even on a large fishing boat like the *Flying Scud,* it was a dangerous trip. As the rescue mission waited to leave, Musgrave wrote to his wife outlining his reasons for putting himself back in harm's way. With his typical humility, he explained that he felt 'an incumbent duty and in common humanity I felt myself bound to comply'. No doubt Musgrave truly felt this kind of humanity was common to all people, but in reality, selfless duty and compassion under such circumstances are extremely rare.

After the rescue of Musgrave's friends, Henry Forgès and George Harris ('my boys' as he called them), his thoughts returned to his suspicion that there had been another shipwreck to the north.

As the *Scud* sailed up the coast of the island, Musgrave searched for other castaways. As we know, Captain Dalgarno, Robert Holding and Andrew Smith of the *Invercauld* had already been rescued, but Musgrave did stumble upon someone else. In the ruins of a hut, he found a fully dressed corpse lying sprawled on a makeshift bed. Musgrave deduced (correctly) that it was an injured sailor who had been left to die by the *Invercauld* survivors several months earlier.

> *Looking at this poor abandoned corpse, we felt a deep compassion…We were unwilling to leave it unburied. Next day we dug a grave and reverently interred it; and, after saying a few prayers over its last resting place, we planted there a wooden cross.*

The men from the *Invercauld* had simply left their shipmate, James Mahoney, to a lingering and lonely death from cold and starvation.

Ernest Shackleton, trapped with his men on a small ice floe

off Antarctica in 1916 after the loss of their ship *Endurance*, also showed an instinctive compassion. In the middle of the night, Shackleton had an 'intangible feeling of uneasiness' and got up to check the floe was sound. Sensing a problem, he rushed to let the watchman know. As he hurried past one of the tents, the ice under it cracked and split, dragging a man, still in his sleeping bag, into the icy water. Disregarding his own safety, Shackleton threw himself down at the edge of the crack and reached down into the water for the sleeping bag: 'I was able to grasp it, and with a heave lifted man and bag on to the floe. A few seconds later the ice-edges came together with tremendous force.'

Shackleton was lucky not to have his arm crushed, but his quick thinking saved his companion. This was typical of Shackleton, who felt the heavy weight of responsibility for the safety of all his men. In return, he received extraordinary love and loyalty from his crew. Expedition member Frank Worsley later wrote of the men's absolute trust in their leader, 'their loyalty to Shackleton and their absolute conviction that whatever he did was for the best'. They admitted they would have followed him anywhere.

# THE DOGMA OF RACE

*We've got to have rules and obey them. After all, we're not savages.*
*We're English; and the English are best at everything.*
*So we've got to do the right things.*

JACK, *LORD OF THE FLIES*

**IF WE COULD** summon the ghosts from a failed group and ask
them what factors contributed to their downfall it's unlikely
they would consider race. Nevertheless, racist attitudes have
often swirled around disasters—and they can materially affect
a group's chances of survival. The more confident a group is of
its inherent superiority, the less likely it is to survive.

William Golding was well aware of its effect and at pains
to highlight it in *Lord of the Flies*. A quick look at R. M.
Ballantyne's *The Coral Island* shows why.

The three teenage English boy-heroes of Ballantyne's novel
(Jack, Ralph and Peterkin) have an inherent sense of their
racial superiority, and a well-established belief in 'wild beasts
and savages, torturings at the stake, roastings alive, and such

like horrid things.' When they first see the 'savage chief' he is described as 'the most terrible monster I ever beheld'.

Golding makes two direct references to *The Coral Island*, the most poignant when the boys are rescued by the English officer on the final page. The man is confused how these filthy, warring children 'with the distended bellies of small savages' can be English. He hopes it's just fun and games: 'Jolly good show. Like Coral Island.'

Golding's approach to the violence in his book stems from the atrocities he witnessed in World War II. As he explained in an interview,

> *There were things done during that period from which I still have to avert my mind lest I should be physically sick. They were not done by the head-hunters of New Guinea, or by some primitive tribe in the Amazon. They were done skilfully, coldly, by educated men, doctors, lawyers, by men with a tradition of civilisation behind them, to beings of their own kind.*

Marooned on the island, Golding's boys are confident that their Englishness will ensure their survival, and fail to see they are sliding towards a moral black hole. Golding reinforces the point at the end of the book when the English officer lectures the boys: 'I should have thought that a pack of British boys— you're all British aren't you?—would have been able to put up a better show than that.'

A similar sense of superiority lingers over many real-life survivor accounts. The implicit message is: no Englishman/ Frenchman (substitute here any race not immediately involved in any given disaster) would resort to such dreadful acts in order to survive. It seems that the more safe and comfortable a country, the more likely its inhabitants are to see steadfastness in adversity, fortitude in peril, calm and basic common decency as national traits.

The *Medusa* disaster caused national hand-wringing in France. When a report by Corréard and Savigny was leaked to a newspaper, detailing the incompetence of the captain and the appalling behaviour that followed the wreck—the establishment went into denial as a wave of revulsion swept the nation. France was a civilised nation: surely its people could not sink so low?

The English, naturally, couldn't get enough of the salacious detail—such as the fact that Captain de Chaumareys had not even been the last man off the *Medusa*. British reports emphasised and enforced the conviction that no such behaviour would have occurred on a British ship. The preface to the 1827 English edition of Charlotte Picard's book on the *Medusa* tragedy contains a smug comment: 'There is also something peculiarly gratifying to an Englishman in the reflection that such a disaster could not have befallen almost any British crew.'

Shortly after the *Medusa* disaster its events inspired a hit play in London: *The Fatal Raft*, by William Moncrieff. Moncrieff injected a (fictional) heroic character into the action: an English sailor called Jack Gallant who repeatedly rallies the people on the raft and, when they contemplate cannibalism, reminds them they have 'the hearts of human beings' and should take their 'passage to heaven together'. Jack doesn't hesitate to point out the moral superiority of his race over the French, at one point asking: 'When did [one] ever find a British officer desert his men in this way?'

This sense that certain races are above barbarity, while others are only too willing to embrace it, continued for some time. J. G. Lockhart, in his 1939 book *True Tales of the Sea*, gives a wonderful racy (and racist) description of the scene on board as the *Titanic*'s passengers realise their ship is sinking:

*The people were behaving splendidly. The first and second class passengers were mostly British and American, and could be trusted to meet the crisis with the courage of their race. But, like all ships crossing the Atlantic, the* Titanic *carried a big steerage, emigrants mainly from South and South-Eastern Europe—Poles, Russians, Italians, Roumanians, and so on, whose conduct was less assured. How might these folk behave when they learnt that at least half their number was doomed? Already there had been one ugly rush, quickly checked by officers and crew; and a little later on, as one of the boats was being lowered, the officer in charge was compelled to fire his revolver in order to scare away a bunch of Italians who were crouching on the bulwarks like wild beasts ready to spring and who threatened to leap into and swamp the boat.*

In accounts of other disasters, indigenous companions are frequently referred to as 'savages', even when they are doing most of the work.

Dr John Rae, an intelligent and resourceful Scotsman, trekked across the Arctic twice to find out the fate of Franklin's lost expedition. Basing his report on what the Inuit told him they had seen a few years earlier on the west coast of King William Island, Rae came to a grim conclusion: 'From the mutilated state of many of the bodies and the contents of the kettles, it is evident that our wretched Countrymen had been driven to the last dread alternative—cannibalism—as a means of prolonging existence.'

When Charles Dickens, the most famous English writer of his time, heard of these Inuit reports he took up his pen. Spurred along by Franklin's redoubtable widow, Lady Jane, he started a propaganda campaign against the man who had first reported the rumours.

Dickens lambasted Rae, and characterised the Inuit as 'covetous, treacherous and cruel'. He refuted the claims of cannibalism. 'The noble conduct and example of such men, and of their great leader himself [Franklin]...outweighs by the weight of the whole universe the chatter of a gross handful of uncivilised people, with a domesticity of blood and blubber.'

He went on to claim the Inuit had probably murdered the whole party. After a response by Rae in the press, *The Times* came out all guns blazing: 'Is the story told by the Esquimaux the true one? Like all savages, they are liars.' Dickens also contributed a general comment on 'the uncivilised', writing:

*It is impossible to form an estimate of the character of any race of savages, from the deferential behaviour to the white man when he is strong. The mistake has been made again and again: and the moment the white man has appeared in the new aspect of being weaker than the savage, the savage has changed and sprung upon him.*

Such attitudes are problematic for two reasons. As Golding pointed out, the belief that one's group will remain civil simply because they are 'civilised' is completely false. Consequently, many survivor groups are blindly optimistic, and have no social mechanism in place to deal with outbreaks of hostility and aggression. When the first Biosphere crew told their replacement crew to be wary of factionalism, fighting and hatred, their warning was laughed off: 'Come on...We all know each other. We're friends. We know how to deal with this. It's no big deal.' The new crew suffered from many of the same problems.

In the 1970s social psychologist Irwin Altman and his colleagues highlighted the surprising perils of optimism in a series of experiments to ascertain the effects of confinement stress on pairs of male subjects. The volunteers were placed into a 3.6 metre by 3.6 metre furnished room for eight days. Even though they were comfortable and supplied with food, games and books, more than half the participants 'aborted the experiment' and were unable or unwilling to finish. Altman attributed the high failure rate to some of the participants being over-confident in their ability to withstand the stress. Consequently, they 'did not undertake effective group formation processes necessary to cope with the situation'. The aborters tended to be 'thrill-seeking', alpha-male types.

The other big problem associated with an assumption of racial superiority is a tendency to dismiss or ignore the practices of any indigenous races in the vicinity. The starving men of the *Wager* watched the local Patagonian tribe harvesting 'sea eggs' (sea urchins) in large numbers. Sea urchin roe is highly nutritious and is a delicacy in many cultures, but the *Wager* crew never considered trying to get any sea urchins for themselves. Nor did they try to construct the sort of simple tidal fish traps used by the indigenous people. Instead they starved.

Many explorers, including Franklin, saw the Inuit wearing sealskin or caribou-skin pants and fur parkas, which were waterproof, wind-resistant and warm. Even so, most of the

Europeans didn't consider replacing their thin European wool and flannel clothing. Nor did they seem to appreciate that the Inuit had been surviving and prospering in this harsh environment for generations. Instead, the explorers had an almost religious faith in the power of tea: 'that soothing, cheering, invigorating emblem of civilisation—T-E-A,' as the nineteenth-century Arctic explorer Charles Hall put it.

John Rae, hailing from the Orkney Islands (where they know a thing or two about extreme cold), adapted to the harsh Arctic conditions and respected and learned from the local population: 'My small party passed the winter in snow houses (igloos) in comparative comfort, the skins of deer shot affording abundant warm clothing and bedding.' Rae survived to die of old age in London, while Franklin's two expeditions resulted in the deaths of 140 men.

It was an ironic twist, considering that Franklin himself had little respect for the Orcadians. On his first expedition, Franklin had scoffed at the way four recruits from the Orkneys had painstakingly scrutinised every detail of his expedition plan before they agreed to be hired. How different from his fellow countrymen, he wrote. 'An English seaman enters upon an enterprise, however hazardous, without inquiring, or desiring to know, where he is going, or what he is going about.'

Rae not only discovered the grim fate of the doomed expedition, he also explored further and more successfully than Franklin. Yet it was Franklin who passed into legend a knight of the realm, while Rae died in obscurity, the victim of a great injustice. His crime was that he had exposed the folly and inferiority of the tea-drinking, tally-ho approach to polar exploration.

The inspirational *Grafton* five were the original motley

crew: an English-born Australian captain leading an Englishman, a Frenchman, a Portuguese and a Norwegian. There seems to have been no race-based assumption that any one individual was superior or more important than the others. This probably contributed to the remarkable tolerance and harmony that sustained them during their nineteen months in the sub-Antarctic.

# THE DARK

*Soon the darkness was full of claws, full of
the awful unknown and menace.*

LORD OF THE FLIES

**SURVIVOR GROUPS OFTEN** struggle with a problem that is hard
to comprehend in our well-lit twenty-first century. During
the day they have to contend with hunger, thirst, in-fighting,
shelter and other pragmatic issues, but as night comes on a new
issue emerges: the darkness itself. The inability to see their
surroundings and their companions has a shocking effect on
some survivors.

Nyctophobia (fear of darkness) is the most common fear
among children, with symptoms peaking around five years of
age. Under normal circumstances, it is very rare in adults. From
an evolutionary perspective, nyctophobia makes perfect sense.
We are undoubtedly much safer in the light: a predatory attack
is much more likely to be successful in darkness, and wandering

around at night will increase the chance of an injury.

Once again, this is an area where the primitive amygdala takes over, so we have little conscious control over our responses, and they can be far from rational.

In 2008 forty-year-old Hayden Adcock, an experienced hiker from Australia, became lost in dense jungle in Laos. He had set out on a short hike expected to take a few hours, and was carrying neither a torch nor matches. On the first night, lost in the pitch-black, he got spooked by the darkness, ran wildly through the forest and injured himself falling down a steep ravine. He spent the rest of the night in a riverbed where he felt safer. As the next night approached, Adcock felt the darkness overwhelm his mood: 'It just went from being exhausted and disappointed to just freaking out...I pretty much completely lost it.' Consumed by a fear that he would die, he retreated once more to the riverbed, despite the cold. He was rescued after eleven days.

Israeli adventurer Yossi Ghinsberg experienced something similar when he became lost in the Bolivian jungle in 1982. Separated from his companions, Ghinsberg felt his mind filling with desperate, frightened thoughts of death as the darkness grew. When daylight returned his fears disappeared, but 'when it began to grow dark, I was overtaken with fear'.

Hundreds of years separate these two men from the survivors on the *Medusa* raft, but the reactions were similar. On the raft, the darkness stirred up a potent mix of terror, despair and mindless aggression. Their second night adrift was almost as if someone had opened the door into hell and shoved them all through. 'The soldiers and sailors, terrified by the presence of inevitable danger, gave themselves up for lost.'

This unleashed an orgy of destruction in the darkness, directed both at the raft, which they tried to chop up, and other passengers. People were hacked or beaten to death and thrown into the sea. If no weapons were at hand the 'deranged men' used their teeth and fists: 'In their delirium they were entirely deaf to the cries of reason.' By morning more than sixty people were dead, but 'as soon as daylight beamed upon us, we were all much more calm'.

The survivors passed the following day in a state of shock. They managed to get through the next twenty-four hours unscathed, but on the fourth night, 'darkness brought with it a renewal of our disorder in our weakened state. We observed in ourselves that natural terror...greatly increased in the silence of the night.' In a repeat of the nightmare, some of the men became filled with 'afflicting thoughts' and 'horrid rage' and the slaughter recommenced. By the next morning, when the insanity had retreated, only thirty of the 147 who had boarded the raft were still alive.

Very frequently, castaways adrift on lifeboats or rafts will claim that, as soon as darkness descends, the swell becomes rougher, the wind picks up and the waves become higher. On the *Medusa* raft:

*When the night came, the sky was covered with thick clouds; the wind, which during the day had been rather high, now became furious, and agitated the sea, which, in an instant, grew very rough.*

There is no meteorological basis for seas that routinely become rougher at night. A more likely explanation is that the darkness amplifies the perception that the situation has become more dangerous. When daylight arrives, according to survivors, the conditions reverse: 'At day-break, the sea grew calm.'

One of the best ways to see the irrational horror of darkness is to look at survivors who had prolonged exposure to it. Of course, Corréard, Savigny and the other *Medusa* crew experienced only eleven hours of the 'Dreadful night!' at a time. In the polar regions, darkness goes for months.

Polar explorer William McKinlay, aboard the icebound *Karluk* in 1913, noted the disturbing effects of the long nights: 'Darkness added to our worries...The nights lengthened, and the sense of insecurity, aggravated by the storm, was intensified by the eeriness of the dark.'

At the opposite pole, on the *Belgica,* the darkness was to cause catastrophe. The ship carried a Belgian expedition, one of the first to explore Antarctica at the end of the nineteenth century. On board were Norwegian first mate Roald Amundsen, American Renaissance man Dr Frederick Cook (surgeon, anthropologist, writer, photographer and possible con-man), a Belgian captain, a decidedly mixed crew and the ship's cat, Nansen. In March 1898, the *Belgica* became hopelessly trapped in the ice, 'held by the increasing grip of the too affectionate pack'.

The *Belgica*'s crew went into the seventy days of darkness in relatively good health with a good stove to keep them warm and adequate provisions (although, not surprisingly, they were sick of eating their *fiskabolla:* canned Swedish fish balls). Within weeks there was a marked physical and mental decline. Their skin took on a greenish hue, their hair grew rapidly, the skin grew over their fingernails, their heart rates became alarmingly erratic and their appetites failed.

Mentally they became lethargic, isolated, apathetic, introspective and filled with despair. Dr Cook grew to loathe the 'soul-despairing darkness' and came to view it as their bitter enemy: 'the death-dealing darkness is doing its devilish work'. After just three weeks of the polar night one of the crew, Emile Danco, died. In the doctor's opinion, 'the prolonged darkness... sent him to a premature grave.' Unable to bury him, the men hacked a hole through the ice near the ship, tied weights on his feet and dropped Danco's corpse into the sea beneath.

Even the cat was having trouble. Previously Nansen had been friendly and playful, adored by all on the ship. The men drew enormous comfort from their pet, who could usually be found near the stove or sleeping on the bed of whichever crew member had been lavishing the most attention on him. As the polar night continued, Nansen became withdrawn and took to hiding in corners of the ship. His appetite diminished and he became aggressive—'the long darkness has made him turn him against us'. Desperate to revive the cat, the men caught a penguin to keep Nansen company, but even that didn't work. After a final few days of stupor when the doctor felt the cat's mind was wandering, Nansen died, to the immense grief of all. The cat had endured five weeks of darkness.

Within the following weeks, one sailor reached the verge of insanity, and a previously fit man was showing symptoms similar to those that had killed Danco. The other men were in the grip of a terrible depression, convinced that they would all perish. Desperately worried, Dr Cook instigated his 'baking treatment': he had the men strip and sit directly next to the fired-up stove for one or two hours daily. With an increased ration of fresh penguin meat and the gradual return of the sun, the men began to recover. They eventually freed the *Belgica* from the ice and the expedition continued.

The boys in the Robbers Cave experiment intuitively understood the power of darkness and chose to launch the most destructive raid at night. The fear generated by the night raid was enough to completely immobilise all but one of the Eagle tribe.

The description of the raid, complete with commando-style face painting, is an uncanny echo of Golding's scene in *Lord of the Flies* when, under the cover of darkness, Jack's tribe attack Ralph's encampment. The boys are beaten viciously, their shelter is smashed and Piggy's precious glasses are stolen. The scene is particularly frightening because it is so easy to relate to: everyone has been badly frightened by an unidentifiable noise in the dark. Nyctophobia is always there somewhere in our psyche, even if it's just in our memory, and once the brain has hit the neuro-chemical panic button, there is no rationalising our way out of it.

In 1884 Edwin Stevens, who survived the wreck of the *Mignonette,* summarised the effect of the darkness on those in the lifeboat: 'The nights were our worst time. They never seemed to end and we dreaded them very much.'

William Golding was one of the few adults who suffer from nyctophobia. For him, the darkness was 'full of the awful unknown and menace' and of nightmares, terror, loneliness and memories. Rational thoughts and plans are for daylight; primitive instincts lurk in the dark and as stranded communities deteriorate, other nightmares emerge to plague them.

# THE BEAST

*I don't believe in the beast of course. As Piggy said, life's scientific,
but we don't know, do we? Not certainly, I mean—*

MAURICE, *LORD OF THE FLIES*

**IN BALLANTYNE'S** *The Coral Island* the boys are frightened by
a mysterious noise in the night—a prolonged, hideous cry.
Peterkin and Ralph wonder if it may be a ghost, but Jack
confidently dispels their fears: 'I neither believe in ghosts nor
feel uneasy.' The ever-rational Jack feels they will discover the
source of the noise. Soon they find it was just penguins, 'So
then our dreadful yelling ghosts...have dwindled down to
penguins.' The boys have a good laugh at their fears.

The nineteenth century and the first half of the twentieth century saw a huge wave of scientific advancement—the
geography of the world was essentially known, Einstein discovered relativity, medical knowledge was galloping ahead, and
the secrets of the solar system were being uncovered at a great

speed. Nineteenth-century evolutionary theory had indicated humans were just sophisticated primates, and now biology and palaeoanthropology were confirming the suspicion. Science was marching on like an unstoppable force, sweeping away the primitive, frightening and irrational ghosts of the past. Humans could and would find an explanation for everything; it was just a matter of time. Golding referred to this mindset as 'Victorian', smug and ignorant.

Golding saw a more profound and disturbing vision of what it meant to be human; he would later describe it as 'a realist view of the Ballantyne situation'. When the tendrils of fear start to tear at the boys on Golding's island, there is no simplistic explanation followed by a hearty laugh. When the littluns begin to complain of frightening things in the dark, fear spreads like a disease. Strange noises are heard, inexplicable things are seen.

The 'beast', as Golding calls his monster, grows to haunt the boys with a paralysing terror. Reason is gone, some ill-defined torment in its place.

On the *Belgica*, stranded in the Antarctic, the men were plagued by strange, troublesome thoughts. Dr Cook, not immune himself, explained that in their dire predicament, 'man feels the force of the superstitions of past ages'. The crew were troubled by the human-like groaning of the ice shifting, which they could hear through the hull of the ship. Some thought it might be their dead companion Danco. Dr Cook wrote that the men were tormented by the vision of Danco, 'floating about in a standing position, with the weights to his feet, under the frozen surface and perhaps under the *Belgica*.'

The miners trapped below the Atacama Desert in October

2010 began to catch glimpses of apparitions sneaking around the dark corners of the collapsed mine. Sightings of these human-like figures were so common the men gave them a name—'*mineros chicos*'.

William McKinlay, trapped by ice deep in the Arctic, underwent a paranormal experience while sitting outside the *Karluk* one night: 'Then all at once I became aware of something new and strange, a consciousness of a "presence", a feeling that I was not alone.' Two months later, he experienced the same eerie sensation, but was again at a loss to explain it.

Not all survivors see this supernatural force as a manifestation of evil. In 1916, attempting to cross South Georgia and close to death, Ernest Shackleton and his two companions also felt the presence of the supernatural:

> *I know that during that long and racking march of thirty-six hours over the unnamed mountains and glaciers of South Georgia it seemed to me often that we were four, not three. I said nothing to my companions on the point, but afterwards Worsley said to me, 'Boss, I had a curious feeling on the march that there was another person with us.' Crean confessed to the same idea. One feels 'the dearth of human words, the roughness of mortal speech' in trying to describe things intangible, but a record of our journeys would be incomplete without a reference to a subject very near to our hearts.*

Shackleton, the epitome of a compassionate and caring leader, didn't feel the 'unseen presence' was malevolent. To him it was a guardian angel, there to offer comfort. This tendency for survivors to detect a presence has been named Third Man Syndrome after Shackleton's encounter. So many of the thirty-three Chilean miners felt the presence of God trapped down there with them that they started to call him the thirty-fourth miner.

Supernatural sightings also afflicted many of the *Medusa* survivors. One man on Charlotte Picard's boat, fearful of ghosts, became convinced the sea was on fire around them. Others on the raft saw visions in the sea: fires, phantom ships or vast harbours. While we would explain these as hallucinations, for the sufferers it was just another downward lurch in their inexorable slide.

Perhaps the most frightening episode was described by John Byron after the survivors' long isolation following the wreck of the *Wager* off Patagonia. Byron had noticed the men were disturbed by fears of ghosts and the supernatural, a state 'much heightened by the melancholy condition they were reduced to'. He had considered this a problem confined to the common seamen until a night in December 1741:

> One night we were alarmed with a strange cry, which resembled that of a man drowning. Many of us ran out of our huts towards the place from whence the noise proceeded, which was not far off shore, where we could perceive, but not distinctly, (for it was then moonlight), an appearance like that of a man swimming half out of water. The noise that this creature uttered was so unlike that of any animal they had heard before, that it made a great impression upon the men; and they frequently recalled this apparition at the time of their distresses.

The men agreed the spectre had been sent as a punishment for their failure to bury the corpse of a crewman 'stabbed in several places and shockingly mangled' months before on the aptly named Mount Misery. As soon as they returned to their old camp, the men immediately hiked up to find the corpse and bury it.

Some three hundred years later, Chilean miner Samuel Avalos felt the same fear. 'The Devil was there—we weren't alone. There was an evil presence. I felt that evil presence myself.' In an isolated section of the mine, the group's unofficial leader, Mario Sepúlveda, suddenly felt another presence in the rock nearby: 'I knew it was not God, but that it was the Devil. All the hair on my body stood up.' Sepúlveda shouted at the Devil, reminding him that he too had been a son of God, and the manifestation departed.

In *Lord of the Flies*, Golding describes belief in the existence of the beast as a tipping point: 'The world, that understandable and lawful world, was slipping away.'

In 1959, at a BBC radio interview, Golding explained the appearance of the beast and its meaning:

*It's the things that have crawled out of their own bones and their own veins, they don't know whether it's a beast from the sky, or where it's coming, but there's something terrible about it as one of the conditions of existence.*

Golding's boys tried to appease the beast with violence and sacrifice. In reality, too, violence—either self-inflicted or against another—seemed an easy and inevitable choice.

# BLOODSHED IN VINLAND

**LOCATION:** L'Anse aux Meadows, Newfoundland, Canada
**NATIONALITY:** Viking
**DATE:** Approximately 1010 AD
**FATALITY RATE:** 45%
**DURATION:** Approximately nine months

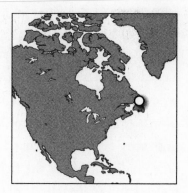

History is punctuated with examples of failed settlements and micro-colonies that imploded with fatal consequences. Early records of such events are rare, but people in ancient and mediaeval times often found themselves in isolated pockets clinging to survival, and must have endured privations and bloodlust on a fairly regular basis.

The Vikings were prime candidates for these disasters for a variety of reasons. Their inheritance laws encouraged the younger sons to make their own way in the world, and many struck out to settle virgin lands, a practice known as *landnam* (land-taking).

Occasionally the heavy hand of the law added to this

pressure to relocate. The family of Eirik the Red was a good case in point. Eirik's father, Thorvald, was responsible for a number of murders in his native Norway and was driven into exile. Following the family's move to Iceland, Eirik himself was twice forced to move on after killing his neighbours. The final murder, over another neighbour's failure to return a borrowed item, resulted in Eirik's family leaving Iceland and heading for Greenland.

The Norse had superb sailing craft and nautical skills, but lacked sophisticated navigation, so they were frequently blown off course and lost. Although some perished in the treacherous North Atlantic, others would sail their well-provisioned boats until they eventually struck land. Consequently the Vikings can take credit for being the first Europeans to sail to Greenland, Iceland and eventually Vinland, on the North American continent. A thousand years later we have a detailed record, thanks to the rich and detailed Norse Sagas. Although there remain some lingering doubts about the veracity of the Sagas, recent archaeological evidence lends weight to the case for treating them as an historical record.

The *Greenlander Saga*, dating from about 1010 AD, describes the voyage to Vinland of Freydis, the illegitimate daughter of Eirik the Red, and her Icelandic companions, Helgi and Finnbogi.

Vinland, now assumed to be Newfoundland, was the location of a tiny Norse colony at a site referred to as Leif's Camp by the Norse (now known as L'Anse aux Meadows). Various members of Eirik's family sailed across from Greenland for a season, harvested wood and 'grapes' (the mysterious 'vin' of Vinland may actually have been native berries) and traded furs from the indigenous population, whom they unflatteringly referred to as Skraelings, a derogatory term meaning 'scruffy' that covered both Inuit and indigenous tribes.

Leif, Freydis's brother, had already built a house on the coast of Vinland. Excavation at L'Anse aux Meadows in the 1960s revealed the remains of a large Norse longhouse, twenty-nine metres by fifteen metres with six rooms, quite possibly the house in question. Leif, however, had returned to Greenland with tales of the rich lands and timber. His half-sister Freydis, who had inherited her father's ambition and infamous, violent temper, had already spent one season at the site. She had earned a reputation for herself during a fight with the Skraelings (described in *The Saga of Eirik the Red*) and it is worth a brief look for the insight it provides into Freydis's extreme personality.

Relations between the Norse and the indigenous tribes in Vinland were patchy at best. The locals appeared sporadically to trade furs for milk and strips of bright red cloth. As the supply ran out, the strips of cloth got thinner and thinner, until they were barely as wide as a finger. One day, during a tense trading session, the local traders were frightened by the loud bellowing of a bull and fled.

Three weeks later the Skraelings returned in force and unexpectedly attacked, armed with *warrslings*. These weapons, unfamiliar to the Vikings, were harmless missiles fired from poles which hit the ground 'with a hideous noise'. This time it was the Vikings who got spooked and they fled into the woods, chased by the tribesmen.

Freydis emerged from the longhouse to witness the unedifying sight of well-armed Norsemen running away to hide.

Filled with scorn, she taunted the men for fleeing from such 'worthless creatures who looked as easy to kill as sheep', then declared she needed a weapon to deal with the threat herself.

Freydis ran into the woods (somewhat slowly because she was pregnant, the Saga notes casually) and came upon the corpse of Thorbrand lying on the path, his head crushed by a large rock. She grabbed his sword, and turned to face the attackers. As they rushed down the path towards her, Freydis exposed her upper body and began to slap her breasts with the flat of Thorbrand's sword.

This astonishing sight proved too much for the attackers, who turned tail and fled. The Vikings then emerged from the woods, 'came up to her and praised her zeal'. Following this encounter, the Norse decided to return to Greenland; even though the land was rich 'there would always be war and terror overhanging them' from the indigenous population. On the way, they happened upon five sleeping locals, whom they killed.

Some years later, Freydis and her husband, Thorvard, decided that despite the danger there was money to be made in Vinland. Freydis visited two Icelandic brothers, Helgi and Finnbogi, and talked them into a new expedition to Vinland. The plan was that they take a ship each, and restrict the number of crew to thirty 'fighting men' per ship, plus women. After a winter in Vinland, they would return home to Greenland laden with wood and furs and split the profits.

The brothers agreed to Freydis's proposition, upon which she went to her brother Leif and asked if she could stay in his house over the winter. Leif agreed to let her use his buildings, but emphasised that they still belonged to him. The two ships were loaded with stores and set sail. Freydis must have anticipated trouble of some kind because she hid five extra men on her ship. Although they had agreed to travel together, the brothers and their Icelandic crew sailed faster and reached Vinland first.

On arrival, Helgi and Finnbogi unpacked their boat and carried their stores up to the main house. It was common for large groups to share the living area of the longhouses, keeping them warmer through the freezing winters. When Freydis disembarked, she discovered the Icelanders already lodged in the longhouse. She demanded to know what they were doing. The brothers replied that they understood Leif had let the house to all of them to share. 'To me Leif lent the house,' she replied tartly, 'and not to you.' Freydis threw them out.

This petty act put the brothers' group at a serious disadvantage. Not only was there the danger of a surprise attack by the Skraelings but winter was fast approaching. Autumn typically sees Newfoundland lashed by Atlantic storms, destructive winds, freezing rain and heavy fog. The lack of immediate shelter put the brothers' party in a perilous position, which they needed to rectify as fast as possible.

Helgi and Finnbogi, now aware that they were outnumbered, declared that in 'malice' Freydis far exceeded them, and stormed off with their crew, taking their supplies with them. Angry at Freydis's duplicity and the unspoken threat of being outnumbered, the brothers moved well away from the small settlement and set about building a longhouse big enough for their party of thirty-seven (the brothers, their men and five women).

A traditional Viking longhouse was substantial and took considerable time to build. The Icelanders had to fell trees and dress the timber for the large wooden frame. After this was constructed, the walls and roof had to be covered with a thick layer of sod. Stone-lined fire pits were built for cooking and warmth. The floor was packed earth. In addition, the brothers' group needed to cut enough firewood to keep their longhouse warm through the winter. Traditionally the fires burned day and night, consuming a lot of wood. In all likelihood, they also had to build fenced areas for their livestock.

Meanwhile, Freydis and her party, ensconced in Leif's house, set about felling and preparing the nearby timber for export back to Greenland. The two groups, trapped together by the harsh winter with no help or hope of external mediation, needed to address their bad relationship.

The Icelanders took the first steps towards reconciliation. The brothers approached Freydis and proposed the groups should 'set up games and have some amusement'. At the time, popular Viking games included wrestling (both men's and women's) and Knattleikr, a team ball game played on ice. Elsewhere in the Sagas, descriptions of the ball game outline a tough, physical game played with sticks that could last all day. Body contact and insults were par for the course, and the aggressive competiveness could descend into violence and injuries: it must have been a bit like modern ice hockey, only without the padding. Spectators would use the games to judge which players were physically the strongest—crucial information in Norse society.

Given the pre-existing bad feelings and mutual suspicion, it's hardly surprising the games ended badly. The Saga explains that, rather than healing the rift, the games finished in 'evil reports and discord'. The attempt to reconcile the two factions was abandoned and all communication was cut off.

There was another problem: they were trapped. The threat of hostile locals and the weather meant they couldn't move elsewhere in Vinland. Nor could they simply pack up and sail home at that time of year. The hostility continued throughout winter, no doubt with each side growing more apprehensive as time wore on. The vexing question of surrendering half the trading profits to the other party must have been running through the minds of both groups.

Then early one morning, Freydis took matters into her own hands. She got up, put on her husband's cloak and walked to the brothers' longhouse. Finding the door open, Freydis boldly walked in, waking Finnbogi up in the process. When Finnbogi asked what she was doing, she calmly asked him to come outside and talk to her privately. Finnbogi did as requested. When Freydis asked how Finnbogi thought things had been going, he answered, 'I think the land has much to offer, but I don't like the ill-feeling between us'. He added that it was difficult to understand how it had gone so wrong. Freydis agreed, then she surprised him by saying that she wanted to leave Vinland, and 'I want to exchange ships with the two of you, as you have a larger ship.'

According to Freydis, Finnbogi readily agreed to this outrageous demand. Perhaps he was glad at the prospect of seeing the back of them, or perhaps Freydis fabricated the entire conversation. Clearly she was plotting something more sinister.

Returning to her longhouse, Freydis woke up her husband, Thorvard. He asked why her feet were wet and Freydis told him that she had visited the brothers to discuss buying their boat, but they had 'beat me and used me shamefully'. Freydis demanded Thorvard seek revenge for her dishonour, and threatened to leave him if he refused. Thorvard woke and armed his men and marched rapidly to the brothers' camp.

Bursting in, they caught the men still sleeping. Helgi, Finnbogi and all thirty men were seized, bound and marched out. Freydis, waiting outside, had each man killed as he walked out of the longhouse. Finally, only the five women were left cowering inside. Freydis demanded that they, too, be killed, but Thorvard and his men refused. Despite the blood already on their hands, killing Norse women was unacceptable.

Exasperated by their refusal, Freydis demanded an axe, entered the longhouse and hacked up the five women, only stopping when she was certain all were dead. The group left the scene of the massacre and returned to their camp, Freydis appearing very pleased with her morning's work.

She lined the men up and demanded their silence, threatening to kill anyone who spoke of the murders after they returned to Greenland. If anyone asked of the Icelandic brothers' whereabouts, Freydis ordered, her men were to say that the brothers' party had decided to stay in Vinland.

By early spring, Freydis had the brothers' larger boat stacked up with as much as it could carry, and the whole group sailed back to Greenland. At first, all went well. Adopting a kind of carrot-and-stick policy towards her men, Freydis not only threatened them, but also bought their silence with rich gifts.

However, whispers of the murders began to leak out, and eventually reached Leif. Fearing the worst, Leif summoned three of Freydis's men and had them tortured. All three told exactly the same story. Although convinced, Leif still couldn't bring himself to have his sister punished. Instead, he put a curse on their future prosperity, and from that time on Freydis and her husband were publicly loathed, and eventually banished from Greenland.

Of course it is possible to dismiss the entire episode as folklore, but the archaeological discoveries from L'Anse aux Meadows have revealed some tantalising supporting evidence. The *Greenlander Saga* has been dated at about 1010 AD. A piece of worked lumber found at the site was radiocarbon-dated to AD 1000 (+/−10 years). The size of the architectural remains and various Norse artefacts discovered at the site, such as a bronze cloak pin, a spindle whorl and stone fire-lighting kits, indicated a small settlement (seventy to a hundred) of mainly men, but also some women.

A scientific analysis of the jasper fire-starting stones by geochemical fingerprint identified that four of them came from Greenland, and five from Iceland, suggesting a mixed group of inhabitants from Iceland and Greenland. Other evidence pointed to a short-lived settlement. A considerable amount of the wood found in a bog at L'Anse aux Meadows was the discarded by-products of timber, cut with metal tools, proof that extensive woodwork had indeed occurred on the site.

There is also a lake about one kilometre inland from the primary archaeological remains at the shore, which fits perfectly with the account.

The sorry end of the Vinland settlement established a pattern—breakdown to bloodlust—that has been repeated all too often among small groups stranded in difficult circumstances on distant shores. Worse was to come.

# SUICIDE

*It wasn't really committing suicide. It was to not continue suffering.*
CHILEAU MINER VICTOR ZAMORA, 2010

**THE INITIAL REACTION** of almost everyone in a disaster is an overwhelming urge to survive. When people seek to kill themselves, it is generally a sign that things have become completely desperate, that any makeshift community has collapsed and that suicide is preferable to continuing survival.

Occasionally, the suicides begin very quickly: four of those cast adrift on the *Medusa* raft attempted suicide within the first twenty-four hours; three were successful, and one was prevented by Henri Savigny. Over the next few miserable days there were about twenty suicides, most at night.

It is possible to see suicide not just as an escape from miserable circumstances, but also as a way an individual can wrest back some control in situations where he or she has lost all other autonomy.

Sometimes it can be a fleeting impulse. Captain James Riley, captured by Bedouins and enslaved in the Sahara after the loss of his ship, the *Commerce*, was caught in such a moment in 1815. Starving, dehydrated, naked and shoeless, he was severely blistered from sunburn and had lost the skin off his thighs by being forced to ride a camel bareback. The days were scorching, the nights freezing, and he was treated appallingly by his captors. All that he saw before him was a short, wretched life in slavery.

> *It was here that my fortitude and philosophy failed to support me...I would have put an immediate end to my existence, but had neither knife nor any weapon with which to perform the deed. I searched for a stone, intending if I could find a loose one sufficiently large, to knock out my own brains with it; but searched in vain.*

Failing to find a rock in the desert sands, Riley decided to put his trust 'in Providence' instead. When his suicidal urge passed, Riley, like many others in similarly desperate situations, described feeling more at peace, less despairing and more resolved to face what was to come. The act of making the decision to stay alive seems to empower and sustain them, at least in the short term. Perhaps the ability to make any kind of choice counts as control when you have nothing.

The most destructive form of suicide is when the entire group reaches a collective conclusion that it is their only option. In Numantia, at the end of the long siege in 133 BC, almost the entire population inside the walled city decided to commit mass suicide by poison or fire rather than surrender to the Romans. Once the three days of wholesale killing had finished, a few survivors emerged. The Romans were horrified by their shocking condition:

> *Their bodies were foul, their hair and nails long, and they were smeared with dirt. They smelt most horribly, and the clothes they wore were likewise squalid and emitted an equally foul odour.*

Appian, who based his account on Polybius's eyewitness record, wondered what forces had reduced these noble and courageous people, who had stood equal to the Romans, to this state. The emaciated survivors had a look in their eyes that terrified the seasoned Roman soldiers, 'an expression of anger, grief [and] toil'.

Scipio seized the survivors to parade in his triumph back in Rome and completely razed what was left of the city. Numantia, once the scourge of Rome, was obliterated.

A similar mass suicide took place more than two thousand years later in a closed community in the jungle of Guyana. Jonestown, as the isolated encampment in the jungle was known, was a quasi-religious community built by the apparently normal, well-meaning, educated American followers of the Peoples Temple cult. Ironically, the Peoples Temple had started its life in the late 1950s as an organisation devoted to social justice and racial equality, but its ideology was a curious amalgam of Pentecostal religion, socialism, faith healing and paranoia. Eventually it degenerated into a totalitarian, brutal personality cult.

Jim Jones, a messianic pretender and founder of the Peoples

Temple, had begun sending his followers to develop a large jungle property deep in Guyana. Things in the United States had become too uncomfortable for the cult following media articles outlining fraud, abuse and violence, so in July and August 1977, over five hundred members moved to the jungle compound. Once there, it became almost impossible for the followers to leave: talk of returning to America was considered 'blasphemy' and a punishable offence.

Once the community was isolated, Jones, mentally unstable and given to serious drug abuse, became increasingly controlling and manipulative. Families were split up, violence increased and people were set to spying on and denouncing each other. With his paranoia escalating, Jones built up a cache of weapons and a massive supply of pharmaceuticals. The information flow in and out of the compound was stifled and guards armed with guns and crossbows patrolled the perimeter. It was almost impossible to leave.

One of the more sinister activities at the compound was the so-called 'White Nights', when Jones would call his followers, who now numbered more than nine hundred, to all-night meetings. Initially the White Nights were elaborate rehearsals for defending the compound if hostile forces arrived to wipe them out. During these twice-monthly sessions the concept of fighting to the death was reinforced, but one night in February 1978, the plan changed abruptly as the residents were told to drink from vats of fruit juice that Jones told them were poisoned. People were allowed to raise objections but those who did were sent to drink first. When someone enquired what would happen to the babies in the nursery, 'Jim said they had already been taken care of.'

Standing in the long queue to reach the vat, sixty-three-year-old teacher Edith Roller realised she didn't want to die:

> However it was a new sensation, and in a certain and peculiar way, I was enjoying it, just the experience. Everything was very vivid. I was fonder of those around me than I had ever been. It was remarkable how disciplined and obedient they were. The look in their eyes showed they knew the importance of what they were doing. I especially noticed the children, who were very quiet.

To enhance the deception, some of the residents had been secretly instructed to collapse. Eventually Jones announced it wasn't poison, but it might be in the future. He was testing the limits of his control over the group, which he explained in statements such as: 'All the power you said God had, I have.' His followers were disturbingly easy to manipulate: they were deprived of adequate food or sleep, and had been taught the harsh penalty for questioning his orders.

Back in the US, increasingly alarmed relatives of the cult members contacted a Californian Congressman named Leo Ryan. In late 1978 Ryan announced an investigation and flew down to Guyana with a small team, including a few of the relatives. What they witnessed during their short time in Jonestown in November 1978 was a carefully scripted performance by the cult: the people declared publicly all was well, and Ryan appeared satisfied, until notes were surreptitiously passed indicating that individuals were being held against their will.

As the horrible truth began to ooze to the surface, Jones realised his elaborate charade had failed. With the

Congressman's party preparing to leave from the nearest airstrip, Jones's henchmen attacked, killing five (including Ryan) and wounding nine. Simultaneously, back at the compound, Jones announced to his followers that the US Government would come down and wipe them out as punishment: 'They'll torture some of our children...they'll torture our seniors. We cannot have this.'

With the entire community assembled in the central pavilion, Jones issued a stark command: 'If we can't live in peace, then let's die in peace.' Jones's control was so complete that almost no one raised any objections; they lined up calmly and drank from vats laced with tranquillisers and cyanide. Parents squirted poison down their children's throats, in what Jones declared was an act of 'revolutionary suicide protesting the conditions of an inhumane world'. The entire final meeting and suicide were recorded (one of Jones's many macabre habits). At the end of the day, 909 people—including hundreds of children—lay dead, scattered facedown around the compound, a huge carpet of corpses.

It has been called the largest mass-suicide in modern history. Although the recordings show only one follower publicly objecting to the impending poisoning, a few who managed to escape into the jungle have argued that Jonestown was a massacre, not suicide. Certainly for the children it wasn't a voluntary act. Jonestown survivors point to Jones's absolute control, the elaborate planning, the White Nights and the stockpiling of cyanide. As one of the survivors, Tim Carter, argued, 'We were just fucking slaughtered.'

# ABUSE AND VIOLENCE

*He took a step, and able at last to hit someone, stuck his*
*fist into Piggy's stomach. Piggy sat down with a grunt.*
*Jack stood over him. His voice was vicious with humiliation.*
*'You would, would you? Fatty!'*

LORD OF THE FLIES

**ABUSE IN A** closed community often starts out in a verbal form.

At the Robbers Cave site, the boys quickly began to throw insults: *communist, sissies, dirty bums, ladies, cheats* and worse were used (the researchers censored the results, excluding the rudest ones, presumably in deference to 1950s prudishness).

When already desperate situations deteriorate, there is often a marked rise in threats—threats of corporal punishment, threats of future court martial, threats of beatings, threats to banish or abandon people and death threats.

These may be from individual to individual or authorised by the group's leader. When John Franklin's men threatened to abandon his first expedition in 1820, he informed them he would deal with the next troublemaker by (in surveyor

George Back's words) 'blowing his brains out'.

Muzafer Sherif and his wife eventually conducted three Boys vs. Boys group experiments along the same lines as the Robbers Cave Experiment. By the end of the last experiment, the researchers realised that, once the two groups moved into a state of conflict, leaders would often threaten low-status members of *their own group* if they felt the individual was underperforming. If a leader failed to be aggressive enough during conflict, their status crashed. In contrast, violence between the groups (verbal or physical) was often instigated by the low-status members as a way of improving their standing within the group.

In the no-man's-land between verbal and physical violence lay smashing and destroying objects. Sherif's boys smashed windows, tore up posters, destroyed clothing, burned group banners and smashed dishes. Objects were thrown: garbage, cutlery, crockery and food. Shipwrecked sailors are often described pointlessly smashing up anything they come across, as happened aboard the *Wager*: 'They fell to beating every thing to pieces that fell in their way.'

The next step is violence directed at people, and often insignificant things can provoke conflict. The trapped Chilean miners fought over sheets of cardboard. Outbreaks of shouting and shoving were commonplace at the *Wager* and Greely campsites, in Biosphere 2, and among the *Karluk* survivors on Wrangel Island and the *Invercauld* group on Auckland Island. Even at the Andes plane crash site in 1972, tempers became frayed, leading at times to shouting and shoving.

Spitting at people is also common. Jane Poynter, of Biosphere 2, recalled two incidents of spitting by fellow residents in one day: 'I watched as she [Gaie] collected a big wad of saliva in her mouth and spat in my face. She turned and walked away without a word.'

Left unchecked, this kind of conflict can quickly degenerate into physical attacks, ranging from slaps in the face to punches in the stomach or head. Violence appeared among the Robbers Cave boys, the survivors on the *Medusa* raft and the *Invercauld*. Within the Greely and the *Wager* camps, violence became almost commonplace, but tapered off as severe starvation set in and the men became too weak to fight. In Vinland, the games designed to bring the factions together had to be cancelled when they descended into violence.

The infamous bloodshed among the *Batavia* survivors off Western Australia in 1629 was an exception, because it was not the result of accumulated tension and starvation, but was instead planned almost from the start by the chief villain, Jeronimus Cornelisz, and his gang of henchmen. After the violence had commenced, no one among the large group on Batavia's Graveyard island tried to resist—probably because they didn't want to attract the ire of Cornelisz. Their passivity fuelled further weeks of murder.

The passivity of the group in Jonestown seems to have been a factor in the escalation of violence there too. In the jungle of Guyana, we have an accurate snapshot of brutality and abuse unleashed, thanks to extensive tape recording and accounts from defectors. Jones employed an arsenal of abuse, frequently involving public humiliation. Women were made to strip naked in front of the group assemblies and were then criticised by the crowd. On 'family nights' children and adults were publicly spanked with a paddle, to the point where these events were really beatings. Audience participation was encouraged. Organised boxing matches between the children led to violent adult bouts. People were beaten for a range of offences. One follower who managed to escape prior to the carnage, Deborah Layton, described daily life at the compound:

> Keep your head down and don't talk unless it's absolutely necessary. For each person showing weakness by speaking of his or her fears, another would become more trusted for reporting it. There were no enduring friendships—everyone soon learned that it was too dangerous to run the risk of confrontation or public beating.

Others were punished by having a snake draped around their neck, or by being locked in a pitch-black packing case. Teacher Edith Roller described how her students were taken to listen to the terrified howls of an eight-year-old girl locked in the 'isolation facility' crying out for water. Other children were left in overnight, and a twenty-three-year-old was left in the box for a week.

Children deemed to have transgressed were lowered into the well at night, a ritual described to them as 'meeting the tiger'. Unbeknownst to them, men were hiding inside to grab at them or make frightening animal noises. The well was conveniently located near Jones's cabin so he could hear the screams. To avoid being lowered twice it was necessary for the children to scream for 'Father's' (Jones's) forgiveness with suitable contrition.

Serious sleep deprivation, forced labour, the stripping of personal property, control over followers' sex lives, and the separation of families all took a terrible toll. Recalcitrant followers were heavily sedated and confined for long periods to a sick tent. To enforce discipline, Jones had a group of roaming spies and a gang of enforcers, who were feared for their violence and cruelty. The range of punishments seemed endless: a child was forced to eat his own vomit, people were poisoned with pieces of cake, heads were shaved, men were forced to write public letters saying how they had enjoyed being sexually abused by Jones, or how they had abused their own children.

The extent of the abuse is revealed by a tape-recorded dressing down of Tom Partak, a depressed thirty-two-year-old Vietnam veteran who had been refused permission to leave. Jones stood him up in front of the congregation, simultaneously abusing and striking him:

> *You miserable, goddamn person…You miserable goddamn, self-centred, son-of-a-bitch. I'm going to give you more and more. You're going to stay awake twenty-four hours. You're going to be crazy, goddamn you!*

The transgression that had provoked this extreme vitriol was a suicide attempt by Partak. Jones then invited members of the crowd to continue the physical and verbal abuse. Eventually, Jones made Partak apologise and then justified the process as 'a rage of love'.

Jones undoubtedly derived pleasure from watching and hearing people suffer. He tried to convince others that the victims of his sexual abuse had been pleading for it, and that he had derived no pleasure from it. Jones also stated that all the men in the compound, with the exception of himself, were actually gay and wanted to have sex with him.

The level of violence and abuse within the cult increased

once the followers became isolated in the jungle. Jones's spiralling drug use increased his paranoia, which in turn fuelled the abuse.

Within a group, the harshest punishments are often reserved for the person perceived as a traitor. In the Robbers Cave groups, the boys identified as 'sell-outs' or 'quitters' were subjected to verbal abuse and physical violence for misdemeanours such as not trying hard enough during the games, or failing to pull their weight during a punch-up. This punishment was inflicted by members of their own group.

Other survivor groups have punished people by abandoning or stranding them. When the dysfunctional *Wager* group decided to punish a thief, he was first whipped severely and then, in freezing weather, 'put alone upon a barren island, which afforded not the least shelter'. When they rowed out two days later, 'we found him stiff and dead'.

With the notable exceptions of the *Batavia* and Jonestown, sexual abuse is not mentioned in survival situations as frequently as might be expected. Of course, many of the episodes we examine involved only men; but just as importantly, starvation very rapidly extinguishes sex drive.

However, where starvation is not a big issue for the perpetrators, as with the *Batavia* wreck and Jonestown, the disappearance of social constraints can be accompanied by rape or sexual subjugation in which it certainly doesn't pay to be female—or, occasionally, a weaker male.

Rape became a way of life for the *Batavia* mutineers off the coast of Western Australia: all the youthful female survivors were forced into sexual slavery. The victims had no choice but to submit, because this offered their only chance of survival.

Judick Bastiaensz, the oldest daughter of the *Batavia*'s *predikant* (pastor), agreed to become the 'concubine' of one of the chief mutineers: she was the only one of the *predikant*'s seven children to make it off the island alive. Creesje Jans, a great beauty of high social standing, was forced to become Cornelisz's personal sex slave. While most of the other women, particularly the old or pregnant, were killed, seven women were kept alive to face daily rape by the mutineers.

In addition to the appalling suffering of the victims, the effect of this bloated and institutionalised violence was to desensitise the entire community, dividing the group into perpetrators and potential targets. Moreover, as the group turned on themselves, individual members were plagued by a very real dread: who would be next?

# THE LAST RESORT

*No person can tell what he will do when driven by hunger.*
ALEXANDER PEARCE, 1824

**IN STRANDED COMMUNITIES,** social mores and customs erode as
the group unravels. Attitudes to sickness, death and corpses
undergo a rapid transformation.

Two short journal entries from Adolphus Greely's Arctic
journal say a great deal more than he intended:

> *January 3rd (1884)—A brilliant aurora from 3.30 to 5 P.M.
> today. Brainard wounded a fox but he escaped. Such incidents
> always depress a man. Dr. Pavy cut off one of Elison's fingers.*

> *May 24th—The tent is much more comfortable. The tempera-
> ture reached 39° [3.9 degrees Celsius] inside it this morning.
> Whistler unconscious this morning and died about noon.*

The group had become complacent about, almost accepting of, death. The corpses of their companions were regarded almost like rubbish, frequently left lying around— perhaps dragged a few feet away—and rarely mourned.

Such desensitisation to corpses creates the problem of starving men in close proximity to fresh meat. Robert Holding recalled the aftermath of the fight between Harvey and Fritz at the *Invercauld* camp:

> *In the morning I found Fritz laying there quite cold and dead...We did what we could for him by taking him under a tree and covering him with boughs. Two or three days after this...I found Harvey had been eating some of Fritz.*

For some of the groups, 'the last resort' seems almost a logical step. John Byron recorded that the *Wager* survivors had been catching and eating the vultures that had been gathering to feed on the corpses washed up on the beach. From there it wasn't a great step for the survivors to start eating the corpses themselves, and some did.

Captain Riley, marching across the Sahara after the wreck of the *Commerce,* faced a slightly different problem:

> *Hunger, that had preyed upon my companions to such a degree as to cause them to bite off the flesh from their arms...I was forced in one instance to tie the arms of one of my men behind him, in order to prevent him gnawing his own flesh.*

Advanced starvation produces a craving for protein. No one writes of wanting corn or rice—they want meat. This was Nando Parrado's epiphany in the plane wreckage in the Andes:

*My gaze fell upon the slowly healing leg wound of a boy lying near me. The centre of the wound was moist and raw, and there was a crust of dried blood at the edges. I could not stop looking at that crust, and as I smelled the faint blood-scent in the air, I felt my appetite rising.*

He caught several others stealing glances at the wound. Parrado suddenly realised they were surrounded by food. And the plane crash survivors' situation *was* dire: freezing conditions, dead and dying people and no rescue in sight. There was no food: just a few scraps in their pockets, some make-up and toothpaste (soon consumed) in the wreckage; no animals, vegetation, birds or even insects in the surrounding landscape. After Parrado's realisation that the frozen corpses scattered around the wreckage might be a larder, he quietly discussed the possibility of eating them with some of the others.

Eventually an open discussion began. Medical, theological and just plain practical issues were debated. Parrado's argument was particularly strong: 'If the bodies of our friends can help us to survive, then they haven't died for nothing.' Others compared it to the Eucharist—since after all this was a group of Catholics—and claimed God had provided the food in order that they survive. Then, having found the necessary moral justification, some of them began, tentatively, to cut strips of flesh off the corpses of their companions.

Cannibalism is the last taboo. Naturally, groups often lie about it afterwards, but sometimes it takes only a simple timeline of deaths to reveals the truth.

At the Greely camp on Cape Sabine in 1884, the entire

expedition was dying; it was just a matter of how long it would take.

On April 5 and 6, Sergeant David Linn and the Inuit Thorlip Christiansen died of starvation.

On April 9, George Rice died, exposure and starvation. Lieutenant James Lockwood also died of starvation.

On April 12, Sergeant Winfield Jewell died of starvation.

The next death wasn't until a month later. Evidently, something had changed.

When the expedition was finally rescued in June 1884 by Commander W. S. Schley, Greely tried to dissuade him from exhuming the bodies from their shallow graves (in some cases, hands and feet protruded from the thin soil), claiming they ought to remain in the ground 'consecrated' by their greatest achievements. Schley disagreed, feeling the families would want the bodies back. At first nothing looked amiss, until Schley realised the flesh had been removed from under the clothes of six men.

When confronted with the grim facts Greely at first denied them, then claimed the flesh had been used for bait to catch tiny shrimp called sea fleas (*Onisimus edwardsi*).

An analysis in 2001 by Professor Jan Marcin Weslawski and Dr Joanna Legezynska revealed that if the expedition had lived just on their recorded diet of rations, sea fleas and occasional game, they would have sustained a deficit of two million kilocalories between them, which would have resulted in the loss of the entire group. In order to maintain minimal energy requirements under the conditions, the men must have consumed at least 240 kilograms of human flesh.

As it turned out, the first corpse to have been stripped was Jewell's. The next day, Greely increased the meat ration to one pound of meat each. Following Jewell's death, the next five to die were eaten. The skeletal remains of the first six corpses eaten were then buried, but the next four men to die had their remains dumped into an ice crack. They were never recovered. At least ten expedition members seem to have been eaten. (Curiously, once the cannibalism had commenced, only one of the dead—Edward Israel, who died on May 27—was not eaten. The reason, apparently, was that he was Jewish.)

When the news broke in the American press, Greely's reputation was battered, but other explorers have managed to pull the wool over the world's eyes fairly successfully. Franklin's first expedition to northern Canada made him famous, but there were some strange anomalies.

The expedition swung wildly between farce and tragedy. Poorly planned and provisioned, the group wandered about the treacherous Northwest Territories, lost and desperate for food. Two of the explorers almost got into a duel over the affections of a sixteen-year-old Indian girl named Greenstockings. This was averted by the timely removal of the charge from the men's pistols, but Greenstockings went on to bear a child to one of the men.

Starvation, exhaustion, exposure, mutiny and in-fighting took their toll. People were abandoned and left to die; the group split innumerable times. The struggle proved too much for three of the explorers—Robert Hood, John Hepburn and Dr John Richardson—and their guide Michel. With Hood near death, the four decided that they couldn't go on and made a camp in the snow, with no food.

According to the account written by Dr Richardson, Michel (the strongest of the four), disappeared for a considerable time and turned up with a package of 'wolf meat', which the four devoured. Suspicions mounted over the origins of the meat (it was probably from another member of the expedition who had fallen elsewhere). Michel, who was behaving erratically, allegedly shot Hood when the other two were out of the campsite. Several days later, Richardson killed Michel 'by shooting him through the head'—essentially an execution.

After that, Richardson and Hepburn claimed that they walked through deep snow for eight days to find Franklin's camp having eaten nothing but a few partridges, part of a buffalo-skin jacket, the putrid marrow from an old deer spine and *tripe de roche*.

Franklin held *tripe de roche* in high esteem as a food source; in fact, it was lichen. Unsurprisingly, modern research has shown the human stomach does not contain the enzymes necessary to digest lichen—at best it will simply pass through, at worst it will cause severe stomach cramps and diarrhoea. Obviously, Richardson and Hepburn had been consuming something else that they did not want on the official record.

One plausible explanation is that when Hood died, the other three ate him. When that source of meat ran out, the two explorers killed Michel, dismembering his body to serve as rations on their trek back to Franklin's camp.

Winston Churchill said, 'History will be kind to me, for I intend to write it.' In much the same way, Richardson's account became fact when Franklin added it to his bestseller. Calls from William Wentzel, the expedition interpreter, for Richardson to stand trial were quietly suppressed. There was no official inquiry. Despite the deaths of more than half of his party, Franklin got a promotion and became a national hero. His glittering fame gave him a platform for organising and staging his tragic final expedition twenty-three years later.

If a group overcomes their squeamishness over the consumption of human flesh, the first step will be tiny strips of muscle from the arms, legs or buttocks. Frequently these are dried in the sun (on the *Medusa* raft, strips were suspended from ropes), air-dried (they were laid out on the fuselage of the plane in the Andes) or, if possible, cooked. Anything that will disguise their origins.

Once the psychological barrier has been breached, reservations disappear rapidly. The Andes survivors went from tiny strips of muscle to 'kidneys, and hearts…lungs, parts of the hands and feet, and even the blood clots that form in the large blood vessels of the heart'. They harvested calcium by meticulously shaving the bones to powder using a piece of glass. The final step was hacking open the skulls to consume the brains. These could be eaten only if they hadn't turned putrid. Other body parts were still edible when rotten and, the survivors said, tasted like cheese when cooked.

Lacking in utensils, they used the upper part of the skulls to make four bowls, and fashioned spoons from the bones. They became so accepting of their new food source that they left the uneaten remains lying in piles around the fuselage. The same observation was made at the Franklin expedition campsites on King William Island in the Arctic Circle.

Sir John Franklin's 'Lost Expedition' of 1845 was an even bigger catastrophe than his first venture into the Arctic. It took decades to piece together the fate of the 129 men because little evidence remained. The two ships had disappeared without a trace and the expedition itself was a barely distinguishable smear on the frozen landscape: a few bones and incongruous odds and ends, and a verbal record from the Inuit of white men dropping dead as they walked, carrying boots filled with cooked human flesh.

In the twentieth century more solid evidence emerged. Forensic scrutiny of bones found scattered around several campsites revealed cut marks consistent with de-fleshing. Furthermore, the skeletal remains of a European male, found at Booth Point, showed an array of bones clustered at one end of a circle of stones that had secured a non-Inuit, canvas tent. The anthropologists who examined the site found leg, arm and cranial bones—but nothing from the torso. The logical conclusion was that the body had been dismembered and the torso eaten elsewhere. (The bones also indicated the presence of scurvy and high levels of lead, probably caused by the lead solder in the expedition's stock of tinned food.) At another site on King William Island, the skeletal remains of at least eleven men were found: twenty-five per cent of the bones had de-fleshing marks consistent with the use of a straight metal cutting implement. Several large bones had been smashed open, probably to extract the marrow, a detail which matched the Inuit accounts.

Right across King William Island, the scattered bones were in such a state that only three bodies have ever been identified. Far more silver cutlery was identified than expedition members.

Such details make unpleasant reading. But many of these

survivors were faced with a stark, simple choice—eat the dead or die themselves. In the Andes Nando Parrado, after swallowing his first morsel, felt neither guilt nor shame: 'If I felt any strong emotion at all, it was a sense of resentment that fate had forced us to choose between this horror and the horror of certain death.'

The Andes survivors agreed on a pact—'"If I die, please use my body"—that attitude made it feel less like a profanity.' This approach clarified the whole issue. If it is acceptable for people to give their bodies as food, then it should be acceptable for others to receive it as food.

One characteristic which appears almost universal is the habit of eating strangers first, friends next and family last. The Andes survivors agreed not to eat Nando Parrado's sister and mother unless absolutely necessary (a promise which they upheld).

Even in America's Donner–Reed wagon-train group—now infamous in the annals of cannibalism—this reluctance to eat family members was apparent. The Donner–Reed party, a group of eighty-seven immigrants who set out west in a wagon train from Illinois in 1846, were destined to become one of the most famous American pioneer stories, not least because only forty-eight of the group made it to California. Convinced to take a supposed shortcut across Utah and Nevada, the group of men, women and children laboured through the Wasatch Mountains and the Great Salt Desert, shedding horses, cattle, wagons and people on the way. Autumn and winter saw them trapped in the Sierra Nevada mountains, deeply divided, resentful, mutually suspicious and very, very hungry. A group of fifteen set out in snowshoes to try to reach California, but became disoriented. When the decision was made to eat the bodies of those who had succumbed to starvation and cold, the parcels of meat were meticulously labelled so that two daughters wouldn't have to eat their father. Just seven members of that group survived.

In the little cabins back at Truckee Lake (now Donner Lake), things were just as grim for the rest of the wagon party. It was a spectacularly cold winter and the people, scattered around in groups, were dropping from cold and malnutrition. The families were reduced to eating mice, then strips of an ox-hide tent boiled into a glue-like jelly. The inevitable wasn't far away, even after spasmodic outside help had begun to arrive.

When the various relief parties finally reached the snowbound camps, terrible reports started to circulate of the survivors eating the corpses of their companions. Accounts by those who had been trapped in the mountains were more pragmatic: Patrick Breen's diary did not dwell on the utter misery, but it's clear from his entry of February 26 just how desperate things were even after the first relief party had taken out some people. 'Hungry times in camp…Mrs Murphy said here yesterday that she thought she would commence on Milt & eat him.' 'Milt'—Milton Elliott—had died a couple of weeks before. His cannibalised remains were later found in the Murphy cabin.

After the fourth relief expedition rescued the last survivor, Lewis Keseberg, most of the public opprobrium fell on him. Many thought the German had been guilty of theft and murder, and believed he had eaten human flesh out of choice rather than necessity. While he admitted to the cannibalism, Keseberg categorically denied enjoying the fare, describing it as 'loathsome, insipid and disgusting'.

A year afterwards, Sergeant Daniel Tyler and other members of a disbanded Mormon battalion reached the deserted site. Tyler wrote that they were:

*horrified at the sight which met our view—a skull with hair lying here, a mangled arm or leg yonder, with the bones broken as one would break a beef shank to obtain the marrow from it; a whole body in another place covered with a blanket, and portions of other bodies scattered around in different directions.*

During the many famines that have racked China over the centuries, a practice was recorded of village families swapping children to eat. (While this sounds like wild propaganda, it should be noted that there are extensive records of cannibalism occurring in Mao's great famine of 1958-1962. In Anhui Province, for example, official records detail 1289 cases of cannibalism in 1961.)

There are other instances in which family members have been eaten. In a famine inside the besieged city of Sancerre in France in 1573, two parents were discovered to have eaten their daughter. And in the failing colony of Jamestown in Virginia, a starving colonist salted and ate his pregnant wife in 1609. He was later tortured and executed.

But as terrible as these cases sound, absolute moral decay starts when the starving run out of bodies to eat.

# KILLING FOR FOOD

*The lad was dying before our eyes, the longing for his blood came upon us...the master hastened his death by bleeding him.*
EDWIN STEVENS, THE LIFEBOAT OF THE *MIGNONETTE*, 1884

**THE WHALESHIP *ESSEX*,** commanded by Captain George Pollard, was hunting a pod of whales 1500 nautical miles west of the Galapagos Islands in 1820 when a huge male sperm whale slammed into the side of the ship with such force the *Essex* began leaking. The first mate, Owen Chase, frantically started the pumps, then caught sight of the whale heading straight at the ship for a second strike:

> *Apparently with twice his ordinary speed, and to me at that moment, it appeared with tenfold fury and vengeance in his aspect. The surf flew in all directions about him and his course towards us was marked by a white foam...his head was half out of the water, and in that way he came upon us and again struck the ship.*

Within minutes the ship was lost. The crew of twenty piled into three small boats, which proceeded to drift slowly south. As the supplies dwindled and the men despaired, weeks passed on the open ocean. Eventually the boats chanced upon a tiny, uninhabited island (one of the Pitcairn group) which they stripped almost bare of resources in one week before deciding to sail on. Three men couldn't face the thought of dying at sea and chose to remain on the island, which at least had a scant supply of fresh water.

The other seventeen returned to the boats, hoping to sail east to Easter Island (rather than towards Tahiti, which they wanted to avoid because they'd heard it was full of cannibals). Two weeks later, a man who had been ill before the shipwreck died and was dropped overboard. Several days after that, rough weather separated the boats. Owen Chase found himself alone with four other crew.

Meanwhile, on the other two boats, supplies of hard tack were almost gone. After the third death from starvation the men decided to eat the corpse of their African–American crewman, Lawson Thomas. Two days later another African–American died and was eaten, followed by two more black crew over the next week. Mysteriously, none of the whites died. On January 9, on a particularly dark night, Captain Pollard's boat lost track of the third boat, carrying three crew. They were never seen again.

The four men on the captain's boat, having run out of African–Americans, began to have 'horrible thoughts in our minds'. Finally it was sixteen-year-old Charles Ramsdell who voiced the unspoken thought that had been plaguing the men: lots should be cast and the loser killed and eaten. Always a desperate option, the 'custom of the sea' was well known to all sailors, spoken of often and occasionally resorted to. Standard practice called for two ballots, one to choose the victim and one for the executioner.

For Pollard, even contemplating this was unbearable. The other three on his boat were teenagers from his close-knit community of Nantucket. One of them, Owen Coffin, was his seventeen-year-old cousin entrusted into Pollard's care by his mother, Pollard's aunt, less than six months earlier. After the *Essex* sank, Pollard had made sure the young friends were placed on his boat so he could keep a watchful eye on them. Now he would most likely have to see one of them murdered, possibly at his own hand.

Despite the captain's initial refusal, the starving youths talked him round. Pieces of paper were placed in a hat, and to Pollard's eternal horror, his cousin pulled out the victim scrap. Owen's childhood friend, Charles Ramsdell, drew the executioner's.

The captain was distraught. Initially he refused to allow the murder, and Ramsdell also rejected his assigned role as the killer. Apparently, the only person reconciled to the disastrous turn of events was Owen Coffin, who allegedly said of his fate, 'I like it as well as any other.' When the others were finally persuaded, Owen uttered a final message for his mother and calmly put his head down on the boat's gunwale. Charles shot him in the head. Owen's corpse sustained them for a while, but just five days later, one of the remaining three died of starvation, leaving only Pollard and Ramsdell on the boat.

Nearly two weeks later, as the captain and Ramsdell lay more dead than alive in the bottom of the boat, a ship pulled alongside. From the deck of the *Dauphin*, the crew looked down in disbelief at the contents of the small, drifting boat. The two incoherent, emaciated men, with ulcerated skin, lay on a devil's nest of human bones. During the final week they had survived by smashing open the bones and sucking out the marrow. The human body contains 206 bones, and the two men had consumed three bodies. The senior naval official in the vicinity, Commodore Charles Ridgely, later recorded in his journal:

> *They were ninety two days in the boat & were in a most wretched state, they were unable to move when found sucking on the bones of their dead Mess mates, which they were loth to part with.*

The men's pockets were found to be stuffed with finger bones and other skeletal fragments. Incredibly, both made a rapid recovery. As soon as he was sufficiently well, Captain Pollard was compelled, presumably by overwhelming guilt, to make a detailed and graphic description of how they had survived. One witness to his harrowing tale described it as 'the most distressing tale, that ever came to my knowledge'.

In Valparaiso, the two men were reunited with three other survivors from the *Essex,* including the first mate, Owen Chase. The men left behind on the island were also rescued, barely alive. Twenty years later Chase's son gave Herman Melville a copy of his father's account of the disaster. It inspired Melville to write the novel *Moby-Dick.*

No charges were laid, and most of the community of Nantucket stood quietly behind Pollard. Owen Coffin's mother was the exception; she avoided him for the rest of her life.

Melville met Pollard in person years later and described him as a brooding man who never smiled. Pollard continued with his compulsion to confess the horrible details of the voyage to strangers for decades.

No one questioned the suspicious maths of all the African–American crew dying, while eight white men survived from a total of twenty crew. (The odds of this happening by random chance are one in sixty.) The first four men eaten were all African–American.

The *Essex* wasn't the only case where it was dangerous to be an outsider among a hungry crew. On the American sloop *Peggy*, adrift in 1765, the crew sidestepped short straws entirely. Instead, they reached down into the cargo hold to haul out a terrified slave from between the casks of wine and the brandy. The slave, named Wiltshire, was one of a number who had been exported *from* America to the West Indies slave markets, but had failed to sell. A disappointed Captain Harrison had decided to take him back to New York.

By the thinking of the times, Wiltshire was an article of trade goods. Despite half-hearted objections from the captain, the crew shot the slave in the head. Then:

> *They ripped him open, intending to fry his entrails for supper, there being a large fire made ready for the purpose;—but one of the foremast-men whose name was James Campbell, being ravenously impatient for food, tore the liver from the body and devoured it raw as it was.*

Campbell paid dearly for his 'extravagant impatience' in consuming raw liver: he went insane and died three days later. The others, fearing the insanity might be contagious, refrained from eating Campbell's corpse and threw it overboard.

Meanwhile, Wiltshire's body was further butchered, affording the crew a 'luxurious banquet' that went on well into the night. The following day, the men voted on what to do with the rest of the body. 'It was unanimously agreed to cut the body into small pieces, and to pickle it; after chopping off the head and fingers, which they threw overboard, by common consent.'

The whole horrendous tale only came to light when Captain Harrison rushed to a notary in London after their rescue to make a legal statement. The purpose of this statement was not to absolve him of complicity in murder and cannibalism, but to make an insurance claim for the lost cargo consisting of:

*Twenty pipes [large casks] of brandy...seventy three pipes of wine...and one negro slave, or black man; the casks of brandy and wine being marked with the mark AM and the negro or black, called or named Wiltshire.*

(Captain Harrison later wrote an account of the *Peggy* disaster and its aftermath, but the only time Wiltshire was referred to by his name was in the insurance claim.)

A similar fate awaited the two Native American Miwok guides of the Donner–Reed wagon train. After finishing off four white companions who had died from starvation, the would-be California pioneers shot and ate their two Miwok guides, Luis and Salvador. These 'Indians' were not part of the original group; they had in fact trekked in to try and help the stranded pioneers.

It is possible to look at these scenarios in a theoretical context where 'the ends justify the means'—in that one life taken saves multiple other lives. In reality, however, most were a case of survival of the fittest.

As the city of Numantia descended into anarchy, the stronger began to hunt down and eat the weak. Many of the victims were women and children. According to Appian, 'No form of misery was absent. They were rendered savage in mind by their food, and their bodies were reduced to the semblance of wild beasts.'

History has shown that, in any isolated group of starving people, it does not pay to be a member of a disempowered minority. Things rarely go well for slaves, children or any ethnicity different from the majority. Cabin boys, for example, were statistically far more likely to become targets of cannibalism than other crew members. In the *Mignonette* dinghy—'the Master selected Richard Parker boy as being the weakest.'

Because the public might look askance on the consumption of minors, the accounts of such episodes by survivors tend to be carefully censored, spun and packaged. This occurred when the British collier the *Euxine* sank in the South Atlantic in 1874.

Adrift on one of the lifeboats were seven men. As they became hungrier, it was proposed that they follow the 'custom of the sea' and draw lots. After their rescue, the second mate, James Archer, testified that the ballot was drawn three times and each time the youngest and smallest crewman, an Italian named Francis Shufus, lost.

According to the deposition, another crewman then gallantly offered to die in Shufus's place, a proposal the Italian nobly declined:

*Shufus bore it with great calmness and showed the utmost resignation...(he) prepared himself to meet his fate by praying and speaking in Italian...and laying himself down in the bottom of the boat gave himself up to be tied...He did not struggle nor scream.*

The men slit the Italian's throat, cut his heart and liver into small pieces, and ate them mixed with a little seawater and Shufus's blood.

Several hours later, the survivors were rescued and taken to Singapore. The presence of a torso and limbs in the lifeboat's locker made it hard to deny what had occurred, and curiously the crew reported another cabin boy had been lost when the lifeboat overturned four days before Shufus's demise.

Unfortunately, another version of what happened to Shufus—believed to have come from the other men—swept through Singapore in November 1874. Related in a letter by Captain George Harrington, it ran as follows:

*He [Shufus] then jumped overboard and attempted to drown himself, but was seized by his shipmates, dragged into the boat, his throat was mercilessly cut, and portions of his body were devoured by his former shipmates.*

Of the two versions, human nature suggests Harrington's account is more believable.

A study published in 2012 by researchers Mikael Elinder and Oscar Erixson from Uppsala University in Sweden reinforced the dangers of being disempowered in the aftermath of a disaster. Elinder and Erixson assessed the likelihood of surviving a maritime catastrophe based on gender by analysing eighteen major shipwrecks that had occurred between 1852 and 2011.

During this relatively modern timeframe, conventional wisdom held that the principle of 'women and children first' (known as the 'Birkenhead Drill', after a famous shipwreck in 1852 where this protocol was followed) should indicate a higher rate of survival for these two groups. However, the researchers concluded: 'Women have a distinct survival disadvantage compared to men. Captains and crews survive at a significantly higher rate than passengers.'

Contrary to common perception, the *Titanic* was one of only two cases in the Uppsala University study where women and children had a survival advantage over men. From the fifteen thousand individuals analysed, crew members had a 61 per cent chance of survival, women had a 26.7 per cent chance and children a pitiful 15.3 per cent.

Elinder and Erixson concluded, 'Our findings show that behaviour in a life-and-death situation is best captured by the expression "Every man for himself".'

# A MORAL ABYSS:
## The Lifeboat of the *William Brown*

**LOCATION:** Atlantic Ocean, west of Nova Scotia

**NATIONALITY:** Mixed, but primarily Irish & American

**DATE:** 20 April 1841

**FATALITY RATE:** 40%

**DURATION:** 32 hours

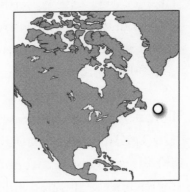

In 1841, about four hundred kilometres off the coast of Newfoundland, a shipwreck occurred that could have been a dress rehearsal for the *Titanic* disaster of 1912. Though painted on a smaller canvas, the picture that emerges from the wreck of the *William Brown* is infinitely more disturbing.

The *William Brown* was carrying emigrants from Ireland and Scotland to the New World when it struck ice in the Atlantic.

In truth, the 559-ton sailing ship was a little long in the tooth. It had been constructed in the shipyards of New York in 1824 by a company with the unlikely but ominous name of Blossom, Smith & Demon. The ship regularly ran the route between Liverpool and Philadelphia in the 1820s and '30s—manufactured goods and migrants left England, and raw materials came back.

By 1841 the recently sold *William Brown* was still running migrants and cargo across the North Atlantic. The ship was in a legal limbo as its new owner, Joseph P. Vogel, had not yet taken delivery of it. Nevertheless, on March 13 she set sail from Liverpool with seventeen crew, sixty-four passengers including families with small children, and a full cargo of salt, coal and £10,000 worth of china crockery.

The captain, George L. Harris, was a forty-eight-year-old Philadelphian with at least eighteen years' experience at sea. On April 19 the *William Brown*, like the *Titanic*, was sailing at full speed in the dark through an icefield. Other vessels in the vicinity of this busy shipping route at the edge of the Gulf Stream had slowed to a crawl, but the *William Brown* was sailing at ten knots when she hit ice about 8.45pm. There is conflicting testimony, but it appears the ship struck twice: first a small scrape along a flat icefloe, followed by a direct hit straight into an iceberg some fifteen minutes later.

The shock of the impact was enough to knock Mary Carr, the only passenger not in bed, off her feet. Below deck, twelve-year-old Owen Carr was thrown from his bunk. Another passenger, Bridget McGee, was horrified by the violence of the collision and rushed out, fearing 'the ship had broken in two'. Indeed, the iceberg had fatally damaged the ship, and after surveying the destruction to the hull, Captain Harris quietly ordered the crew to lower the two boats and abandon ship.

The passengers were kept in the dark, even lied to, until one of them discovered the truth, rushed below and spread the news. Some passengers immediately ran up to the deck in their nightgowns. Others made the mistake of pausing to dress or pray before escaping. By the time these passengers reached the deck, the only two boats, a small jollyboat and a larger longboat, were already full.

In the scramble for the few places, all the crew secured spots. Captain Harris, eight sailors and one passenger were in the relatively uncrowded jollyboat. The rest of the crew and the faster passengers rushed into the longboat. Fearing overcrowding, the crew ordered two teenage girls (Bridget McGee and Biddy Nugent) and another female passenger out of the longboat and back onto the sinking ship. The crew singled out the younger females who didn't have a father or husband to fight for them, but the women refused to give up their precious seats, even when Biddy was manhandled. Young Owen Carr had the good fortune to be knocked into the longboat by another passenger, who quickly followed him in.

As the crew hastily lowered the longboat, other passengers desperately scrambled in, many leaving family members behind on the doomed ship. Nineteen-year-old Sarah Carr raced below deck to find some warm clothing: 'I went below for my cloak, when I returned the longboat was in the water alongside the vessel. I jumped.' She hit the sailor Charles Smith, who ordered her to return to the ship. Sarah refused.

Mrs Margaret Edgar, a formidable Scot, shepherded three of her daughters into the longboat but another, Isabella, fell over on the deck and failed to make it into the boat. Hearing the little girl's cries for help amidst the howls of the other thirty-one passengers trapped on the deck of the crippled ship, Mrs Edgar cried out, 'Someone! Save my daughter for pity's sake.'

From his seat in the longboat, twenty-six-year-old Swedish sailor Alexander Holmes stood up and asked the crew to manoeuvre the boat back to the *William Brown*. Holmes, who held the rare distinction of being liked by both passengers and crew, was described by the second mate as 'a kind, orderly and sober man'. Going back alongside the ship was a risky exercise and other crew members tried to dissuade him, but Holmes was determined. As soon as the longboat was in position, he climbed up a rope onto the deck, and found Isabella.

Later, Isabella described her rescue: 'He carried me down by the rope into the longboat. I held on by one hand to his neck and he swung down by the rope, holding it with one hand.'

The second mate later said, 'there was great danger in this, both of him and the female; he was a strong man; no man of moderate strength could have done it.' It was a rare moment of heroism on a night filled with displays of self-serving cowardice.

Isabella testified that, as Holmes was carrying her off the deck on his shoulders, a wealthy female passenger rushed up to him with a Faustian proposition. Mrs Anderson was the wife of a doctor. She was travelling to Cincinnati with her three young children to join her husband, James, who had left Ireland seven months earlier to establish himself. With the ship sure to go down, Mrs Anderson tried to bribe Holmes with 'as much money as he could earn in a twelve-month' to save her life. She made no mention of her three children, also trapped on the deck of the ship. Nor did Mrs Anderson apparently care that, in order to carry out her wishes, Holmes would have to dump Isabella back onto the deck.

The pragmatic woman clearly thought her life was worth the loss of four children, three of them her own. A disgusted Holmes refused the bribe, saying, 'Money is not the object. It is lives I wish to save,' and continued his rescue of Isabella.

The longboat and the jollyboat rowed away from the *William Brown* but remained tied to the ship by two long ropes, unable either to help or to leave. Instead, the occupants sat and watched, listening to the cries for help. Abruptly, around midnight, the howling and pleading from the deck ceased and the freezing air was filled with an 'eerie silence'.

Minutes later, the ship pitched forward, tearing off her masts as she sank. The horrified sailors hacked frantically at the ropes, and the two orphaned boats were left alone on the open ocean. The twenty children, seven women (including Mrs Anderson) and four men left on board the *William Brown* died.

The longboat was crowded, and some of the passengers had to sit on the floor at the front of the boat. Alexander Holmes took off his blue overcoat and turned to a shivering twenty-two-year-old Julie McCadden: 'He put his jacket on my shoulders and told me to keep it till he wanted it.' Several other crew members also gave their jackets to the underdressed female passengers. (The seamen always slept in their clothes, which had two advantages—they had got to the boats first, and now they were adequately clothed. Many were also carrying their knives.)

The two boats rowed together for the rest of the night. At one point, a peg in the bottom of the longboat was accidentally dislodged, and a small amount of water flowed in. This peg, the diameter of a chair leg, was in effect a small plug. One of the passengers used some cloth from her pocket to temporarily plug up the hole while Holmes cut a new peg with his axe. The hole was safely sealed, and the leak stopped.

Throughout the first night, the crew took turns rowing and the passengers bailed when it was necessary. It rained intermittently, heavily at times.

The dawn light revealed an uncrowded jollyboat and the longboat crammed with thirty-two passengers and nine crew. The boats converged for a conference. Captain Harris announced his intention of sailing for Newfoundland in the jollyboat. He put Francis Rhodes, the first mate, in charge of the longboat. Rhodes and two of his passengers tried to persuade the captain to take a few more people, but Harris refused. Rhodes told the captain that the longboat was unmanageable and that unless some passengers were transferred to the jollyboat, he might have to take drastic action. One witness recalled the captain saying: 'Don't speak of that now. Let it be the last resort.' In his later deposition regarding the longboat, Captain Harris said he thought 'the chances of her being picked up, were ninety-nine to one against her'.

In fact, this wasn't a realistic assessment at all. The shipping route they were floating in was always busy in spring. European and British immigrants were pouring in their thousands across to North America in sailing ships and new-fangled steamboats. In 1841, 54,000 people left the British Isles for the New World, and the majority of them were at sea during April and May as that was the fastest time to cross.

Then, as now, time was money, so ships crossing the North Atlantic stuck to the swift-flowing channels in or by the Gulf Stream. Add to this the fishing boats and the many other migrant ships from the rest of Europe, and it was clear the two boats stood a reasonable chance of being spotted fairly quickly.

There was food, navigation equipment and charts on both boats and no shortage of fresh water: the boats were surrounded by bits of brash ice. True, the longboat had no sail and its rudder was damaged, but it had oars and twenty-four men to take turns rowing. Both boats had experienced sailors in charge. The longboat's occupants merely needed to remain in the shipping lane and keep a sharp eye out for passing ships.

The longboat was crowded, but it wasn't small. At 6.85 metres long and 1.8 metres wide, it was just fifteen centimetres shorter than the open longboat William Bligh had sailed 6700 kilometres across the Pacific to Timor some fifty years earlier. And Rhodes certainly wasn't in the middle of nowhere, as Bligh had been. The longboat from the *Medusa,* just 2.3 metres longer than the *William Brown*'s, had carried ninety people.

Unfortunately, the sight of the jollyboat sailing off to the north-west shattered Rhodes's confidence and he tried to resign his command.

In the longboat, the crew occupied the middle, with most of the passengers split into two groups at either end. This splitting of the passengers into separate groups probably contributed to what followed. Owen Riley, a young man who was migrating to join his wife and start a new life in Philadelphia, sat at the front of the boat with young Isabella and the rest of the Edgar family.

During the first day, the crew continued to take turns rowing and the passengers bailed. There was some rain and spray coming in, and the floor of the boat remained wet, but the peg held. By nightfall, the weather seemed to deteriorate. It was raining, and the frightened passengers thought the waves were coming closer to the gunwales. There were ominous mutters from the increasingly nervous crew about what needed to be done: they seemed to have forgotten they had all survived the previous night's rain and rough seas without mishap.

About 7pm, several of the crew lost their nerve. They stood up and seized one of the male passengers. He struggled and shouted, 'Let me be! This isn't the way. You don't just take a man and shove him into the sea!'

The crew members let go and sat down, fearing a struggle would cause the longboat to capsize.

The boat sailed on for a few hours with the same combination of rowing and bailing. At some point the peg was knocked out again in the darkness, and more water began to appear in the bottom of the boat. Nobody bothered to check if the peg had been dislodged. Rhodes said later that, surrounded by ice and with the boat taking on water, he

> Thought it improbable that she could hold out, unless relieved of some of her weight. I then consulted the sailors, who were all of the opinion that it was necessary to throw overboard those who were nearly dead, until we had room enough to work the boat and take to our oars.

This testimony contradicts the accounts of several passengers, who said that conditions on the longboat at the time had been no worse than on the previous evening.

Nevertheless, huddled in the darkness, Rhodes shouted: 'Men you must go to work, or we shall all perish.' Four of the crew stood up and made their selection from the group in the bow: a passenger who, significantly, had no other family on the longboat.

Julie McCadden heard the crew address Owen Riley: 'They first told him to stand up. I thought they were going to make him bail the boat. When he stood up they took hold of him.' After he had been grabbed, Owen realised what was coming and begged Mrs Edgar repeatedly to stop them.

One of the four crew members to stand up was Alexander Holmes. Riley must have felt a surge of relief to see the Swede next to him, and probably thought his pleas for mercy had been answered. He seized hold of Holmes's sleeve, but rather than sparing his life, the Swede pitched Riley into the icy water to drown. As he went overboard, Riley clung desperately to Holmes's sleeve, tearing it as he went.

Nobody knows how long Riley took to die. The temperature for salt water containing ice hovers around zero degrees Celsius (seawater freezes at about minus two degrees depending on the precise salinity level). A healthy, lightly dressed adult can survive immersion at zero degrees for more than an hour, provided he or she can swim. Of course, many adults in 1841 couldn't swim, and nobody on the longboat had any kind of life jacket. Furthermore, after more than twenty-four hours on the longboat, the victims' core temperatures would have already been lowered to a level of mild hypothermia (they were shivering but not confused)—a core temperature of between thirty-two and thirty-five degrees. Provided he could swim, Riley might have been capable of following the boat for five to ten minutes before he lost the ability to use his limbs and drowned.

The rest of the passengers now fell into a state of terror, even though they easily outnumbered the crew. If they had shown collective defiance, they might have halted the murder;

instead, they sat in petrified silence. Those who could covered their faces with their clothing, hid or tried to make themselves small. Nobody wanted to draw attention to themselves.

The next passenger to be seized and thrown overboard was James Todd, a young man from Scotland who was also on his own. He reportedly died without protest or resistance, either from himself or his fellow passengers. The lack of opposition seemed to encourage the crew to continue their mission. Sarah Carr later described the death of the third victim:

> When they got hold of James MacAvoy he asked them to give him five minutes to pray. Some of them refused him, but Murray, the coloured man, said he should have it. He then said a prayer, and they threw him out.

The traumatised passengers later had trouble remembering the order, but the next man to die was probably Bridget McGee's uncle, George Duffy. He begged to be spared but was hurled into the sea as Bridget watched. The longboat was now at least 240 kilograms lighter, but the killing continued. Man after man was pitched into the sea.

Unlike many of the other victims, Frank Askins wasn't alone. He was travelling to America with his two sisters, Ellen and Mary, who sat shivering by his side in their nightgowns. Holmes stood up and grabbed Askins. 'Holmes laid hold of him,' testified Ann Bradley, 'and called for the others to help him, or Askins would have him over.'

When the Askins siblings realised Frank was to be next, his sisters tried to save his life by arguing their lives were as good as over without his protection. Meanwhile, Frank begged for his life and tried to persuade Mrs Edgar to intervene. When that

failed, he offered the crew five sovereigns to let him live until
the next morning, swearing that he would jump overboard
voluntarily should it still be necessary.

Bridget McGee testified as to their response:

> *Frank Askins had two sisters in the boat. One was named
> Mary. She said if they threw her brother over, they might
> throw her over after him. After they threw him over, they
> threw her over too, and then they looked for, and threw the
> other sister, Ellen, overboard.*

Pathetically, the two sisters asked for something warm to
put on before being thrown into the sea.

As the night went on the murders continued, as if the crew
had been seized by an urge that defied both logic and compassion. After ten murders the longboat was considerably lighter
and less crowded. Only passengers were killed. The official
inquiry later noted: 'Not one of the crew was cast over', and
added incredulously, 'One of them, the cook, was a negro.'
At some point, the peg had been replaced and the wind had
dropped. The remaining passengers had fled to the furthest
points possible at either end of the boat, and were attempting
to conceal two men behind their cloaks.

The crew seemed to oscillate between horror at their
actions and a primal impulse to keep killing. 'After they had
thrown out most of the men,' recalled Sarah Carr, 'the sailors
looked for more, as they would not leave a damned soul of
them in the boat.'

When the grey dawn arrived, fourteen corpses lay
somewhere in the freezing wake of the half-empty longboat.
The weather was calm, the rain had stopped, the peg was back

in place, and the boat was about 840 kilograms lighter. But then the crew found the two men who had been concealed by the women. According to Bridget McGee:

> One of them was under a seat, and the other under the stern of the boat; they had hidden themselves there; John Nugent was one of them, I don't remember the other; at daylight these two men commenced bailing the boat; when they had done bailing the boat, the sailors threw them out.

Young Owen Carr said that the other man was Charles Conlin, who had been sitting next to Owen when Holmes seized him. Conlin, who was evidently friends with Holmes, pleaded, 'Holmes, dear, you won't throw me over?' To which Holmes answered, 'Yes, Charley, you must go.' After Conlin had been pitched out, Owen lost consciousness.

About 6am, just thirty minutes after the final murders, the survivors caught sight of a ship. It was another American vessel, the *Crescent*, and her captain, George Ball, quickly ensured the longboat's occupants were rescued and brought on board. Several days later, Captain Harris's jollyboat was rescued by a passing French ship.

In the ensuing weeks, the survivors arrived at various ports around the world, with the majority disembarking in the French port of Le Havre. Details of the killing spree leaked on both sides of the Atlantic, and eventually public outrage caused the American authorities to act. The only crew member not back at sea was Alexander Holmes, and on August 14 1842 he was arrested in a cheap boarding house for sailors and kept in solitary confinement until his trial.

★

The *William Brown* is a perplexing case. Why didn't the passengers fight back? After all, they outnumbered the crew three to one. The answer, as became apparent at Holmes's trial, was that once the killings had started, people were terrified to draw attention to themselves, lest they be next. Jane Johnston said: 'I was so stupefied with fright I scarcely knew what I was doing.'

Fearful of being targeted, the passengers seemed to think it would be safer to try to merge into the woodwork of the longboat. Many tried to hide (difficult on a small open boat), while others desperately avoided eye contact or hid their faces under coats. The lack of opposition probably contributed to the slaughter.

At the start of the killing, no one could have predicted the extent of the depravity. If they had known that so many would lose their lives, perhaps courage—or just a sense of mutual self-preservation—would have rallied a leader from their ranks.

The crew appeared largely united in their actions, but the passengers were reduced to a collection of individuals, each struggling to preserve his or her own life. They paid a huge price for their failure to unite and resist.

A more complex and perplexing question is why Holmes, who was instrumental in many of the killings, had risked his life at the start by returning to the *William Brown* to rescue a sick girl as the ship was going down. How could a man's nature change so drastically within twenty-four hours? Before the killing spree, most of the passengers liked Holmes. During that first night on the longboat he gave his coat to a freezing young woman and handed out food. Soon after, he was helping to kill sixteen helpless passengers.

Holmes's lawyer, David Brown, argued in court that

a social state no longer existed in the lifeboat; instead the crew and passengers existed within 'a state of nature'. Brown declared: 'In such peril, a man makes his own law with his own right arm.' Which was exactly what Holmes and the rest of the crew had done.

Holmes was originally charged with murder, but this was reduced to 'manslaughter on the high seas'. He was found guilty and given six months' hard labour in solitary confinement in the notoriously harsh Eastern Penitentiary of Pennsylvania. As soon as he arrived, a black hood was placed over Holmes's head and he was taken to a cell. He served out his whole sentence without ever leaving the cell or talking to another person. Afterwards he vanished from history.

No one else was ever charged.

# MURDER

*They hate you, Ralph. They're going to do you.*
*They're going to hunt you tomorrow.*

SAMNERIC, *LORD OF THE FLIES*

**IN A STRANDED** and imploding community, murder can appear
in many guises and for many reasons. At one end of the moral
spectrum there is neglect leading to death, which occurs in
many survivor groups. The sick, the young and the weak are
left behind, or denied their share of food, water or shelter. In
extreme circumstances this enfeebled group, along with disempowered minorities, are often the prime candidates to be killed
for food.

Another non-accidental cause of death is deliberate premeditated abandonment, as in the case of the *Medusa*
raft and, repeatedly, in Patagonia with the *Wager* crew. Jean
de Léry's account of his disastrous voyage to Brazil in 1578
includes a vivid account of the captain and crew jumping into

the lifeboat and abandoning the hapless passengers to their fate. On his last voyage, in 1611, Captain Henry Hudson was abandoned in a small boat and cast adrift in Hudson Bay with eight sick crew members, including his son. All perished.

Leaders, often paranoid and desperate to maintain power, sometimes act violently and without evidence against anyone they believe may be threatening mutiny. It was his paranoid fear of insurrection that prompted the *Wager's* Captain Cheap to shoot Midshipman Cozens in the face, then refuse him medical treatment.

Any personal animosity that exists before the crisis occurs is generally exacerbated in the days, weeks or months that follow. When pent-up loathing simmers for too long, it can be fatal. This appears to have happened on the ill-fated *Polaris* expedition to the Arctic in 1871.

The race to the North Pole bore a striking resemblance to the race to the moon. Of little strategic value, both goals became vehicles for fierce national pride. The obsession of individuals was matched only by the vast expenditures of governments. The big difference was that reaching the North Pole took much longer and racked up a far higher death toll.

The American Expedition of Charles Francis Hall used a converted navy tugboat, the *Polaris*. In the gentlemen's world of the educated, well-heeled explorer, Hall was an anomaly—a former blacksmith's apprentice who had gone on to become the publisher of two small newspapers in the American Midwest. Built like a wrestler and with little formal education, Hall was intelligent, fiercely religious and obsessed with the idea of polar exploration. He had already conducted two amateur expeditions searching for Sir John Franklin's missing party and, like

John Rae, had demonstrated an ability to live with and learn from the Inuit, whom he trusted and respected. In particular he befriended an Inuit husband and wife team, Tookoolito ('Hannah') and Ebierbing ('Eskimo Joe'), who acted as translator, guide and cook.

These minor triumphs had filled Hall with a burning desire to attempt the journey to the North Pole. After obtaining funding and support from the US Government, he wrote of the expedition—'Glorious is the prospect of the future.' Tookoolito and Ebierbing were hired to accompany him once again. Unfortunately, Hall's tunnel vision blinded him to the problems of the *Polaris* expedition, which, from the outset, had no absolute commander.

Hall considered it to be his expedition, but the *Polaris* itself was captained by an experienced whaler named Sidney Budington, who was not just a dipsomaniac, but an old antagonist of Hall's. To make matters worse, there was a scientific contingent headed by a German academic, Dr Emil Bessels, who exhibited outright contempt for the self-educated Hall.

The expedition, comprising Germans, Americans and some Inuit, sailed from Newfoundland in 1871, and those aboard quickly split along national, class and professional lines. The navigator, George Tyson, felt the expedition was headed for trouble, but Hall's polar fixation drove him on: 'He was willing to die, but not to abandon the expedition.' (Ultimately, Hall did both.)

The scientific faction and some of the crew showed 'insolence and insubordination', Tyson recalled, and openly expressed the view that 'Hall shall not get any credit out of this expedition'. While Hall was intent on pushing north, others, including Captain Budington, refused. Bitterly disappointed, Hall set up a winter camp at a site he named Thank God Harbour in northwest Greenland (he had already planted a flag and taken possession of Greenland 'in the name of the Lord, and for the President of the United States'). With the camp established he set off north by dogsled, leaving the malcontents behind to raid the scientific alcohol supplies using homemade skeleton keys.

Hall returned two weeks later, flushed with success (even though he had travelled only eighty kilometres) and determined to restock and return north. The navigator commented how well and happy Hall appeared, but within hours the situation changed. Tyson recorded: 'Captain Hall is sick; it seems strange, he looked so well...he is lying in his berth and says he feels sick at his stomach. This sickness came on immediately after drinking a cup of coffee.'

Stomach pains and vomiting progressed to delusions and paralysis. Dr Bessels diagnosed apoplexy, administered several quinine injections and declared that Hall would never recover. Hall stammered that the strange, sweet-tasting coffee had been poisoned. The others assumed he was just ranting, but he soon refused to have any more treatment from the doctor, and ate only food prepared by Tookoolito. He made a rapid recovery and, after only a week, was up and talking of his next trip north.

The chaplain pleaded with Hall to let Dr Bessels give him more quinine injections, and eventually Hall agreed. Soon he was experiencing vomiting and breathing difficulties and accusing Dr Bessels of poisoning him.

One of the last coherent things Hall asked was how to

spell 'murder'. Four days after the injection, he was dead. Seaman Noah Hayes reported that Dr Bessels was light-hearted and laughed about Hall's death, and even went so far as to say it 'was the best thing that could have happened for the expedition'.

Hall was buried in a shallow grave at Thank God Harbour and, as one of the crew remarked later, 'the expedition died with Captain Hall'. Morale and discipline crashed; Captain Budington, who 'was drunk very often', allowed the men to do as they chose, which meant all-night drinking and cards. To add to the chaos, the captain issued firearms to all the men. The carpenter went insane and crept about the ship, hiding in corners fearing he, too, would be murdered. Theft became widespread, and Budington and Dr Bessels came to blows over some stolen grog. Finally, to stop the men from stealing his scientific alcohol, Dr Bessels adulterated it with an emetic. Ebierbing later testified, 'everyone watching one another...all afraid somebody put down poison in water, bread or something.'

Eventually the expedition made its way back to civilisation, but not before Captain Budington had run the ship aground and abandoned nineteen people—Tyson, the Germans, Tookoolito, Ebierbing, their daughter and another Inuit family with three young children and a baby—on a massive ice floe. The Germans all moved into one large igloo and refused to speak English, which isolated the Americans and the Inuit. The party drifted for more than six months, with the Inuit feeding the indolent, complaining scientists, who repaid this favour, Tyson wrote, by eyeing the Inuit children hungrily. Surviving on some meagre supplies and passing seals, the starving group was eventually rescued by a passing ship, the *Tigress,* after drifting more than three thousand kilometres.

Rumours of foul play dogged the returned expedition. An inquiry into the failure of the *Polaris* venture revealed more than was officially comfortable—a vast web of conflicting testimony, lost official logs and destruction of evidence. Eager to save national face over the failed expedition that had been backed by the US Government, and in the absence of physical evidence, the investigation found that Hall had died of apoplexy. The testimony of the Inuit was largely ignored, and they were ordered not to speak to the press about the matter. America breathed a collective sigh of relief—the English couldn't officially gloat if the *Polaris* expedition wasn't officially a disaster.

Hall's body lay in the permafrost for ninety-seven years until it was exhumed by his biographer Chauncey Loomis, who took samples of the explorer's remarkably well-preserved fingernails and hair. The Toronto Centre of Forensic Science, which examined them, reported 'an intake of considerable amounts of arsenic by C. F. Hall in the last two weeks of his life'.

The *Polaris* crew had not suffered many of the stress factors that debilitate other survivor groups; they were relatively comfortable, had adequate food and were not permanently stranded. Yet someone—most probably Dr Bessels, who had arsenic in his medical supplies—apparently decided to murder the expedition's commander, putting everybody's lives at risk.

This incident highlights the potential consequences of pent-up hatred within a closed group. Once the group has begun splitting, and fear grows to fill the space once occupied by trust, nerves become frayed and hostility rises until, like a pot of boiling water, it spills over.

Hall had been through such a scenario before. Three years earlier, he had hired five whalers to help with his expedition around King William Island searching for traces of Sir John Franklin's lost party. The men began to resent Hall's orders, and he thought they were malingering and weren't attending to their hunting chores. Food was plentiful (the men had just netted 175 salmon), but aggression was building and Hall feared one of the men, Patrick 'Pat' Coleman, was leading the others towards a rebellion.

One evening, Hall got into an argument with Coleman. There were 'mutinous' comments from Coleman, followed by raised fists. At this point Hall, who was outnumbered, dashed back to his tent, 'and seized my Baylie revolver, and went back and faced the leader of the mutinous crowd, and demanded of Pat to know if he would desist in his mutinous conduct? His reply being still more threatening, I pulled the trigger and in a few minutes he staggered and fell.'

Hall had shot an unarmed man at point-blank range. Coleman took two weeks to die from his injury. The incident bears an eerie resemblance to the shooting of Cozens at the *Wager* campsite. Both commanders, fearing mutiny, took what they considered a pre-emptive strike—and, in both cases, the rest of the men turned against their leader as a result. (Because of legal and jurisdictional problems with the case, Hall was never charged over the killing.)

The first murder can be a terrifying watershed for an isolated group clinging to survival. In situations where all society's usual constraints have been swept away, the first murder can trigger a bloodbath, often for no discernible reason—as happened on the *Medusa* raft, when on two separate occasions, a single killing, at night, sparked wholesale slaughter.

But when it comes to a bloodbath scenario, no account demonstrates the Lord of the Flies principle more starkly than the *Batavia* shipwreck off Western Australia.

The *Batavia* was on its maiden voyage when it left the Netherlands in October 1628 bound for Java. The huge square-rigger was carrying 332 men, women and children, as well as a valuable cargo of silver, gold and precious jewels (including a massive cameo destined to be sold to the Mogul Emperor). After crossing the Indian Ocean, the ship sailed full tilt into the Abrolhos Island cluster eighty kilometres from the mainland.

What followed—a psychopath taking advantage of a catastrophe—is the stuff of nightmares.

About 230 people decamped to a dry, rocky, uninhabited pair of islands. The ship was left stranded on a coral fringing reef, with seventy men still aboard—drinking, looting, fighting and frolicking in piles of other people's money. After nine days, the remains of the ship suddenly disintegrated, and another twenty men made it to shore.

Meanwhile, the *Batavia*'s commander had taken the biggest longboat, along with forty-seven people and the senior representative of VOC (the Dutch East India Trading Company), and sailed to Indonesia to get help. Unfortunately for most of the 208 remaining survivors, the ship's third-in-command, the undermerchant Jeronimus Cornelisz, was left in charge.

Cornelisz, who was about thirty, proved to be a near-perfect example of the psychopathic killer. Articulate, persuasive and highly intelligent, he was bolstered by a personal philosophy

Major General Adolphus Washington Greely served in the American Civil War, and was promoted to First Lieutenant of Cavalry in 1873. Unfortunately his military experience proved little help in the Arctic. (*Courtesy of NOAA*)

Lt. Greely and his dying companions found in a tent, Cape Sabine, 1884. Sgt. Ellison's amputated limbs were too disturbing to include in this newspaper illustration. Inset: Greely, following his recovery.

A posthumous sketch of Alexander Pearce, escaped convict and murderer, following his hanging in Tasmania in 1824. Artist: Thomas Bock.

Mugpi, aged three, was caught up in the *Karluk* disaster and the epic trek to Wrangel Island. She survived with nothing more than a scratch on her chin. (*Photo: Lomen Bros. Courtesy of the Frank and Frances Carpenter collection, Library of Congress*)

The *Belgica* trapped in ice in the Bellingshausen Sea near Antarctica, 1898 (*Courtesy of NOAA*)

RIGHT: This 1849 poster offered a huge reward, the current equivalent of over $3,000,000, for anyone who might help rescue Sir John Franklin's missing expedition.

**20,000 POUNDS STERLING (100,000 Dollars) REWARD!**

TO BE GIVEN BY

**HER BRITANNIC MAJESTY'S GOVERNMENT**

to such private Ship, or distributed among such private Ships, or to any exploring party or parties, of any Country, as may, in the judgment of the BOARD OF ADMIRALTY, have rendered efficient assistance to

**SIR JOHN FRANKLIN,**

HIS SHIPS, OR THEIR CREWS,

and may have contributed directly to extricate them from the Ice.

**H. G. WARD,**
Secretary to the Admiralty.

LONDON, March 23, 1849.

The attention of WHALERS, or of any other Ships or parties disposed to aid in this service, is particularly directed to SMITH'S SOUND and JONES'S SOUND, in BAFFIN'S BAY, to REGENT'S INLET and the GULF of BOOTHIA, as well as to any of the Inlets or Channels leading out of BARROW'S STRAIT, particularly WELLINGTON STRAIT, or the Sea beyond, either Northward or Southward.

VESSELS entering through BEHRING'S STRAITS would necessarily direct their search North and South of MELVILLE ISLAND.

NOTE.—Persons desirous of obtaining information relative to the Missing Expedition, are referred to EDMUND A. GRATTAN, Esq., Her Britannic Majesty's Consul, BOSTON, MASSACHUSETTS; or ANTHONY BARCLAY, Esq., Her Britannic Majesty's Consul, NEW YORK.

ABOVE: Defleshing cut marks found on ninety-two bones from at least eleven members of Sir John Franklin's expedition. The concentration of cuts to the finger bones remains a mystery. None of the bones had been burned. (Courtesy Prof. Anne Keenleyside)

RIGHT: Dr John Rae discovered the tragic fate of the Franklin expedition and paid the price for revealing the truth. He was the only major Arctic explorer not to be knighted. Artist: Stephen Pearce.

**Living the Utopian dream:** Jonestown residents in a promotional brochure entitled 'A feeling of freedom' 1978. (*Courtesy Jonestown Institute*)

**Grim reality:** Authorities who arrived at Jonestown two days after the mass suicide in November 1978 found the compound carpeted with more than 900 bodies. Only four people at the site survived.

that held that anything he did was sanctioned by the Almighty: 'for God, said he, was perfect in virtue and goodness' wrote Francisco Pelsaert later, 'so was not able to send into the heart of men, anything bad, because there was no evil or badness in Himself.'

Even before the shipwreck, mutiny had been fomenting on board the *Batavia*. On the island, Cornelisz set about reviving plans to steal the company's gold and jewels and escape to a life of piracy once a rescue ship appeared. His first step was to quietly recruit a band of willing henchmen. Then, at the head of a small council, he set about organising the camp. Most of the survivors were on a tiny island, barely 200 metres by 150 metres, they had named Batavia's Graveyard.

The group wasn't too badly off: it had rained, the weather was mild, the sea around the island was rich in fish, and there was a large seal colony, thousands of birds and even 'cats' (actually tammar wallabies, the first ever seen by Europeans) on two nearby islands. They had supplies from the ship, plenty of planks from the wreck, tools, small boats, guns and fishing nets. Their biggest problem was the lack of a permanent source of fresh water.

Cornelisz secretly convinced his followers (whom he moved into two separate tents) that there were too many mouths to feed. But Cornelisz knew that he was likely to meet opposition from the large number of soldiers who were loyal to the VOC.

To overcome this problem, Cornelisz, who was Machiavellian to his core, decided to dump dozens of people on three nearby islands, where he hoped they would die of dehydration or starvation. Most importantly, he planned to rid himself of likely opposition by rowing twenty able-bodied men, including most of the 'boldest soldiers', to High Island with no weapons, ostensibly to look for water. (The search was a ruse. Cornelisz had taken the precaution of secretly ordering a reconnaissance beforehand, and was convinced the island was dry.)

In total, seventy-five men, women and children were ferried off Batavia's Graveyard and distributed over three small islands.

Among those ferried to High Island (now East Wallabi Island) was a soldier called Wiebbe Hayes. His group was told to light three fires if they found water. In the second week of July, Hayes's men lit the beacons on the island slightly to the southwest (now West Wallabi Island), to which they had walked at low tide. Cornelisz had been mistaken, the island had two well-hidden sources of water. But no one came to pick them up.

With the group on Batavia's Graveyard reduced to a more manageable 130 or 140 people, Cornelisz set about making sure that he and his henchmen would survive until the rescue boat arrived and they could sail off to a life of riches.

At the beginning of July the murders began. The first execution—of a soldier who had been caught illegally tapping a wine barrel—was almost justifiable within the normal code of survivor discipline. Then it was the turn of two carpenters, whom Cornelisz accused of plotting to sail off in a makeshift boat. Despite a lack of evidence, and 'although neither had done any misdeeds whatsoever', they were killed by two of Cornelisz's followers.

Within days, another seven men had been tricked into sailing off to hunt for water. The real plan was to take the men out of sight of Batavia's Graveyard, and drown them. Andries de Vries, an assistant in his early twenties, and another man begged for their lives and were spared, on the proviso that they joined the mutineers.

The killings of these five victims near Traitors Island was probably witnessed by the group of fifteen who had been stranded on that outcrop. No doubt shocked and terrified, the group rapidly constructed two rafts, intent on escape.

On July 9, 'Pietersz Jansz provost with still another fourteen people, women as well as men, had made two rafts on Traitors Island, with which they had the intention to sail to High Island, and to prevent that, it has been decided by Jeronimus and his council to drown or kill them.'

As the two rafts desperately paddled towards the safety of High Island, the current carried them within shouting distance of the main island. They were quickly overtaken by a boat filled with heavily armed mutineers. Some dived off the raft to try to escape, while the rest—including two children—were thrown into the deep channel. Only four men managed to reach the main island but when they emerged from the sea and begged for protection, Cornelisz ordered them to be killed on the beach, in full view of the other survivors.

The cat was now out of the bag, so there was no more need for subterfuge by the mutineers. Over the next few days the murders started in earnest, beginning with the sick and the lame. Initially, Cornelisz had at least the semblance of a reason for the slaughter, claiming there were too many to feed, too many 'useless mouths'.

The reign of terror carried the *Batavia* survivors into the final stage of the Lord of the Flies principle.

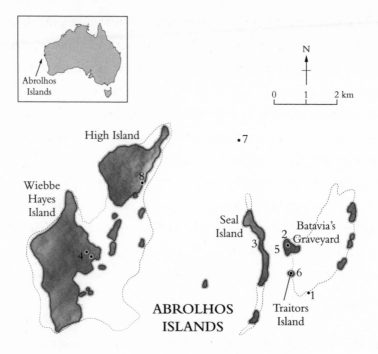

1. The location of the *Batavia* shipwreck
2. Batavia's Graveyard—the main camp and site of most of the murders
3. Seal Island—forty-four murders and later the mutineers' execution ground
4. Wiebbe Hayes Island, their two forts—the site of four murders and the final battle
5. The deep channel where fourteen people were killed by drowning
6. Traitors Island—five murders, on or near the island
7. Approximate anchorage of the rescue yacht *Sardam*
8. High Island—the surgeon was killed on or next to the island

In the end, there was only one rule—self-preservation. Rather than be hacked to death or drowned, some of the men defected. The ranks of the mutineers swelled, as men realised the only way to escape the slaughter was to join the killers. Opportunistic as these defections were, Cornelisz didn't know how many of these converts he could trust. He devised two strategies for testing them.

The first was to have the men sign an oath of allegiance to the cause, such as this one from July 11, where the men agreed to 'remove all distrust that may be amongst us…making to each other the greatest oath that anyone can take, to be faithful in everything…(to) assist one another in brotherly affection in all matters that may happen'. A new oath was written every few days, with the later ones insisting the men refer to Cornelisz as their 'Captain General'.

Cornelisz's other technique was far more diabolical. He would present the new recruits with a stark option: kill to prove your loyalty. About July 10 one of the men who had been spared off Traitors Island, Andries de Vries, was summoned by a posse of the mutineers, who were following orders from Cornelisz. They 'have taken Andries de Vries and brought him to all the huts of the sick, and ordered him to cut their throats, which he did'.

Four days later, de Vries cut the throat of carpenter Hendrick Clauss, under orders from Cornelisz. But the new acolytes were still in a perilous position, as de Vries found out later that day, when he was murdered as a punishment for speaking to Cornelisz's 'concubine'.

Cornelisz also sent a party of followers over to nearby Seal Island, to wipe out a group of boys who had been exiled there earlier. The boys proved to be tricky prey, and the men hunting them split into groups. One fifteen-year-old cabin boy was caught by the murderous David Zevanck. 'Boy, you must help lustily to kill or be in a fix yourself,' Zevanck told him. The cabin boy duly ensured his own survival by catching a boy his own age, wrestling him to the ground and stabbing him to death.

The deliberate taking of lives within a group, individual against individual or faction against faction, breaks the final bonds with the normal world, and it appears to be the tipping point where some intangible but essential component has vanished from the integral structure of the group, and from its bedrock of beliefs.

The *Batavia* survivors—supposedly civilised people, who came from a strict and conservative corner of Europe—had already witnessed or descended into senseless spasms of murder. But the final stages of group collapse laid bare what William Golding called 'the darkness of man's heart'.

# THRILL KILLS

*Kill the beast! Cut his throat! Spill his blood! Do him in!*
LORD OF THE FLIES

**OCCASIONALLY A STRANDED** group reaches the final rung of depravity: casual murders, committed for enjoyment.

In normal societies, it is almost unheard of for groups of people to kill others for entertainment. However, that changes when the victim is not human but animal. The Wisconsin Department of Natural Resources documented and studied twenty thrill-kill cases of animals in 2005 and seventeen cases in 2006. Most involved groups of two to five people; several had ten or more perpetrators. The men came from backgrounds no different from the average population (except that there was an over-representation of rural participants), but there were two strong common denominators—youth and boredom. The report concluded:

*Thrill killing usually involves adolescents or young adults*
*abusing one or several animals purportedly for entertainment*
*or the relief of boredom, and it usually is a group activity.*

When the Wisconsin DNR interviewed the young men about the reasons for these offences, responses included:

*'At the time, it was something to do.'*
*'I don't know. It's exciting, I guess.'*
*'I have that power, why not use it?'*

When the victim is human, social and cultural conditioning provides an almost insurmountable barrier. Even in warfare, many soldiers show an extreme reluctance to kill the enemy, particularly in close-quarter combat. Research by psychologist Dave Grossman into the use of bayonets in combat has revealed that, even if soldiers find themselves in life-threatening situations, their instinct is not to use the bayonet as a stabbing implement, but to club the victim with the butt of the gun: 'The average human being has a strong resistance to piercing the body of his own kind with a hand-held edged weapon.'

This was certainly not the case on Batavia's Graveyard, where the progression and escalation of murders was telling. The first few murders at the beginning of July 1629—a month after the shipwreck—were ostensibly executions of men for theft or conspiracy to steal. Within days another five men were tied up and drowned, as Cornelisz began to weed out his potential enemies and reduced numbers. Around July 8, a six-year-old girl was strangled. From that day on, the number of murders and their brutal nature escalated, and no victim was too innocent or too inconsequential to kill.

July 9 saw twelve, possibly thirteen victims, including

two children and three women. Cornelisz's gang of killers began to prefer murders that involved bodily mutilation and blood loss rather than a simple clubbing over the back of the head. Bloodless drowning gave way to slashing, hacking or stabbing with a sword, or running through with a pike (or both). Although Cornelisz's men had guns, there was only one victim on Batavia's Graveyard who was shot dead.

The vast majority of the killings took place at night. On the evening of July 10, eleven people in the sick tent had their throats slit. To get an inkling of the aftermath of the massacre, bear in mind that the average person contains five and a half litres of blood. The tiny island was literally becoming soaked in blood as the killers warmed to their work and 'smirched their hands with the shedding of human blood'. The term 'overkill' seems apt. When Cornelisz decided one night to get rid of a gunner, a sick boy and a lame carpenter named Jacop Drayer, he sent four henchmen to their tent. The later confession of one of the killers describes Drayer's brutal murder inside the small tent, with one man holding him down as another:

> stabbed 2 knives to pieces on his breast; also 2 knives on his throat, whereupon Lucas Gellisz handed him one of his knives, but he could not bring him to death, so that at last he cut his throat with a piece of knife, after that did likewise to the boy.

It was a frenzied assault: four knife blades broke on the bones of the carpenter's upper body.

While he personally ordered almost every single murder, Cornelisz joined in only once. Even then it was a curiously bloodless crime against a totally defenceless victim. Cornelisz decided to poison a baby whose crying was bothering him. He gave the baby's young mother, Mayken Cardoes, a potion on the pretext that it would help to quieten the infant. (The undermerchant was, after all, an apothecary by trade.) The mercury-based potion was poisonous, but the baby lingered on in a coma, so Cornelisz sent one of the weakest mutineers to finish the infant off with 'a little noose'.

From then on, Cornelisz relied on his henchmen to do all the killing.

By mid-July, after almost fifty murders, the number of inhabitants on the island had been drastically cut and there was no longer any semblance of excuse for further reductions. Throughout the entire episode the excuse of insufficient food looked flimsy; while there is little in the records about what the survivors ate, there are some indicators that they had enough food. The night the pastor's wife and six children were killed in their tent, they had seal meat cooking on the fire for dinner. They had been on the island for almost seven weeks, and this family would have been towards the bottom of the island hierarchy, but they evidently still had a pot of seal meat. At Cornelisz's trial, Pelsaert asked him:

> *Why he allowed the devil to lead him so far astray from all human feeling (to do that which had never been so cruelly perpetrated amongst Christians) without any noticeable hunger or thirst, but solely out of cold bloodthirstiness to attain his wicked ends.*

It is also significant that despite an ample supply of corpses, there was no cannibalism.

Pelsaert attributed the bloodshed to Cornelisz's innate

wickedness, possibly aided by Satan: 'through the Devil he has denuded himself of all humanity...and he was more evil than if he had been changed into a tiger, so that he had let flow so much innocent blood'. The evil had then corrupted Cornelisz's followers, both the hardcore murderers and those who had only dabbled: 'some, more hardened are already impregnated with the bad life, whilst others have only sipped a little of the poison'.

Poison seems a very fair metaphor. There was enough food and rainwater to go around, and the surviving non-mutineers were working hard and staying quiet. But with nothing to do, the killers grew bored. One of the youngest killers, Jan Pelgrom, was itching for another murder. Pelsaert's account records that the eighteen-year-old took to roaming about the tiny island 'more like a beast than a human being' and calling out, 'Who wants to be stabbed to death? I can do that beautifully, and many more of gruesome, devilish blasphemies.'

Every day Jan Pelgrom begged Cornelisz 'that he should be allowed to kill someone, because he should rather do that than eat or drink'.

Soon more than a hundred murders had been committed. This caused another problem: the killers were running out of victims. Even many of those with practical skills that would have been useful to survival on the island had been killed. (The surgeon, for instance, had been run through with a pike, smashed in the head with a spiked club, hacked in the head with a sword, and finally run through again for good measure.) By mid-August, the lack of victims meant a whole week went by without any bloodshed.

Finally Cornelisz organised a murder for everyone's

entertainment, using a new and brutal method. The victim was selected—a boy named Cornelius Aldersz whose job had been to repair the fishing nets. The undermerchant gave a sword to a delighted Jan Pelgrom and offered him the chance to decapitate the net-maker. Another man objected, saying scrawny Pelgrom was too weak to carry out the killing. Mattijs Beer, another enthusiastic killer, asked to be allowed to murder the boy. The net-maker was seized, blindfolded and surrounded. Cornelisz told the boy to 'sit quiet, they are only joking with you, whereupon Mattijs Beer cut off his head, at which Jeronimus, Zevanck and the others were laughing'. Pelgrom was the only one not enjoying the show. He was in tears at missing his chance to decapitate someone.

A month later the bloodshed was brought to an abrupt halt by a pitched battle between Wiebbe Hayes's faction and the mutineers—and the fortuitous arrival of a rescue ship carrying Commander Pelsaert. By then Cornelisz and his gang had 'drowned, murdered and brought to death, with all manner of cruelties, more than 120 persons, men, women and children'.

William Golding illustrated snowballing violence and the descent into brutality for the sake of gratification with great insight. In Lord of the Flies, accidental death gives way to beatings, followed by the frenzied group stabbing of Simon. Just like Jan Pelgrom, some of the boys begin to enjoy inflicting pain. When Roger rolls a boulder on top of Piggy, killing him instantly, it is in a state of 'delirious abandonment'. In the final hunt for Ralph, the boys are intent on spearing him to death, decapitating him and displaying his head on a stick. Golding describes the hunters as 'laughing excitedly' and cheering loudly. They are caught up in what American child psychologist Bruno Bettelheim called 'the dark beauty of violence'.

In 1955 Muzafer Sherif, mastermind of the Robbers Cave experiment, and his wife happened to run into one of the boys who had participated in the 1949 'summer camp'. Far from recalling a savage spiral of pack aggression and violence, the young man looked back on the experience as 'terrific'.

A common characteristic of the thrill-kill group is that it tends to be headed by a charismatic, intelligent, persuasive leader who likes to leave the actual killings to others but whose ego feeds on the bloodshed and the ability to murder by proxy. Jeronimus Cornelisz certainly fits this profile, as do Jim Jones and Charles Manson. Cornelisz and Jones were also well educated.

Manson and his followers were hardly fighting for survival on the edge of civilisation, but he did his best to isolate his tribe by holing up in remote ranches in Death Valley and rural California. He talked a group of followers into a series of brutal and senseless murders in the late 1960s in California, culminating in the notorious Tate–LaBianca murders in 1969.

Manson's followers were young, disaffected counter-cultural Americans, many female, who fell under his spell and joined his quasi-communal cult, known as the 'Family'. Like Jim Jones (who was prone to bouts of faked stigmata), Manson implied to his followers that he was some kind of Jesus figure. He encouraged his followers to go out at night in groups and 'creepy-crawl' the houses of strangers. They would select a house, break in and quietly move around inside as the owners slept. When the thrill of this wore off, they escalated the buzz by standing around the owners' bed as they slept and moving objects around the house to frighten the residents in the morning.

Finally, in the summer of 1969, Manson instructed four of his followers to enter the house of Roman Polanski at midnight and kill whomever they found. The five murders, carried out by twenty-four-year-old Charles Watson and three twenty-one-year-old women, were brutal. On entering the house, Watson told the terrified residents, 'I'm the Devil and I'm here to do the Devil's business.' The pregnant actress Sharon Tate was stabbed sixteen times; another victim was shot twice, bludgeoned and stabbed fifty-one times. Nothing was stolen.

The following night, Manson took six of his followers to another residence, where he tied up the two inhabitants and ordered three of his followers to murder them. The group followed orders, leaving Leno LaBianca with twenty-six stab wounds, 'any six of which could in and of itself have been fatal'. A carving fork was left protruding from his stomach and a knife from his throat.

His wife, Rosemary LaBianca, was stabbed forty-one times.

One of the killers, Susan Atkins, later described to her cellmate what 'a rush' it had been to stab her victims: 'the more you do it, the better you like it.' It was, she said, better than sex. Leslie van Houten, twenty-one, told another Family member, 'the more you stabbed, the more fun it was.'

Such extreme violence, when not driven by a battle for survival, requires a total break with decades of social conditioning. One way that has been used to achieve this is to alter one's appearance, even to dress up.

As we have seen on shipwrecks that involve looting, sailors will often dress up in lace and frills as soon as the mayhem commences. On Batavia's Graveyard, Cornelisz went so far as to produce a uniform:

> To all his followers, whom he could best trust, and who were most willing to murder, he gave clothes made from red laken [a fine wool cloth] trimmed with 2 or more gold passementen [lace], creating a new mode of cassock.

The murderers were still wearing these ridiculous outfits the day the rescue ship arrived.

Golding refers to transformation of appearance repeatedly in Lord of the Flies. First Jack, then his hunters, shed most of their clothes, tie their long hair back and make face and body paints from clay and charcoal. No doubt from his experience as a naval officer in World War II, Golding understood the dangers of a uniform. Firstly it imparts what he described as 'the painted anonymity of the group', unifying the group into a cohesive mass, and providing a sense of shelter from individual responsibility.

It also accelerates the group slide into barbarity, as Jack finds the first time he paints his face into a mask: 'He began to dance and his laughter became a bloodthirsty snarling. He capered towards Bill and the mask was a thing on its own, behind which Jack hid, liberated from shame and self-consciousness.' Golding knew painted Jack was perfectly capable of a moral depravity that unpainted Jack would baulk at.

Golding hammers his point home in the final pages of his novel. The naval officer who rescues Ralph is appalled at the mob of 'little boys, streaked with coloured clay, sharp sticks in their hands'. He expresses surprise that British boys should have sunk to this dire level.

In his book *Men in Groups*, anthropologist Lionel Tiger points out, 'The English officer is sketched no differently than the boys; he wears epaulettes and a uniform in the way the savage children tie their hair and paint their skin.'

In 1961 director Peter Brook noticed the same tendency when he was filming *Lord of the Flies* on a tropical island off Puerto Rico. Brook discovered 'many of their [the child actors'] off-screen relationships completely paralleled the story'. The boys playing the other characters were bullying and threatening the actor playing Piggy. As the young actors slid into a state of hostility that mirrored the plot, Brook discovered how to maintain order: 'We had to cake them in mud and let them be savages by day, and restore prep-school discipline by the shower and the scrubbing by night.'

As we have noted, on the night of their most violent dash, bash and smash raid, the Robbers Cave Rattler boys covered their face and arms with dark paint, commando-style. The raid proved a destructive, painful and terrifying event for the Eagle group.

Charles Manson insisted his cult members don a uniform of black clothes and a knife before they went on 'creepy-crawly' missions, even when violence was not intended.

Another consistent thread running through the thrill-kill groups is the age of the perpetrators. From the animal kills in Wisconsin to Batavia's Graveyard and Manson's 'Family', the hands-on killers are almost exclusively in their late teens and early twenties, considerably younger than their Svengali-like leaders. Cornelisz was thirty-one, Jim

Jones was forty-seven and Charles Manson was thirty-four.

Thrill killings appear to be premeditated, excessively brutal, senseless—and addictive. Sometimes, as happened with the Family and on Batavia's Graveyard, external forces arrive and stop the killing. But there is one last scenario: near-total annihilation of the entire group.

# LAST MAN STANDING

*Each strove to catch the other off his guard, and kill him.*
*ALEXANDER PEARCE, 1824*

**IF A GROUP** has the good fortune to be rescued at the death knell, the few remaining survivors are often in an appalling state.

Scanning a freezing, desolate Arctic coastline for any survivors from Aldolphus Greely's expedition, the rescue party led by John Colwell spotted the figure of a man stumbling slowly along the ice-covered rocks. 'He was a ghastly sight. His cheeks were hollow, his eyes wild, his hair and beard long and matted...As he spoke, his utterances were thick and mumbling, and in his agitation his jaw worked in convulsive twitches.'

The man pointed Colwell to a half-collapsed tent nearby. Cutting the tent open with a knife, the rescuers were not prepared for what they saw:

*It was a sight of horror. On one side, close to the opening, with his head towards the outside, lay what was apparently a dead man. His jaw had dropped, his eyes were open, but fixed and glassy, his limbs were motionless. On the opposite side was a poor fellow, alive to be sure, but without hands or feet, and with a spoon tied to the stump of his right arm.*

The other survivors in the tent had 'the hand of death upon them'. They were barely conscious, frostbitten and unable to stand. A few could no longer talk or even comprehend that they had been rescued. Even the healthiest men were petulant, rambling, fitful, incoherent, delusional and begging for food. Outside the tent, Colwell found the shallow graves of the cannibalised corpses, the body of another man lying where he had dropped dead and another mutilated body at the edge of the campsite, shot through the chest.

If a dysfunctional stranded group fails to be rescued or rescue itself, social annihilation is inevitable.

This also occurred with the *Bounty* mutineers on Pitcairn Island. After seizing the ship and abandoning Captain William Bligh and his loyal crew members in a longboat, the mutineers set off under the command of Fletcher Christian to make a new life for themselves in the tropical paradise they had glimpsed in Tahiti. But from the start, the mutineers had trouble finding a suitable place to settle. Initially they chose Tubuai Island in French Polynesia, but friction with the locals added to conflict within the group itself. Besotted with the local women, the men began to argue and chafed at being under Christian's command. Two men went AWOL, declaring, 'we are now our own Masters'. When they returned, Christian, attempting to enforce his crumbling authority, placed a pistol at their heads and threatened to shoot them.

A prolonged argument ensued: 'Three days were spent in debate, and having nothing to employ themselves in, they demanded more grog. This he [Christian] also refused, and they broke the lock on the spirit room and took it by force.'

Under pressure from the locals, they left Tubuai, but the group soon fractured. More than half the men insisted on being dropped off in Tahiti: the nine mutineers who sailed off again in the *Bounty* took the opportunity to kidnap eighteen women (six of whom were soon abandoned for being 'ancient') and six Polynesian men.

The *Bounty* eventually made its way to Pitcairn, an uninhabited island where Christian felt they could remain hidden from the long, vengeful arm of the Royal Navy—a task made easier because the island was incorrectly located on the contemporary charts by 290 kilometres.

They started their new colony in January 1790, after burning the *Bounty* to the waterline to avoid attracting attention from passing ships. The mutineers arrived well prepared with adequate supplies—crops, livestock, tools and slave labour in the form of the kidnapped Polynesians. The island had plenty of fresh water, a mild climate, mature coconut and breadfruit trees (left from a previous Polynesian settlement) and fertile soil.

It should have been the paradise the men had dreamed of, but instead the embryonic colony turned on itself in a familiar pattern. There are many versions of what transpired, but the most reliable is probably an account from one of the kidnapped Polynesian women, Teehuteatuaonoa (known as Jenny by the

Europeans), who was consort to one of the men, Isaac Martin. Unlike the mutineers, she had no reason to fabricate her story to avoid British naval justice.

Teehuteatuaonoa recorded that the Europeans took one woman each to be their wives, leaving the three remaining women to the six Polynesian men, who were also not given any land. At first everyone was busy, constructing houses and planting vegetable plots. Many of the women gave birth, but disaster struck when two of the mutineers' wives died, prompting the widowers to help themselves to two of the Polynesian men's wives as replacements.

The disgruntled husbands planned to kill the mutineers but the plot was discovered, and the two Polynesians, Oha and Tararo, fled into hiding. Christian seized another Polynesian and forced him, on pain of death, to hunt down and kill the two conspirators. He obeyed.

Two years of relative peace followed before intractable problems between the Polynesians and Europeans boiled over. The Polynesian men, who had just one 'wife' between them, were mistreated and overworked by the mutineers, who regarded them as slaves and beat them for any misbehaviour. Eventually the Polynesians decided to kill all the mutineers and began to arm themselves.

In late September 1793 they put their plan into action. They shot dead a man who was working on his fence. Proceeding to Fletcher Christian's garden, 'they went up behind him and shot him between the shoulders—he fell. They disfigured him with an axe about the head, and left him dead on the ground.'

Next they confronted two more mutineers, Mills and McCoy; Mills was shot dead but McCoy escaped to the mountains. The Polynesians moved on, wounding Isaac Martin, then hunting him down at William Brown's house, where he had taken refuge. They finished him off with a hammer. Brown was beaten with a rock, then killed with a shot through the back of the head as he begged for his life. John Adams, barricaded in his house, was hit in the hand by a musket ball, breaking two of his fingers, but his life was saved when some of the women intervened. Another mutineer, Edward Young, was also spared, and Matthew Quintal was not in the settlement at the time.

By now, five mutineers lay dead, one was wounded and one was in hiding. The victorious Polynesians quarrelled over the divisions of the spoils (and the women): one of them, Teimua, was shot dead by another, Manarii. That night, McCoy and Quintal sneaked into the settlement and, at the urging of the women, killed Manarii. The two remaining Polynesian men fired at the mutineers, but McCoy and Quintal fled unharmed. The following day, one of the women and Young sneaked up on the remaining two Polynesian men:

> About noon, while one of the Otahetian men was sitting outside of the house, and the other was lying on his back on the floor, one of the women took a hatchet and cleft the skull of the latter, at the same instant calling for Young to fire, which he did and shot the other native dead.

Nine people—more than half of the Europeans and all of the Polynesian men—died in two days of violence. The women refused to bury the five slain mutineers, so the corpses lay around until they decomposed.

A tense calm followed, but the women were still unhappy

at their treatment and continued to suffer beatings from Quintal and McCoy. Things got worse when McCoy discovered how to distil a potent alcohol from the sweet roots of the local cordyline shrub. Drunk, Quintal became even more hostile, proposing to the other men 'not to laugh, joke, or give anything to any of the girls'.

After four years on the island, paranoia and hostility were still simmering. The men discovered a plot by the women to murder them, and the women tried to escape on a homemade boat. The men purported to forgive them, but secretly agreed to kill the next woman who got out of line.

However, the next fatality was one of the men. McCoy, who had injured himself in a fall, had taken to drinking heavily and was depressed and unstable: in 1797 he killed himself by jumping off a cliff. Quintal, also drinking to excess, became fearful of the other two men and decided to kill them along with Fletcher Christian's children. Young and Adams got to him first, however, hacking Quintal up with an axe in what Teehuteatuaonoa described as 'a drunken affray'.

When a passing American ship, the *Topaz,* chanced upon the settlement a decade later, they discovered the last man standing: John Adams, surrounded by nine women and dozens of children.

Of the fifteen men who had landed, twelve had been murdered, one had committed suicide and Young had died from an asthma attack. As successive ships visited the island over the following years, Adams's version of events changed drastically, always casting him in an innocent light.

Pitcairn shows the extreme natural progression of a failed group: mutual annihilation until just one man is left.

Even though the *Bounty* mutineers were ensconced in a 'paradise' of their own choosing, with plentiful food and water, the community tore itself apart—albeit a little more slowly than groups clinging to existence in far harsher circumstances. Finally, with just one adult male left alive on Pitcairn, the murders stopped and the island settled into a surprising idyll.

When a group is whittled down until just two men remain, the dynamic is particularly chilling.

In 1822, a convict named Alexander Pearce escaped from the brutal Australian prison settlement of Sarah Island in western Tasmania with seven other prisoners. The tiny band unwittingly absconded into some of the worst terrain in Australia, with almost no supplies. Within a week they were out of food, struggling through impenetrable forests in freezing weather.

As soon as the food ran out, co-operation evaporated. Arguing about whose turn it was to get firewood, the eight men lit eight separate fires one night to avoid sharing fuel. One of the convicts, Robert Greenhill, who had been serving a fourteen-year sentence for forgery, quietly suggested killing one of the company to eat.

He didn't wait for consensus. 'About three o'clock in the morning, Dalton was asleep; then Greenhill ran and took an axe and struck him on the head.'

The body was dismembered and divided up. As soon as the group set out again, two of the weaker members, terrified they might be next, dropped to the back and fled. From that point, the group was playing a high-stakes game in which sleep could equal death. When the meat ran out, Greenhill picked a new target, once again hitting the victim in the head with his axe. Several days later, with the men scared to fall asleep and keeping a vigilant eye on the axe, the putrefying human flesh they were carrying made one of the survivors violently ill: 'he then began to vomit. Greenhill started up and took the axe, and hit him on the forehead.'

The pattern continued until just Greenhill and Pearce remained alive. The terrain improved, but the fear was paralysing: they were terrified to stay together, but separating would put one at risk of a surprise attack from the other. All they could do was watch each other constantly. Sleep was out of the question so they stayed awake for several days. In this deadly standoff, Pearce was at a grave disadvantage because Greenhill had the axe.

At the end of the third day, exhausted, cold and weak, they stopped and lit a fire for the night. Towards dawn, after about sixty hours without sleep, Pearce saw his chance: 'I found he was asleep; I run up and took the axe from under his head, and struck him with it and killed him.'

Pearce chopped off Greenhill's arm and thigh, and continued into the wilderness. One of the persistent paradoxes of human desperation then presented itself: having fought desperately to stay alive within a group, as soon as he was alone Pearce began to consider taking his own life. He contemplated hanging himself with his belt, but fought off the urge. Several days later, he was found by a farmer in a paddock at the edge of the bush with a half-devoured raw lamb in his hands.

Pearce's confession was so disturbing that the authorities refused to believe it and convinced themselves the other seven escapees were living as bushrangers. Pearce was let off scot-free for the murders and the cannibalism, and returned to his old work camp.

Within a year he escaped again with another convict, Thomas Cox. Ten days later he was caught with Cox's body parts in his pockets. This time Pearce was hanged. Trial observers commented that the man in the dock did not look like a cannibal.

Sometimes when stranded survivors are found alone, such as Philip Ashton (on an island off Honduras in 1724), they will claim that the second-last survivor just up and left or died of natural causes. Indeed, it seems safe to say that the truth definitely dies with the second-last victim. On other occasions, no one is found. Vanished groups and colonies mysteriously dot the pages of history.

Twenty-seven years after the *Batavia* came to grief off the West Australian coast, the *Gilt Dragon,* another ship belonging to the Dutch East India Company, suffered a similar fate. Seventy-five passengers and crew made it to the Australian mainland, about ninety kilometres north of present-day Perth. The captain, mindful of the *Batavia* disaster, decided to stay with the survivors and ordered a junior officer and several crew to sail to Jakarta for help.

When three rescue ships arrived over the following eighteen months, there was no trace of the sixty-eight people who had been left behind. All the rescuers found was a semicircle of planks set in the sand.

What had happened? The captain would have known that he simply had to stay put for a few months and keep a signal fire burning. The first rescue ship arrived a mere three months after the wreck had occurred. The would-be rescuers reported an adequate food supply of seals and birds in the area. The autumn weather was mild, with an average four centimetres of rainfall a week. But some catastrophe had clearly struck, leaving not even a single survivor. Their fate remains a mystery.

When R. M. Ballantyne and William Golding imagined their tropical paradises, they conjured up visions of lush, coconut-fringed islands with a warm lagoon and a coral reef teeming with fish. The Pacific Ocean is dotted with hundreds of uninhabited islands very like this description (minus Ballantyne's penguins). But archaeology has revealed evidence of a surprisingly large number of small-scale settlements that have simply vanished. All that remains of them are traces of stone tools and cultivation, introduced crops such as banana and taro now growing wild, the scattered remains of houses and graves, and traditional *marae* (large ceremonial areas bordered by stones). The *Bounty* mutineers found such traces on Pitcairn; indeed three of the four islands in the Pitcairn group bear the remains of lost settlements.

Colony collapse from a simple lack of food or resources tends to leave a trace—animal species will suddenly go extinct, or forests disappear. But, in the absence of a written record or a survivor account, annihilation by the hand of man is more elusive and harder to detect. On the charnel ground of the Abrolhos Islands, there is very little trace of the extreme violence. Blood, even in vast quantities, washes away and very few graves of the 120 *Batavia* victims have been discovered. One mass grave (three adults, a teenager, a child and an infant) was found in the 1980s. But of these six victims, only one showed a detectable sign of a violent death. If the *Batavia* killers had been allowed to continue, it is likely the outcome would have been another question mark on the page of history, much like that of the *Gilt Dragon*.

# SCARS

*With filthy body, matted hair and unwiped nose,*
*Ralph wept for the end of innocence, the darkness of man's heart...*
LORD OF THE FLIES

**SOME INDIVIDUALS SURVIVE** their ordeals and return home, to attempt a resumption of normal life. For others, the rule of law may arrive to reimpose order, justice and retribution.

When Francisco Pelsaert's rescue yacht, the *Sardam*, finally reached Batavia's Graveyard on September 17 1629, the blood-soaked islands looked like the final scene from a Greek tragedy.

The mutineers (now minus Jeronimus Cornelisz, who had been captured) had again attacked Wiebbe Hayes's men. The mutineers had fewer fighters, but they had guns, and a pitched battle had been raging for two hours when the *Sardam* sailed into the view of both factions. Its appearance sparked a desperate race to reach the ship.

Commander Pelsaert tacked around the islands before

dropping anchor. With several of his crew, he rowed towards land, scanning for any survivors, when he saw a yawl pull into view. Wiebbe Hayes, who had just won the race of his life, was yelling: 'Go back on board immediately, for there is a party of miscreants on the islands near the wreck, with two sloops, who have the intention to seize the yacht.'

Pelsaert listened to just enough of Hayes's summary to be convinced. He headed back to the *Sardam* and was barely back on board when the mutineers' boat, with eleven men brandishing weapons, pulled alongside. Pelsaert turned his poop guns on them and, after a brief standoff, the mutineers surrendered.

Interrogations began the same day, testimony and confessions spilling out of each mutineer until Pelsaert ascertained that more than 120 people had been murdered and that Jeronimus Cornelisz had been the ringleader. Cornelisz was brought before Pelsaert. He blamed everything on the others: 'with evident lies he tried to talk himself clean with his glib tongue.'

Cornelisz was subjected to a horrendous water torture so that the truth could be ascertained. He was tied up and fitted with a large, watertight collar that covered his head. It was filled to above his nose, so the only way to avoid drowning was to drink the water, whereupon it was topped up again. It was simple but devastatingly effective.

He made multiple confessions, recanted, prevaricated and then, finally, on September 28, signed some statements. Through the torture and confessions of other mutineers, and the statements from the few innocent survivors, the whole grim story emerged—although there had been so many murders, the killers had trouble recalling the exact order and dates.

Retribution was swift and harsh. Cornelisz had both his hands cut off with a hammer and chisel before he was hanged. Four other mutineers had one hand struck off before hanging. Three others were simply hanged. Seven men were keel-hauled three times each. (This punishment involved being dragged in a harness under the hull of the ship from one side to the other, resulting in lacerations, head injuries and occasionally drowning.)

Eight other men were sentenced '3 times to be dropped from the yard'. Under this punishment, a rope about fourteen metres long was attached to a man's wrists and bound behind the man's back. Weights were tied to the feet and the victim was dropped from the ship's yardarm. After a free-fall equivalent to the height of a four-storey building, the rope would snap taut. The shock would break bones and dislocate shoulders. This punishment was then repeated twice, regardless of the men's injuries. The keel-hauled and 'dropped' men also received one hundred lashes, after salt water had been poured on their backs to increase the pain.

Nine other mutineers were taken to Java for further interrogation and nineteen oath signers were freed. Two men, including eighteen-year-old Jan Pelgrom, were dumped on the Australian mainland. Centuries later, tales of blond Aborigines in Western Australia have sometimes been cited as evidence that the murderous pair may have survived to become Australia's first white settlers.

But what of the survivors, such as the seven women kept alive as sex slaves on Batavia's Graveyard? People in these desperate situations must have clung to the belief that rescue would arrive and end all their suffering. No doubt many survivors cherish the same naive hope expressed confidently by Commander Winfield Scott Schley when he rescued the six living members of the Greely expedition: 'The survivors were got on board safely...They were saved and had left behind them Camp Clay and its horrors.'

In some cases it is true that the survivors return to their families and homes and tried to resume life, outwardly not greatly affected by the trauma and terrors they have endured. Creesje Jans, who was forced to become Cornelisz's concubine on Batavia's Graveyard, remarried shortly after the rescue and apparently lived another fifty-two years.

But other survivors bear deep scars, both physical and psychological. In the past, traumatised individuals were rarely encouraged to gush about the suffering they had endured. But if we look at how some survivors spent the rest of their lives, it is possible to glean clues about the long-term effects of their experiences.

For a few months following a rescue, many survivors were busy with inquiries or trials or engaged in a frenzied rush to write about their experiences. Much more revealing insights tend to come from studying what occurred to them after this period.

When Lieutenant Greely and five others were rescued after three disastrous years in the Arctic, they had survived near-mutiny and starvation. They were the only survivors of the twenty-five who had set out on the expedition. All but one made a rapid recovery on the voyage back to civilisation, with rescue commander Schley noting a fast improvement in the men: 'Their muscles filling out, their voices were strong.'

The weather was fine but foggy, and 'the invalids suffered somewhat from the dampness and the summer heat, which produced a temporary prostration. Except for this, and for their aching joints and muscles, they were all fairly convalescent.' By the end of the six-week voyage back to civilisation, Greely had put on twenty-two kilograms and was pretty much back to his normal weight.

Photographs taken three months later show the expedition survivors looking remarkably well fed and jovial—although Greely said the health of two of the men had been totally broken by the ordeal. It may have been some consolation that the men were officially greeted as heroes. Public opinion shifted when, in August 1884, the *New York Times* published graphic accounts of the state of the bodies that had been repatriated, concluding: 'The secrets of those awful days are locked in the hearts of the little handful of survivors.'

Soon after, Greely wrote a long account of his 'Three Years of Arctic Service'. He dedicated the book to the men of his expedition—'to its dead who suffered much—to its living who suffered more'. Greely always insisted that, as far as he knew, no cannibalism had occurred. He did, however, note the heavy cost on the other survivors: two dead, two with 'broken health' and one who 'lies...helpless in a city hospital, aided by private charity, his pension not even awarded'.

Greely, however, went on to enjoy a series of promotions and a stellar career in the US Army. In 1925 he was described by the *Boston Sunday Post* as 'a tall, soldierly figure, erect and strong despite his eighty-four years...General Greely's voice is clear and penetrating, his beard as white as any patriarch's...A calm, courteous, kindly man.' He died at the age of ninety-one and is buried in Arlington National Cemetery.

Robert Holding, the most resourceful of the nineteen men who made it to shore after the *Invercauld* was wrecked on Auckland Island, seemed to regard the year he spent there as an adventure, even though he was one of only three survivors. 'Thus the first day of June found me up on the island again in search of food and adventure,' he wrote cheerily in a memoir penned much later. Holding appeared to suffer no long-term psychological effects and went on to lead a long and productive life. He did, however, keep a memento of the disaster: the last three matches he possessed on the island.

The ultimate unscathed survivor would have to be little Mugpi, who boarded the *Karluk* aged just two, and survived the 120-kilometre ice trek over the frozen East Siberian Sea, and six months of starving isolation on Wrangel Island. She carried just one single scar: a scratch on her chin from the ship's cat. According to her family, Ruth Makpii Ipalook lived a positive and cheerful life before she died in Alaska in 2008, aged ninety-seven.

Greely, Holding and Mugpi seem to be exceptions, however. There are many more stories of survivors suffering physical breakdown, personality shifts and nightmares. Today we have a name for it: post-traumatic stress disorder.

PTSD is a debilitating anxiety disorder that can result from exposure to a terrifying ordeal. Even after the danger has long passed, suffers of PTSD may feel afraid, angry, depressed, jumpy, isolated or emotionally unresponsive. They are sensitised to danger and will overreact to minor stimuli. Intrusive memories of the trauma, such as flashbacks and nightmares, and physical reactions such as a racing heart can cause grave problems for PTSD sufferers. Often they will try to avoid anything that reminds them of the ordeal, and may become socially isolated. Typically such symptoms will appear within three months of the trauma and may last a lifetime.

Many factors increase an individual's likelihood of developing PTSD, including the severity and duration of the ordeal and the combination of psychological and physical trauma. Women and children are at increased risk of developing PTSD, and being pregnant heightens that risk. Counterintuitively, being intoxicated at the time of the trauma also seems to *increase* one's chance of getting PTSD—bad news for many of our shipwreck survivors.

On a neurological level, PTSD is astonishingly complex and not well understood, but it is clear the amygdala, the hippocampus and the mPFC (medial prefrontal cortex) play a major role. In PTSD, the amygdala responses are greatly elevated; even something as inconsequential as a slammed door can send the person into full physiological and neurological panic mode. A normal response in that kind of situation might be to jump at the loud noise but then calm down when other parts of the brain instruct the amygdala, 'Don't worry, it's just the wind. We are perfectly safe.' In PTSD, not only does the amygdala overreact in the first place ('It's a gunshot!'), but the neurological instructions to inhibit the fear reactions are disrupted, so it keeps pressing the panic button.

Between the lines of reports about survivors, or in their own written memoirs, many PTSD symptoms can be discerned. Of the three *Invercauld* survivors, Andrew Smith went on to suffer pain and numbness in the legs. And according to a report in the *Aberdeen Argus* on October 13 1865, Captain Dalgarno had been aged greatly by his ordeal and was not faring well:

> *His health is still very delicate, owing to the extraordinary privations to which he had been exposed, and his medical adviser has forbidden him to speak to anyone on the subject of the wreck, as any recurrence on his part to the sad events always brings on a nervous attack.*

You might expect to find the resourceful crew of the *Grafton* to have coped better, but they, too, were scarred. Captain Thomas Musgrave and François Raynal wrote bestselling accounts of their ordeal, but neither found life easy.

Musgrave's book outlines his depression, the guilt he felt over his family and his crew, and his need for solitude. All these symptoms indicate that he was suffering from PTSD while trapped on the island (which makes his remarkable strength, perseverance and achievements even more impressive). After returning to Australia, Musgrave promised his wife he would never go to sea again. He became a harbour boat captain in Victoria's Lakes Entrance for a short time and then a lighthouse keeper, taking his wife and numerous children to extremely remote locations. According to his daughter:

> *My father Capt. Thomas Musgrave once remarked when looking up passing the Promontory in his ship 'I wouldn't live there for a thousand a year'. Years later, after his crew had been wrecked on Auckland Island for 20 months... Father gladly accepted the position of lighthouse keeper on the same promontory, at a salary very much less than a thousand a year.*

After nine years on Wilsons Promontory, he moved from one remote spot to another, eventually dying at Point Lonsdale lighthouse in 1891, aged fifty-nine, soon after the death of his wife. It might seem puzzling that, after almost twenty months of desperate loneliness and isolation on Auckland Island, he should choose a career that meant twenty-two more years of the same. But this wish for social isolation is quite typical in PTSD. As a lighthouse keeper, Musgrave spent up to eight hours alone every day, staring out to sea. In all likelihood, he was afflicted with PTSD until his death.

Raynal fared somewhat better. He left Sydney in 1867 and returned to Paris. His book *Wrecked on a Reef* became a bestseller in France and was translated into many languages. (The book influenced Jules Verne, who used it as the inspiration for *The Mysterious Island*, a somewhat confused novel centred on an isolated island with snow, flesh-eating dugongs, pirates and Captain Nemo's secret lair. It features a group of five castaways, led by a resourceful and brilliant leader who is an amalgam of Musgrave and Raynal.)

After the publication of *Wrecked on a Reef*, Raynal landed a good job with the Paris municipal council and went on to have a successful career as a bureaucrat. He retired on the grounds of ill-health in 1888, but his mental state was apparently sound. He became a member of the Geographical Society of Paris, lectured at France's Academy of Science, and was the recipient of various honours, both scientific and literary (including the Académie Française's Montyon Prize). He died at the age of sixty-eight.

William McKinlay, survivor of the *Karluk* disaster in the Canadian Arctic in 1913–14, 'lost almost all his teeth as a result of the starvation diet'. Robert Williamson, another survivor of the march to Wrangel Island, later wrote: 'It does no good raking up the past...therefore I do not care to say or write about our life on Wrangel Island.'

There is evidence that the *Medusa* survivors suffered both psychologically and physically for decades after their thirteen horrifying days on the raft. Alexandre Corréard and fellow survivor Henri Savigny wrote a bestselling book about the expedition. However, Corréard suffered from 'scorbutic wounds' that kept opening up long after his rescue, causing him great pain right up to his death forty years later. More poignantly, after his wife died, Corréard took to clothing a dressmaker's dummy in her garments and sitting it at the window of his home. He would give her a fresh change of clothes each day.

Corréard fought hard to keep the *Medusa* story in the public eye, at a time when the government would have preferred it forgotten. He opened a bookshop, and published 'subversive' pamphlets that brought him to the attention of the police, with the result that he spent time in and out of jail.

Savigny married his sweetheart and became mayor of his village, but he was depressed, bitter, 'racked with grief' and 'frequently ill and haunted by horrific dreams'. When his wife died, the keepsake she had given him as a 'Godspeed' when he departed on the expedition went into the coffin with her.

The sinking of the *Essex,* which had collided with a sperm whale in the southern Pacific in 1820, was followed by weeks of appalling thirst and cannibalism in lifeboats. The events clearly traumatised the survivors. Captain George Pollard, seemingly recovered, went back to sea in 1822, commanding the ship *Two Brothers.* On his new ship he hung a net of food directly over his bunk, so he could see food all the time. Calamity struck the following year, when this ship was also wrecked, sending the captain into an unresponsive stupor that almost stopped him leaving the sinking vessel.

This second disaster pushed him into a depressed state, anxious and guilt-stricken. A missionary who met Pollard in April 1823 reported that the captain insisted on repeating his well-known tale from the *Essex* in excruciating detail, even though it caused Pollard to sob, 'my head is on fire at the recollection'. Soon after, he retired to Nantucket and became a nightwatchman—another solitary and lonely occupation—and lived there until his death in 1870.

Owen Chase, first mate on the *Essex*, wrote *The Narrative of the Most Extraordinary and Distressing Shipwreck of the Whale-Ship Essex* in 'the hope of obtaining something of remuneration by giving a short history of my sufferings in the world'. Chase, who married four times, spent another nineteen years at sea but 'he was prey to the deepest gloom'. He was haunted by memories, and suffered nightmares and terrible headaches. Years later, he took to dressing in rags and reportedly bought huge quantities of food, hoarding stores in the rafters of his home in Nantucket. In 1868 he was formally declared insane, and died the following year.

Benjamin Lawrence, another member of the *Essex* crew, kept a thirty-centimetre piece of twine he had made in his ninety-three days on the first mate's boat. At his death, it was passed on to the Nantucket Historical Association.

Hanging on to mementos is common among survivors. Holding kept his three matches from the Auckland Islands. Captain Tom Dudley of the *Mignonette* kept a grim souvenir—the penknife that he had used to slit the jugular of the unfortunate cabin boy Richard Parker. Dudley even insisted police officer James Laverty (who asked to see the knife while taking Dudley's deposition about the murder) be sure to return it.

The Atacama mine collapse in Chile in 2010 gives a clearer picture of what survivors go through—not just because it unfolded before the eyes of the mass media, but because it occurred when PTSD had become a recognised condition whose effects were less stigmatised, and the thirty-three men were therefore more willing to talk about the consequences of their experience.

The CBS network reported on February 14 2011 that thirty-two of the thirty-three miners who had spent sixty-nine days underground in 2010 were still enduring 'severe psychological problems'.

A year after the mine collapse, about half were still unemployed. Others were battling drug addiction. One had been hospitalised for depression and anxiety. Omar Reygadas, fifty-seven, told the Associated Press he continued to have nightmares:

> I try to read, to tire myself out so that I can sleep well. But if I'm alone in a closed space, it still makes me anxious—I have to get out and find someone to talk with or distract myself with something.

Victor Zamora told CBS: 'I'm still down the mine.' He also said: 'I was a happy guy, but now I'm having nightmares. I'm having problems. I'm not the same person.' He complained he was unable to have a normal relationship with his family, and that he would prefer to be dead.

Zamora said that, while trapped in the mine, 'I wrote two letters. I wrapped them in a plastic bag so that if I didn't get out my rotting body wouldn't affect the paper.' He wrote a letter to his pregnant wife, telling her to marry again. 'Me? I was already dead. To myself I was already dead. I was alive but I was dead.'

Another of the rescued miners, Alex Vega, took to constructing a wall around his house, for no reason that he could explain.

*Whenever I hear a noise, I get scared and look around me. My heart beats faster. I can't go into small spaces. I'm taking five or six pills a day now. If I don't take them, I wouldn't even be able to sit here.*

William Golding had also witnessed and experienced horror in World War II, and later admitted he had been terrified for the duration of his service. (Even the basic training using blank ammunition had frightened the wits out of him.) Serving on board HMS *Galatea,* sailing through U-boat infested fjords, he developed 'a mind so habituated to danger that it ceases to be anything but a continual, only semiconscious worry like a too heavy bill that will have to be paid.'

After the war Golding, who was an anxious person even before he served, developed a veritable Pandora's box of phobias: he was unreasonably afraid of needles, heights, insects, spiders, the dark, being alone, the supernatural and empty rooms. As his daughter Judy Golding later acknowledged, 'The war affected him profoundly.'

In later life Golding became an alcoholic. His biographer John Carey, who had access to Golding's personal journals, thought the author's public mask was very different from the inner man: 'The emotion he felt most vividly and often behind his disguise, was, I think, fear on a scale varying from mild anxiety to terror.'

The author of *Lord of the Flies* had his own demons.

# IMPLICATIONS

*I saw the effects of war: families who lost their men and dislocations of human beings. I saw hunger. I saw people killed on my side of national affiliation; I saw people killed on the other side. In fact it was a miracle I was not killed.*

**THE WORDS ABOVE** could easily sum up William Golding's experiences in World War II; in fact they were written by Muzafer Sherif to explain his fascination with the 'serious business of transaction between human groups'. As an adolescent, Sherif had been caught up in the bloody breakup of the Ottoman Empire following World War I. On May 15 1919, he was standing on the street with a group of Turkish civilians during the invasion of his hometown, Smyrna in Turkey, when a Greek soldier walked up and bayoneted the man standing next to him. Sherif, just thirteen years old at the time, had expected to die next, but the soldier strolled away.

Like Golding, Sherif witnessed an 'intense degree of animosity…and bestial destructiveness'. He also recognised that similar atrocities were being carried out by his fellow Turks— reasonable men whose compassion and self-sacrifice for their own group were equalled only by their vindictiveness towards the enemy.

One World War later, William Golding survived the D-Day invasion of Normandy and later participated in the Battle of Walcheren. He came under sustained fire as the British attacked the small Dutch island of Walcheren, which Golding discovered later had been full of civilians. He described the fierce battle: 'ships blowing up into a Christmas tree of exploding ammunition, ships burning, sinking—and smoke everywhere slashed by sudden spats of tracer over the shell foundations and the drowning, broken men.'

Both men took their experiences and used them: their yesterdays walked with them.

The experiment and the novel are different expressions of the same concept. If either had appeared a few years later, it would have been assumed that one was the father of the other. But on opposite sides of the world, working simultaneously, the teacher and the experimenter were unaware of each other's work.

At the beginning of this book, we asked the question:

*As a template for social decay, how accurate is the Lord of the Flies principle?*

The answer is inescapable—*exceptionally accurate*. William Golding's work followed with almost pinpoint precision all of the main aspects of the implosion of a failed group:

— neglect of the weak and sick;

— a rapid descent into bickering over resources and labour;

— the corrosive, emotional effect of hunger, paranoia and fear;

— the collapse of leadership;

— fragmentation into hostile factions;

— the emergence of personal hatred;

— an absolute loss of compassion and altruism;

— casual acceptance of death;

— violent fights that escalate into murder and, finally, the emergence of killing for entertainment.

The philosopher Thomas Hobbes, who described life in a state of nature as 'solitary, poor, nasty, brutish, and short', would have nodded his head from the first page to the last.

There are a few minor aspects that Golding doesn't cover. The novel doesn't describe the crash: indeed, the boys emerge from the initial disaster miraculously and unrealistically uninjured. Being children, the issue of alcohol never arises, nor do tensions over sex. The boys never resort to cannibalism (although the plans for Ralph's corpse mirror their treatment of the pigs' bodies). The intervention of the naval officer halts the slaughter before it can reach its natural conclusion. If anything, Golding pulled his punches.

Even so, his vision of the progression of social collapse is stark, ugly and realistic. It is a disturbing picture of the naked human condition once the layers of restraint and conditioning— and the thin veneer of civilisation—have been stripped off.

Most accurate of all was Golding's overarching concept that the primary thing from which the group needs protection is itself. When Simon has his vision of the beast in *Lord of the Flies*, the decapitated pig's head mocks him: 'Fancy thinking the Beast was something you could hunt and kill...You knew, didn't you? I'm part of you?…You know perfectly well you'll only meet me down there—so don't try to escape!'

Samuel Avalos, who survived the 2010 Chilean mining disaster, described with shocking frankness how important a functional group dynamic was to their individual survival: 'It's a form of self-protection. It's not about looking after your mates. No…you fuck them over if you can. It's about protecting yourself because you turn into something else down there.' Avalos had experienced that transformation in person when he stole and secretly drank all the saline from the group's medical kit.

Many of the individuals we have examined were torn apart by conflicting forces deep within the human psyche. We all crave company—the idea of living without contact with other people is abhorrent to all sane individuals—but most people aren't very good at living with others. Even families have their fault lines and intractable problems, and the mere existence of the term 'going postal' is proof of how toxic and unbearable some work groups can become.

Australian homicide statistics offer stark testimony to conflict within groups. Over three-quarters of male killers know their victims from group contact (either family, friends, workplace, or through their living arrangements). Only five per cent of all female victims are killed by strangers. Religion can play a part in controlling the more dangerous aspects of social interaction: six of the Ten Commandments are essentially rules for social behaviour.

As our case studies show, when a group is collapsing and conditions are getting steadily worse, many individuals reach the point where selfishness overwhelms their commitment to the group. Many accounts outline the seemingly logical reasoning: resources are scarce, so now it's every man for himself. Unfortunately, once that mindset becomes entrenched, not only is the group itself doomed, but individuals have less chance of survival too.

In other words, self-interest backfires, and absolute selfishness backfires catastrophically.

Without doubt, the cohesive groups—such as the *Grafton*'s crew, or Flight 571, or Shackleton's party—had the best survival rates. These three groups also managed, through their organisation and collective skills and strength, to save themselves.

The surrounding environment is not always critical to success or failure. The *Grafton* crew succeeded brilliantly in appalling conditions; the *Bounty* mutineers failed dismally in a virtual paradise.

We posited another question: *What would I do under the same circumstances?*

Many people might give an immediate response of 'No, I would never descend into such barbarity. And besides, now we have GPS to find our location, and mobile phones to call for help.'

Superficially, this is true. Technology has shrunk the world and made it safer. But this gives us confidence to venture into extreme and inaccessible environments, often for recreation. Sites that were once the domain of hardy explorers—the polar regions, deep caves and remote islands—are now in the sights of casual tourists. But the best laid plans will fail (as they always have)—people will forget the spare batteries or drop the satellite phone on the deck; engines will continue to break down. As long as people choose to travel to remote locations, fate will intervene to conduct its little experiments.

Over four hundred years separate the maritime disasters of Jean de Léry's squall-battered ship and the luxury cruiser *Costa Concordia*, which struck rocks off Giglio Island in 2012. But the two captains' responses were identical—they abandoned their responsibility and their ships with a speed that was disgraceful to behold, unseemly to contemplate and scarcely possible to believe. Terror is an unremitting taskmaster.

We have also seen the 2010 Chilean mine disaster. The Chilean authorities, well aware of the dangerous psychological forces that would plague the miners during their long underground sojourn, called in expert help from NASA to defuse the situation. NASA and the other international space agencies have done extensive research into the fragile dynamic of isolated groups, in preparation for long space missions that lie ahead to distant planets.

Up until now, the era of space travel has been tightly regulated; astronauts have been carefully screened and extensively trained to deal with group conflict. But just ahead lies the last frontier of tourism—anyone with the cash will soon be able to head into space. Furthermore, having paying passengers on board, rather than just crew, alters and complicates the structure of authority on a ship.

This period will open up a new and potentially more catastrophic period of group dynamics. We may have the sophisticated intellects to design craft able to transport people fifty-six million kilometres to the surface of Mars, but those travellers' brains will be carrying destructive prehistoric baggage.

The only significant mistake we may accuse Golding of making is his timeframe—he pictured the social disintegration taking place over months. Peter Brook, the director of the 1963 film of *Lord of the Flies*, watched in horror as life imitated art on the set. Later Brook commented:

*My experience showed me that the only falsification in Golding's fable is the length of time the descent into savagery takes. His action takes about three months. I believe…the complete catastrophe could take place over a long weekend.*

Given that the Robbers Cave boys took only two days to turn violent, and the *William Brown*'s crew lasted just twenty-four hours before they started killing passengers, Brook's assessment seems accurate.

Once the group fragments and the factions turn hostile, there seems to be just one thing that can reverse the poisonous alchemy—the existence of a larger enemy. A violent confrontation on the *Medusa* raft was stopped in its tracks when several great white sharks began circling the raft. In Oklahoma in 1954, Sherif started the reconciliation between the Rattlers and the Eagles by cutting off the water supply. The psychologist also learned the hard way in 1953 when another of his experiments failed. Run along the same lines as the other two, Sherif glossed over the failure in a short statement: 'the study was terminated as an experiment owing to various difficulties and unfavourable conditions including errors of judgment'.

Later Sherif admitted that, during the frustration stage of the experiment, the boys discovered they were being manipulated by the psychologists. Given the degree of violence Sherif had tolerated in his other experiments, something clearly went very wrong this time. There is speculation that, when the boys discovered they were part of an experiment, they joined forces and turned on the adults.

It is easy for people today to feel a sense of disbelief, even disdain, at the failings of survivor groups throughout history. But remember most of the episodes described in this book involved people who were competent at 'useful' activities such as making fires, shinnying up trees and tying knots. The skills valued in modern society—using computers, smartphones and remote controls, or driving a car—are unlikely to be of much help in a survivor situation. Ask yourself: would you fare any better?

No matter how advanced and 'civilised' we believe ourselves to be, human nature has not changed. No one is immune from these forces. If we ever have the misfortune to be landed in a survivor scenario, our biggest enemy could well turn out to be ourselves and our companions. It was for good reason that Golding originally titled his book *Strangers From Within*.

As journalist Meg Greenfield reminded us in 1978 after covering the Jonestown carnage:

*The jungle is only a few yards away.*

# AVOIDING THE LORD OF THE FLIES PRINCIPLE

––––––

1. As soon as disaster strikes, get rid of any alcohol.

2. Acknowledge the situation has changed: the group should be free to choose a new leader—someone they can trust to make decisions for the good of the group.

3. As soon as possible, establish order and a routine.

4. Never allow the weak to die in order to save the strong—survivor maths is a fatal game.

5. Share resources and workloads equally among the survivors, regardless of rank.

6. Use a rotating work schedule.

7. Communicate. Silence is your enemy.

8. Stay busy, even if it seems pointless.

9. The leader must be accountable and replaceable.

10. Fragmentation is almost inevitable, but the leader must control factional discord.

11. Have a plan. If it fails, make a new plan.

12. If one faction begins to dominate and victimise the rest, it is imperative the remainder organise and defend themselves. Once murders commence, they tend to escalate.

13. Fight the mindset of individual self-preservation— we are communal creatures and we survive best in groups.

# INTO THE WOODS:

## THE ROBBERS CAVE EXPERIMENT

**TAKE TWENTY-TWO** eleven-year-old boys. Let them have the run of a paradise of woods, lakes, meadows and creeks, in a place that was once the hideout for the outlaw Jesse James. Give the boys everything they need in terms of food and shelter. Now take away any obvious adult supervision, introduce a bit of friction and watch what happens.

That, essentially, was the starting point of the experiment by psychologist Muzafer Sherif and his wife Carolyn in Oklahoma's Robbers Cave State Park in the summer of 1954.

The boys selected by Sherif and his team were all white, middle-class, Protestant and of above-average intelligence. All were from intact two-parent families, and were deemed to be well adjusted and happy. None had met before. All thought they were attending nothing more than a 'summer camp' and were unaware their behaviour was being monitored by Sherif's team (who posed as camp staff and janitors). The campsite was isolated: a perfect Petri dish for social experimentation.

The boys were divided into two groups that arrived separately. For the first week, each group thought the campsite belonged to them alone. As Sherif's team quietly observed how hierarchies were established in each group, the boys had fun swimming, exploring and playing games. The setting was idyllic and food and shelter were taken care of, but there were no authority figures. The boys had not a care in the world, and the freedom to do whatever they wanted.

One group, the self-styled 'Rattlers', was initially dominated by the largest, strongest boy, codenamed Brown. But he was bossy and played favourites too much, soon wearing out his welcome. Within days, he was supplanted by Mills, a small boy who was a natural clown and a good communicator.

Across the woods in another cabin, the 'Eagles' were slower to bond. On the first night an argument broke out over the correct way to roast marshmallows, and a forceful boy codenamed Craig stepped in to stop it. Craig remained on top during this stage, but his leadership style was heavy-handed and he shouted at or lectured boys he felt were acting up. Two Eagles became so homesick during the first week that they were sent home.

After a week of hiking, swimming, campfires and having fun, the experiment moved into the second phase, during which the researchers hoped to create competition and tensions between the Rattlers and the Eagles. They succeeded well beyond their expectations.

The instant each group became aware of the other's existence, hackles went up as territorial instincts emerged. The boys
talked about how they would challenge or run off the other
group (or 'out-group', to use Sherif's term). Internal group
solidarity strengthened and both groups created their own flag.

When the Eagles heard from the staff that the Rattlers were
intent on challenging them at baseball, they were incensed:
'They can't. We'll challenge them first…they've got a nerve.'

Soon the staff announced a four-day tournament would be
held between the two groups, with various games, contests and
cabin inspections. The secret intention was to maintain a very
close result between the Rattlers and Eagles by tampering with
the scores. The tournament prize was a highly coveted medal
and pocket-knife for each of the winners. For the losers—
nothing.

The prospect of the competition spurred each group into
a frenzy of self-improvement. The Rattlers put up Keep Off
signs around their territory and displayed their flag. Several
members were heard 'making threatening remarks about what
they would do if anyone bothered their flag'.

The initial contest was a baseball match. Both leaders chose
other, more athletic boys to captain their teams. A small but
extremely aggressive boy called Mason was chosen to direct the
Eagles on the field. Mills chose Simpson, who was strong and
athletic, for the Rattlers.

The first time the groups set eyes on each other, the frosti-
ness and suspicion were obvious. For a while they simply sized
each other up, then an Eagle made a harsh comment and the air
was soon thick with insults. The 1950s equivalents of cutting
nicknames were quickly applied—'Fatty', 'Tubby' and 'little

black Sambo'. Because the Eagles were two men down, two Rattlers sat out to balance the numbers. These boys sat on the sidelines, enthusiastically baiting and sledging the Eagles, who went on to lose. Afterwards Craig, who had played poorly, took a Rattlers' baseball mitt and secretly tossed it into the lake.

At lunch the boys ate together for the first time. The meal was punctuated by name-calling and insults.

Trouble emerged during the afternoon tug of war, which the Eagles also lost. Seconds before their defeat their leader, Craig, dropped the rope and walked off, causing anger within the Eagles. In an instant, Craig was out and the aggressive, domineering Mason was their new leader.

The Rattlers were not graceful victors: they teased the Eagles about their double defeat, and returned to their cabin comparing blisters and boasting of their glorious victory. As the Eagles trudged back to their camp, they caught sight of the Rattlers' flag. In a fit of spite, they set fire to it. The burnt remnant was returned to the flagpole to goad the Rattlers. Mason announced: 'You can tell those guys I did it. If they say anything, I'll fight them.' That night Mason threatened to beat up any Eagle who did not try his hardest in the next game.

When the Rattlers discovered their burnt flag the following morning, they began baying for revenge. As soon as the Eagles arrived at the field, hostilities flared. The Eagles' flag was seized and destroyed. A Rattler attacked Craig and got him in a headlock. The Rattlers' Simpson got into a fistfight with a low-ranking Eagle. Alarmed at the violent turn of events, the staff stepped in.

Mason, by now so angry he was crying, demanded that a boy of his own size step forward and fight him. Mills put himself forward, yelling, '*Fight me!*'

Once again staff intervened, and things calmed down enough for the baseball game to begin, amid shouted abuse from both sides. This time the Eagles won. Dissecting their victory, Mason attributed it to prayer the night before and to not swearing as much as the Rattlers. He also proposed that the Eagles never stoop to swearing or communicating with the Rattlers (they had already decided they wanted to eat separately).

At the Rattlers' camp, there were bitter recriminations. Two boys said they wanted to leave the camp, but Mills defused the situation with a joke and focused the group on strategising. Simpson also suggested a raid on the Eagles' camp.

Later that afternoon, the Eagles won the tug of war by literally digging in their heels. The bitterly disappointed Rattlers, who had expected an easy victory, got behind Simpson's earlier suggestion of a night raid on the Eagles' cabin. The Rattlers painted their faces commando-style and, at 10.30pm, launched an attack on their rivals. Mills jumped through the window, while the others rushed in the door. Banging things and shouting, they raced around the dark cabin.

Mason, the only Eagle still awake, desperately tried to rouse his teammates as the Rattlers overturned beds, ripped mosquito nets from the windows and stole things. Other Rattlers waited outside the door, ready to pounce on any boy attempting to escape. But the terrified Eagles were simply too stunned to move. Craig lay in bed, pretending to sleep even after the raid was over.

As the victorious Rattlers raced back to their cabin, Mason vented his fury at his own boys, calling them 'yellow' for refusing to fight, particularly Craig. Once the shock had worn off, the Eagles called for an immediate counterattack. They were arming themselves with rocks when staff again intervened.

Back at the Rattlers' cabin, Mills proudly displayed the comic books and jeans he had stolen. The boys relived highlights of the raid, and were thrilled to discover the stolen jeans belonged to their arch-enemy Mason. Mills vandalised the jeans and tied them onto a stick to parade provocatively the next day.

After just two days of contact, the two groups were enthusiastically on the warpath.

The next morning, the Eagles counterattacked, armed with sticks and baseball bats. While the Rattlers were eating breakfast at the mess hall, the Eagles rushed in to trash their cabin, overturning beds, hurling things about and pouring dirt over the entire mess. Mission accomplished, the Eagles retreated and began filling socks with stones in preparation for the inevitable revenge attack.

Sure enough, when the Rattlers returned from breakfast, there were immediate calls to 'get' the Eagles. The staff defused the situation by reminding the Rattlers that there was to be a cabin inspection that day—they aborted their raid and cleaned up instead. Digging deep into the Cold War lexicon of the day, a furious Simpson declared the Eagles were 'communists'.

Bad weather saw the morning's touch football delayed. Both groups used the time to plan attacks and paint 'raiding flags'. When the game started, the verbal abuse from the Rattlers grew. Two low-status members even turned on the adult staff members who were accompanying the Eagles: shouting at them to 'shut up' and get off their side of the field.

The afternoon's competition saw one victory each. Raiding plans were a hot subject in both groups and the Eagles took the precaution of gathering buckets of rocks just in case.

The final day of the tournament started with a tug of war, which the Rattlers won. Mason instructed his Eagles to take most of the food at lunch, denying the Rattlers their share. Both sides tried to calculate who would win the tournament, and more importantly, the pen-knives. As hope faded for a Rattler victory, talk of an attack against the Eagles increased.

The researchers had decided that victory should go the undermanned Eagles and manipulated the result to that effect. When the decision was announced, Mason cried with joy and the jubilant Eagles ran off to celebrate at 'their' waterhole. The Rattlers were devastated but swiftly hit upon a course of action that cheered them up.

They ransacked the Eagles' cabin, stole all the hard-won medals and knives, and set their boat adrift on the lake.

When the Eagles returned, they ran en masse to take their revenge, with a furious Mason in the lead. Outside the Rattlers' cabin they shouted insults and prepared to fight, but, faced with the impending violence, three of the Eagles (including Craig) lost their nerve and retreated. Back at the cabin, the enraged Mason screamed at his team: 'Come on you yellow-bellies! Are you going to lay down and take this?' This tactic rallied even the cowardly Craig back into the fray.

The numerically superior Rattlers demanded the Eagles get down on their bellies and crawl in order to have their knives returned. Mason yelled that the Rattlers should take out their two biggest boys so the groups could fight on even terms. When the Rattlers refused, fighting erupted. Somewhat belatedly, staff stepped in before anyone was seriously injured. This time they had to drag the combatants one by one back to their cabins.

At this point the psychologists realised their experiment was getting dangerously out of control and changed their plan. The camp director was brought in and the stolen medals and knives were returned. The following day both groups were removed to separate locations to calm down. They spent the day denigrating their enemies.

Sherif and his team attempted to reconcile the warring factions in phase three of the experiment. All competition was removed and after a cooling-down period, the groups were cautiously encouraged to interact during activities tailor-made for eleven-year-old enjoyment, such as setting off fireworks. These 'contact sessions', however, were punctuated by continuing hostility between the two groups, including garbage fights, threats, kicking and verbal abuse.

Sherif resorted to drastic means to finally get the groups to work together. The water supply to the camp was cut off, and the hot and thirsty boys had to co-operate in order to break into a water tanker conveniently left nearby. This was followed by several carefully orchestrated incidents which gradually broke down the intergroup boundaries.

Mason, who had been an excellent leader for the Eagles during wartime, was the most resistant to becoming friendly with the Rattlers during the artificial armistice. But by the time the experiment was over, the boys were able to catch the same bus back home without fighting.

Many have questioned the ethics of the Robbers Cave experiment, pointing out that the children were deceived about the true purpose of the camp, the competitions were manipulated, and the children were vulnerable to physical and psychological harm. Even so, Robbers Cave remains a striking real-life parallel to both Golding's *Lord of the Flies* and incidents among survivor groups in history. The situation at the campsite would almost certainly have become much more dangerous if the adult observers had not stepped in when things began to get out of control.

The Robbers Cave boys displayed hostility to their respective 'out-group' even before the Eagles and Rattlers had set eyes on each other. Unarmed physical violence between the two groups began within twenty-four hours of first contact, and this quickly escalated (in what Sherif called 'rapid spurts') to plans for further violence involving potentially lethal weapons such as baseball bats and socks full of stones. The social restraints of 1950s middle-class America fell away, and the boys were happy to turn to violence, even allowing their hatred to spill over onto adults associated with the enemy out-group.

Nor was the hostility confined to their perceived enemy. Violence and aggression became common within each group, often driving changes in their leadership and hierarchies. In the experiment's peaceful first phase, Brown was demoted as Rattlers leader for 'roughing up' some of his low-status followers. However, once the Rattlers realised that the Eagles (and Mason in particular) were afraid of Brown, his status rose.

Over in the Eagles camp, Mason's inherent aggression helped him displace Craig when the situation became combative.

Sherif observed over the course of the experiment that low-status members would attempt to improve their position in the in-group by demonstrating aggression towards the out-group. Frequently just verbal, it would extend to physical with the backing of the group leader.

During the competitive stage, threats and aggression were much more tolerated than they had been in the experiment's peaceful initial phase. After two straight game losses, Mills roughed up several members of his group, with apparent approval from the others. Similarly, in week two, Mason struck a low-status member of his Eagles group for not helping to keep their cabin clean.

While victory made the winners joyous and boastful, defeat had an extremely negative effect. Sherif noted dryly that 'follow(ing) defeat, heightened solidarity within the group was achieved through united co-operative action by the in-group against the out-group'. All of the fights, vandalism and raids were initiated by the losers. The more physical a contest, the more bitterly the losers experienced the loss.

It could be tempting to dismiss the Robbers Cave experiment as an aberration—except that Sherif conducted two other experiments along the same lines, and with similar outcomes. The 1949 experiment in Connecticut resulted in an even worse escalation of hostilities, with threats, brawls and raids. One combatant went as far as making a spear to use on the enemy and another boy pulled a knife on an opposing boy during an argument. When one of the group leaders tried to broker a truce, his own side turned on him.

Sherif used the results to back his Realistic Conflict Theory, which asserts that competition between groups for desired resources leads to conflict, negative prejudices, and stereotypes.

Perhaps the most disturbing implication of the three experiments is that within a group under stress and without restraints, aggression is often rewarded, and any sign of pacifism is regarded as traitorous weakness.

# PRÉCIS OF *LORD OF THE FLIES*

**WILLIAM GOLDING'S NOVEL,** published in 1954, shocked readers with its depiction of what happens when some English schoolboys are left to govern themselves without any adult supervision. The boys, aged twelve or under, find themselves in an island paradise but, left to their own devices, quickly descend into savagery and murder.

Golding begins the book with a plane crash on a small, uninhabited island. The survivors—evacuees from an unspecified war—quickly realise they must fend for themselves. Piggy, overweight and bespectacled but the cleverest boy in the group, suggests that a conch shell be used to gather the boys together and keep order. The boys elect the charismatic Ralph as their leader. With the naive optimism of youth, they relish their new freedom: 'This is our island. It's a good island. Until the grownups come to fetch us, we'll have fun.'

The group consists of about thirty boys, made up of the 'biguns' (about twelve years old) and the 'littluns' (around six years old). Some of the older children, members of a school choir, form a natural subgroup led by Jack, a confident but aggressive boy. Ralph, who initially likes Jack, appoints the choir to be responsible for hunting food for the entire group.

Ralph, Jack and another boy, Simon, set off to explore the island and settle on a plan to light a fire that will act as a beacon to attract passing ships. They use Piggy's glasses as a lens to concentrate the sun's rays. However, because the boys are playing rather than monitoring the flames, the fire gets out of control and burns through a swathe of forest. In the chaos, one littlun disappears, presumably burned to death.

The boys start off enjoying life without adult supervision, but Ralph wants them to focus less on playing and more on getting organised, maintaining the beacon, building shelters and other serious tasks. Simon supervises the construction of shelters and tries to protect the helpless littluns.

Jack's hunting party is initially unsuccessful in their aim of killing a wild pig, but Jack is becoming increasingly obsessed with hunting and killing. Piggy makes intelligent suggestions about improving their situation, but the communal opinion of him is low. The boys, particularly Jack, have identified him as the perpetual victim and Piggy and his asthma become the butt of everyone's jokes.

The hunters also have responsibility for maintaining the beacon, but when a passing ship is spotted Ralph and Piggy notice that the beacon has gone out. The hunters, however, have caught a pig and their joy at this first kill is celebrated with barbarian frenzy. When Piggy criticises Jack, Jack hits him. Ralph restores order temporarily by blowing the conch shell and making a speech, but the littluns are by this stage very frightened and more of the boys are convinced there is a nightmarish 'beast' somewhere on the island.

The older boys try to reassure them that there is no monster, but the littluns are not convinced. Ralph and Piggy recognise that everything is starting to unravel ('The world, that understandable and lawful world, was slipping away') but they are powerless to stop the drift to anarchy. Meanwhile the littluns are being ignored and neglected, even casually bullied by some of the older boys.

Soon afterwards, Sam and Eric—identical twins who have been assigned night duty tending the beacon—fall asleep on the job. They consequently fail to notice a dying fighter pilot drift down to earth from his wrecked plane to land nearby. The twins wake up to see a silhouetted body and hear the flapping of the parachute. Terrified, they rush back to camp, telling everyone that 'the beast' has attacked them. At a stormy meeting, the frightened boys resent Ralph's boring insistence on rules and keeping the signal fire going. Unfortunately for Ralph, the possibility of a beast and the fear it has generated serves to empower Jack—the hunter—who declares, 'Bollocks to the rule! We're strong—we hunt! If there is a beast, we'll hunt it down!'

Unsettled, the boys organise a posse to look for the beast. Hostility grows between Jack and Ralph as they lead the tense hunting party. Eventually, they chance upon the pilot's corpse, which they mistake for a giant ape, and flee.

Arriving back at their beach camp, Jack immediately calls a meeting. Tempers flare as Jack calls Ralph a coward and seeks to depose him: 'He's not a hunter. He'd never have got us any meat. He isn't a prefect.' When this attempted coup fails, Jack and his hunters leave to form a separate group at the other end of the island. Ralph tells the boys who have stayed behind with him to build a new beacon, this time on the beach, but gradually more and more boys creep away to join Jack's tribe.

The bloodlust of the hunters increases after they become a separate tribe under Jack's leadership. The hunters begin to paint their faces and Jack organises the ritual sacrifice of a pig to appease 'the beast'. Within Jack's tribe, a quiet boy named Roger starts to show sadistic tendencies, making him a perfect second-in-command.

Meanwhile, the original group is being harassed by the growing tribe of Jack's hunters. Simon, who is feeling the pressure, goes off on his own to think—and comes across the decapitated pig's head. Simon has a terrible vision: he believes the pig's head is speaking to him in the guise of the Lord of the Flies, telling him that he can never escape because the beast lives within all men. Overwhelmed by his vision, Simon has an epileptic fit. When he regains consciousness, he sees the body of the dead parachutist. He recognises that it is not a beast, but rather a dead pilot.

Simon rushes back wanting to convey this revelation to the boys, but when he arrives, the entire group—even Ralph and Piggy—are attending a hunting party celebration that has turned into a frenzied ritual dance. In the darkness and the chaos, the group of boys set upon Simon's shadowy figure as he runs onto the beach. They mistake him for the beast and spear him to death, chanting, *Kill the Beast! Cut his throat! Spill his blood!* Simon's battered corpse is carried out by the tide during the night.

The next day, as Ralph and Piggy whisper about Simon's horrible death, the hunters attack them and make off with Piggy's crucial fire-starting glasses, leaving him almost blind. Ralph and his few remaining followers walk to Jack's fort and attempt to reason with him. During the ensuing fistfight between Jack and Ralph, Piggy tries desperately to halt the fighting by brandishing the conch shell.

Perched on rocks high above, Roger rolls a boulder down on them, killing Piggy and shattering the conch. Ralph runs for his life and hides, but the following day Jack orders his followers to set fire to the forest to smoke Ralph out. The twins, who have been tortured and tormented by Jack into joining the hunters' tribe, secretly tell Ralph that Jack is planning to kill and decapitate him.

On the run, desperate, Ralph finds the head of the pig that was sacrificed earlier on. He destroys it, then stumbles onto the beach, dodging spears and expecting to be killed. However, when he looks up he sees not a bloodthirsty mob but rather a British naval officer. The huge fire has attracted the attention of a passing ship.

The other boys arrive at the beach but freeze in shock when they see an adult authority figure. The officer is astonished by the sight of these war-painted, blood-encrusted young savages, and assumes it is all a game. He asks Ralph in jest, 'Nobody killed, I hope?' Ralph's answer, 'Only two. And they're gone,' jolts the officer into the realisation that something unimaginable has occurred on the island. He lectures the filthy crowd of children that, being British, they should have 'put up a better show'. Overwhelmed by the rebuke and the accumulated death and misery, Ralph and the boys begin to sob.

Embarrassed by their tears, the officer looks away, waiting for them to pull themselves together. The surviving boys have been rescued, but their innocence has been shattered by what they have witnessed and endured on the island. The book ends with the naval officer's eyes resting on his trim cruiser moored offshore, a nod by Golding to the ordered, endemic violence that permeates the adult world.

# Acknowledgments

Anyone who writes history must start by thanking the other writers who have covered similar ground. Sources, both secondary and primary, are the backbone of our work, but we are particularly grateful to those primary authors who unflinchingly revealed the truth about the terrible circumstances they were caught up in.

The staff of various libraries have been invaluable. Again and again they would go out of their way to find that lost book, or give advice on which edition was the most reliable. Thanks to the staff of the National Library of Australia, and to the many volunteers who have worked on its invaluable Trove archive. We are lucky in Australia to have such an extensive resource available free of charge.

Thanks also to the staff of Fisher Library, University of Sydney, for their help trawling through their labyrinth of tomes, and to the staff at the State Library of NSW and the Mitchell Library—especially Kevin Leamon—who were so generous with their time, help and advice.

In the same vein, but in a digital form, are the brilliant non-profit organisations Archive.org, Project Gutenberg and the Hathi Trust Digital Library, which provide a vast, priceless digital archive of millions of original texts. As researchers, we are blessed to live in an age when, with the click of a mouse, we can view an entire copy of the first edition of a rare, old book, complete with illustrations.

Thanks to the staff at National Oceanic and Atmospheric Administration and the Library of Congress in the United States for their help with the *Belgica*, Adolphus Greely and Mugpi photographs. Cheryl Yates, of AAP Multimedia, gave much-appreciated advice on tracking down images, particularly of the Jonestown victims. Thanks also to the staff at the Société de Géographie in Paris, the Glenbow Museum in Calgary, Alberta and to the staff at the Western Australian Museum for their help with the *Batavia*.

Some individuals went to a great deal of trouble to check facts, provide detail and qualify information. Special thanks to Associate Professor Anne Keenleyside, Trent University, for her help and advice on the Franklin expedition; to Dr Desmond Lugg, Chief of Medicine of Extreme Environments, NASA (retired) for his correspondence on polar issues; Tess Hines, from the Mary Evans Picture Library in London, for her assistance with our illustrations; and to the staff at the Auckland Libraries for their help with the Franklin reward poster.

Jocelyn Nice kindly took time to share details and information about her gallant relative, Captain Thomas Musgrave. Dr Rebecca Moore and Fielding McGhee of the Jonestown Institute kindly helped us with our work on the subject. Thanks also to Eddie Kelso in Ireland for his help with research on some of the more elusive passengers from the *William Brown*. And to Harry Green and Brian Mulcahy of the Immigrant Ships Transcribers Guild, for their help with the ship itself.

Without the enthusiasm and support of our agent, Fiona Inglis of Curtis Brown, we would never have had the luxury of seeing our book in print. We also thank Michael Heyward, of Text Publishing, for having had faith in this project from day one. And a huge vote of thanks to our editor at Text, Mandy Brett, for her patience and persistence in shaping and polishing *No Mercy*.

We greatly appreciated Rory Tarnow-Mordi's assistance with some complex probability calculations. Thanks also to Patricia Betts in Canada for providing helpful information about both Inuit culture and the Franklin expedition; and to Kevin Todd, a fellow author, who kindly shared some facts regarding the loss of the *Neva*. Also to Roger Steele, at Steele Roberts Aotearoa, Wellington, for his correspondence on Raynal's book.

We would like to apologise to the many family and friends, who have put up with lurid dinner conversations about survivor meals and behaviour. We can see now why so many of you put down your forks.

On a personal level from Eleanor: endless thanks to Eric Betts my ever-patient husband, who tirelessly read redrafts, coped admirably with my outrageous spelling, provided editorial help and countless cups of green tea. Many thanks to my supportive children, Nina and Nicholas, who made practical suggestions, picked up anomalies, checked my maths and listened calmly to my theories on various stomach-churning subjects over dinner. Gratitude also to Anthony Learmonth for his general advice on structure. More thanks and appreciation to Robyn Manser, for acting as a wise and insightful reader near the end of the process. And lastly, to Dorothy MacDonald, who foraged through libraries for elusive texts and gave me my love of history in the first place.

# Sources

(A themed list in alphabetical order by vessel, location or protagonist.)

**The *Batavia***

Ariese, Csilla. 2012. *Databases of the people aboard the VOC ships Batavia (1629) & Zeewijk (1727)*. Special Publication No. 16. Department of Maritime Archaeology, Western Australian Museum, no. 298.

Dash, Mike. 2003. *Batavia's Graveyard: The True Story of the Mad Heretic Who Led History's Bloodiest Mutiny*. Phoenix Paperback, London. (The definitive work on the subject, detailed and exact.)

Drake-Brockman, Henrietta. 2006. *Voyage to Disaster*, UWA Publishing, Perth. (Ms Drake-Brockman's pioneering research on the *Batavia* provided the bedrock for all modern accounts. She was also the first person to correctly predict the location of the wreck.)

Edwards, Hugh. 2012. *Islands of Angry Ghosts*. HarperCollins Publishers Australia, Sydney.

Franklin, D. & Freedman, L. 2006. *A Bioarchaeological Investigation of a Multiple Burial Associated with the Batavia Mutiny of 1629*. Records of the Western Australian Museum. 23: 77–90.

Pelsaert, Francisco. *The Batavia Journal of Francois Pelsaert*. Edited and translated by Marit Van Huystee. Report—Department of Maritime Archaeology, Western Australian Maritime Museum, no. 136, 1994.

Pelsaert, Francisco. 1645. *Ongeluckige Voyagie, van't schip Batavia*. http://acms.sl.nsw.gov.au/album/albumView.aspx?itemID=846587&acmsid=0 (This website contains the original illustrations from Pelsaert's book.)

VOC Historical Society, Perth, Western Australia. www.voc.iinet.au

### The *Bounty* mutineers

Alexander, Caroline. 2003. *The Bounty: The True Story of the Mutiny on the Bounty.* Penguin Books, New York.

Beechey, Frederick W. 1832. *Narrative of a Voyage to the Pacific and the Beering's Strait.* Published by Authority of the Lords Commissioners of the Admiralty. Philadelphia.

Bligh, Lieut. William. 1838. *Narrative of the Mutiny of the Bounty on a Voyage to the South Seas.* William Smith, London.

Morrison, James. (Donald Maxton ed.). 2010. *After the Bounty: A Sailor's Account of the Mutiny and Life in the South Seas.* Potomac Books, Dulles.

Pitcairn's Early History: Before the Mutineers. Pitcairn Island Study Center. http://library.puc.edu/pitcairn/pitcairn/history-pre-mutineer.shtml

Teehuteatuaonoa (aka Jenny) First Narrative. 'Account of the Mutineers of the ship *Bounty* and their Descendants at Pitcairn Island'. *Sydney Gazette*, 17 July, 1819.

Teehuteatuaonoa (aka Jenny) Second Narrative. 'Pitcairn Island—The *Bounty's* Crew'. *United Service Journal.* 1829. pp 589–93.

### The Chilean mine disaster

Franklin, Jonathan. 2011. *The 33: The Ultimate Account of the Chilean Miners' Dramatic Rescue.* Transworld Publishers, London.

'Applied Knowledge: NASA Aids the Chilean Recue Effort.' http://www.nasa.gov/offices/oce/appel/ask/issues/41/41s_applied_prt.htm

'Chilean Miners: 17 Days Buried Alive'. Documentary—director Angus Macqueen. Television Nacional de Chile/ BBC, 2011. (The miners describe their ordeal first-hand—the PTSD is etched into their faces.)

'Chilean Miners Rescued, But Were They Saved?' *60 Minutes.* 14 February, 2011. www.cbsnews.com

'With Drilling Near End, Chile Rescue Enters Risky Phase.' *New York Times.* 8 October, 2010.

### The whaleship *Essex*

Cahill, Tim & Chase, Owen. 1999. *Shipwreck of the Whaleship Essex.* Lyons Press, New York.

Heffernan, Thomas. 1981. *Stove by a Whale: Owen Chase and the Essex.* Wesleyan University Press, Middletown. (Contains Owen Chase's account, and an interview with Captain Pollard.)

Nickerson, Thomas, Chase, Owen & Philbrick, Nathaniel. 2000, *The Loss of the Whaleship Essex, sunk by a Whale—First-Person Accounts.* Penguin Classic, USA.

Philbrick, Nathaniel. 2000. *In the Heart of the Sea: the Tragedy of the Whaleship Essex.* Penguin Books, New York.

Tyerman, Rev. Daniel & Bennet, George. 1832. *Journal of Voyages and Travels in the South Sea Islands, China, India & c.* vol II. Croker & Brewster, Boston.

Nantucket Historical Association Research Library. http://www.nha.org/library/

**Flight 571—the crash in the Andes**

Parrado, Nando. 2006. *Miracle in the Andes: 72 Days on the Mountain and My Long Trek Home*. Three Trees Press, New York.

Read, Piers Paul. 1974. *Alive: The Story of the Andes Survivors*. Book Club Associates London.

Strauch, Eduardo. http://www.eduardostrauch.com/site/index.php?module=hist_ elalud&lang=en (The website, set up by one of the survivors of Flight 571, is a terrific source of both background information on the people involved and the day-to-day account of their ordeal.)

**The Franklin expedition**

Beattie, Owen B. and Savelle, James M. 'Discovery of Human Remains from Sir John Franklin's Last Expedition' *Historical Archaeology*, vol. 17, no. 2 (1983), pp. 100–5.

Brandt, Anthony. 2011. *The Man Who Ate his Boots: Sir John Franklin and the Tragic History of the Northwest Passage*. Jonathan Cape, London.

Browne, James A. 1860. *The North-West Passage and the Fate of Sir John Franklin*. W. P. Jackson, Woolwich.

Cookman, Scott. 2000. *Iceblink: The Tragic Fate of Sir John Franklin's Lost Polar Expedition*. John Wiley & Sons, New York.

Dickens, Charles. 'The Lost Arctic Voyages'. *Household Words*, December, 1854.

Franklin, Sir John. 1823. *Narrative to the Shores of the Polar Sea in the Years 1819–22*. John Murray London, 1823. (Well worth a read, says quite a lot more than the author intended. Also includes Richardson's account.)

Franklin, Sir John. 1859. *Thirty Years in the Arctic Regions*. George Cooper Publisher. New York.

Keenleyside, Anne, et al. 'The Final Days of the Franklin Expedition'. *Arctic*, vol. 50, no.1 (March 1997), pp. 36–46.

Lambert, Andrew. 2009. *The Gates of Hell: Sir John Franklin's Tragic Quest for the Northwest Passage*. Yale University Press, New Haven.

Learmonth, L. A. 'Notes of the Franklin Relics', *Arctic*, vol. 1, no. 2, 1948.

McClintock, Admiral Sir Francis Leopold. 1908. *The Voyage of the 'Fox' in the Arctic Seas in Search of Franklin and his Companions*. John Murray, London.

McGoonan Ken. 2001. *Fatal Passage: The Story of John Rae, The Arctic Hero Time Forgot*. Carroll & Graf Publishers, New York.

Rich, E. E. & Johnson A. M. (eds). 'Arctic Controversy: The Letters of John Rae'. *Geographical Journal*, vol. 120, no. 4 December 1954.

Schwatka, Frederick. 1899. *The Search for Franklin: A Narrative of the American Expedition under Lieutenant Schwatka, 1878 to 1880*. T. Nelson and Sons, London.

Steele, Peter. 2003. *The Man Who Mapped the Arctic: The Intrepid Life of George Back, Franklin's Lieutenant*. Raincoast Books, Vancouver.

'Editorial', *The Times*. October 26, 1854.

'The Arctic Expedition'. *The Times*. May 12, 1845.

'The Fate of Sir John Franklin'. Frank Leslie's *New York Journal*, vol. 1–2. January 1855.

## The *Grafton*

Druett, Joan. 2007. *Island of the Lost: A Harrowing True Story of Shipwreck, Death and Survival on a Godforsaken Island at the Edge of the World*. Allen & Unwin, NSW.

Musgrave, Capt. Thomas. 1866. *Castaway on the Auckland Isles: A Narrative of the Wreck of the Grafton*. Lockward & Co, London, 1866. (Musgrave found the ordeal more painful than Raynal, but his humanity and courage leap out from the pages. The two accounts are very close, with only a few minor discrepancies.)

Raynal, François. 1880. *Wrecked on a Reef, or Twenty Months on the Auckland Islands*. T. Nelson & Sons, Edinburgh. (Raynal was without doubt the real-life MacGyver of his century—the book contains more than seems credible, and at the time readers expressed doubt that it was all humanly possible. But the hut stood for years, the remains are still there today, and Musgrave carried back his double-chambered forge bellows.)

Captain Thomas Musgrave, Lighthouse Keeper, Wilson's Promontory. www.lighthouse.net.au (An excellent account of what became of Captain Musgrave following his ordeal.)

'Auckland Islands—The Return of the Brig *Amherst*.' *Marlborough Express Newspaper*, 18 April, 1868. New Zealand.

'Loss of the *Invercauld*—Letter from the Captain'. (From the *People's Journal*) *Kilmore Free Press*, Victoria, 19 October, 1865.

## The Greely expedition

Greely, Commander Adolphus. 1894. *Three Years of Arctic Service: An Account of the Lady Franklin Expedition of 1881–84, and the Attainment of the Farthest North*. Charles Scribner's Sons, New York.

Guttridge, Leonard. 2006. *Ghosts of Cape Sabine: The Harrowing True Story of the Greely Expedition*. Authors Guild Backprint.Com, New England.

Putnam, William. 2001. *Arctic Superstars: General Adolphus Washington Greely, Admiral George Wallace Melville*. The American Alpine Club, Boulder.

Robinson, Michael. 2006. *The Coldest Crucible: Arctic Exploration and American Culture*. University of Chicago Press, London.

Schley, Commander W. S. & Soley, J. R. 1885. *The Rescue of Greely*. Charles Scribner's Sons. New York.

Weslawska, J. M. & Legezynska, J. 'Chances for Arctic Survival: Greely's Expedition Revisited'. *Arctic*, vol. 55, no. 4 (2002).

The Greely Expedition. PBS. http://www.pbs.org/wgbh/americanexperience/films/greely/
(The website contains extensive and informative information about the disastrous expedition, including maps, journals and photographs.)

'Proceedings of the *Proteus* Court of Inquiry on the Greely Relief Expedition of 1883—United States Congress.' 2012. Cambridge University Press. New York.

'The Shame of the Nation: Dreadful Suffering in the Camp at Cape Sabine. Further Facts about the Ghastly Prison in the Arctic Sea.' *New York Times*. 13 August 1884.

## The *Invercauld*

Allen, Madelene. 1997. *Wake of the Invercauld*. Exisle Publishing Ltd, Auckland. (Written by Robert Holding's great-granddaughter, this book interweaves Holding's account of the shipwreck with Allen's description of the geography, flora and fauna of the Auckland Islands. It does tend to gloss over Holding's failings, but is an invaluable book on the subject. )

Conon, Fraser. 1986. *Beyond the Roaring Forties: New Zealand's Subantarctic Islands*. Government Printing Office Publishing, Wellington.

Smith, Andrew. 1866. *The Castaways: A Narrative of the Wreck and Sufferings of the Officers and Crew of the Ship 'Invercauld' of Aberdeen*. Brown & Sons, Aberdeen.

Aberdeen Built Ships – *Invercauld*. ihttp://www.aberdeenships.com/single. asp?offset=1340&index=110961 (Technical information about the ship and her builders.)

*Auckland Island—The Enderby Project*. Historical Records of New Zealand's South Islands. www.nzetc.victoria.ac.nz/

'Cast Ashore!' (From the *S. A. Weekly Chronicle*). *Sydney Morning Herald*, 13 November, 1865. (Captain Dalgarno's personal account of the ordeal.)

'Wreck of the *Invercauld* at Auckland Islands—Terrible and Protracted Suffering of the Crew'. (From the *Aberdeen Free Press*). *Empire*, Sydney. 17 October, 1865.

## Jonestown

Kilduff, Marshall & Tracy, Phil. 'Inside Peoples Temple', *New West*, 1 August, 1977. (This was the article that exposed the dark side of the Peoples Temple to the American public, causing Jim Jones to flee to Guyana.)

Layton, Deborah. 1999. *Seductive Poison: A Jonestown Survivor's Story of Life and Death in the Peoples Temple*. Anchor Books, New York.

Reiterman, Tim & Jacobs, John. 2008. *Raven: The Untold Story of the Rev. Jim Jones and his People*. Penguin Group. New York.

Reston, James, Jr. 2000. *Our Father who Art in Hell: The Life and Death of Jim Jones*. iUniversity.com Inc. Lincoln, NE.

Scheeres, Julia. 2011. *A Thousand Lives: The Untold Story of Hope, Deception and Survival at Jonestown*. Free Press, New York.

The Edith Roller Journals, 16 February 1978. http://jonestown.sdsu.edu/AboutJonestown/JTResearch/eRollerJournals/
(This archive presents a disturbing mix of mundane diary entries concerning Edith Roller's diet and health, seamlessly blended with her accounts of regular violence, cruelty and paranoia.)

The Jonestown Death Tape, *(FBI No Q 042, November 18, 1978)* @ www.archive.org

Jonestown: The Life and Death of Peoples Temple. Director—Stanley Nelson. 2007. Berkley California, Firelight Media Production for American Experience. PBS.

'Miracle in the Jungle'. *Miracle: The Series*. ABC DVD, 2010. Australia.

## The *Karluk*

Bartlett, Robert (with Ralph Hale). 1916. *The Last Voyage of the Karluk: Flagship of Vilhjalmar Stefansson's Canadian Arctic Expedition of 1913–1916*. McClelland, Goodchild and Steward, Toronto.

McKinlay, William Laird. 1976. *The Last Voyage of the Karluk: A Survivor's Memoir of Arctic Disaster.* St Martin's Press, New York.

Niven, Jennifer. 2000. *The Ice Master: The Doomed 1913 Voyage of the Karluk and the Miraculous Rescue of her Survivors.* Hyperion, New York.

Ruth Makpii Ipalook: 1911–2008. www.nunatsiaqonline.ca

**The raft of the *Medusa***

Alhadeff, Albert. 2002. *The Raft of the Medusa: Géricault, Art and Race.* Prestel Publishing, New York.

Gifford, William, (ed.). 1818. *Quarterly Review, October 1817 & May 1818.* John Murray, Albermarle St. London.

McKee, Alexander. 1975. *Wreck of the Medusa: Tragic Story of the Death Raft.* Signet, New York.

McLeod, Dr John, et al. 1831. *The Shipwreck of the Alceste, an English Frigate, in The Straits of Gasper.* Printed by Thomas I. White, Dublin. (HaithiTrust Digital Library has an original version of this text.)

Miles, Jonathan. 2007. *The Wreck of the* Medusa*: The Most Famous Sea Disaster of the Nineteenth Century.* Grove Press, New York.

Moncrieff, William. 1820. *The Fatal Raft* [play].

Picard, Charlotte. 1827. *Perils and Captivity: Comprising the Sufferings of the Picard Family after the Shipwreck of the Medusa.* Translated by P. Maxwell. Constable & Co., Edinburgh. (The preface contains the English summation and condemnation of the whole squalid affair.)

Savigny, J. B. Henry & Corréard, Alexandre. 1818. *Narrative of a Voyage to Senegal in 1816, Comprising an Account of the Shipwreck of the Medusa.* Printed for Henry Colburn, Conduit St. London. (Charles-Marie Brédif's account is included at the end of Savigny and Corréard's book, and offers the clearest explanation of events on the other *Medusa* boats.)

**The siege of Numantia**

Appian of Alexandria. *Appian's History of Rome: The Spanish Wars.* Translated by Horace White.

Polybius. *The Complete Histories of Polybius, Book 35, The Celtiberian War.* Translated by W. R. Paton. Digireads.com Publishing, 2009.

**Alexander Pearce**

Collins, Paul. 2002. *Hell's Gates: The Terrible Journey of Alexander Pearce Van Diemen's Land Convict.* Hardie Grant Books, Melbourne.

Pearce, Alexander. 1824. *Confession of murder and cannibalism.* (Album View—the website has the original confession along with a transcript.) www.acms.sl.nsw.gov.au

'Alexander Pearce, a convict. The Supreme Court of Van Diemen's Land'. *Hobart Town Gazette.* 25 June, 1824.

'Alexander Pearce's Confession to Rev. Mr Conolly'. *Hobart Town Gazette*, 6 August, 1824.

'Documents relating to the Absconding of Pierce and Cox from Macquarie

Harbour'. Select Committee on Transportation. 313 App. (1) no. 56. House of Commons Papers, vol. 22.

## The *Polaris* expedition

Hall, Charles Francis. 1865. *Arctic Researches, and Life among the Esquimaux: Being a Narrative of an Expedition in Search of Sir John Franklin in the Years 1860, 1861 and 1862*. Harper & Brothers Publisher. New York.

Hall, Charles Francis. 1879. *Narrative of the Second Arctic Expedition of Charles F. Hall: His Journey to the Straits of Fury and Hecla and to King William's Land*. Government Printing Office, Washington.

Hall, Charles Francis. 2011. *Life with the Esquimaux*, vol. 1. Cambridge University Press, New York.

Loomis, Chauncey. 2000. *Weird and Tragic Shores: The Story of Charles Francis Hall*. Modern Library, USA. (Loomis's firsthand account of Hall's exhumation and the evidence of poisoning is particularly enthralling.)

Tyson, George E. 1874. *Arctic Experiences: Containing Capt. George E. Tyson's Wonderful Drift on the Ice-Floe, A History of the Polaris Expedition*. Edited by E. Vale Blake, Harper & Brothers Publishers, New York. (Tyson's account is the best original source, and don't miss the frank admissions from the crew included in the appendix.)

Arctic Profiles—Ebierbing (ca. 1837–ca. 1881) http://pubs.aina.ucalgary.ca/arctic/Arctic39-2-186.pdf

'Scientific Results of the Expedition'. *New York Tribune*, 20 June, 1873.

'The Polar Expedition—Story of Dr Hall and the *Polaris*', *National Republicans*, 22 May, 1873.

## The Robbers Cave experiment

Granberg, Donald & Sarup, Gian (eds). 1992. *Social Judgement and Intergroup Relations: Essays in Honor of Muzafer Sherif*. Springer-Verlag. New York.

Sherif, Muzafer and Carolyn, O. J. Harvey, et al. 1988. *The Robbers Cave Experiment: Intergroup Conflict and Co-operation*. Wesleyan University Press, Middletown.

Sherif, Muzafer & Sherif, Carolyn. 1953. *Groups in Harmony and Tension: An Integration of Studies on Intergroup Relations*. Harper & Brothers, Publishers, New York.

## Vinland

Anonymous. *The Saga of the Icelanders*. 2001. Translated by Keneva Kunze, et al. Penguin Classic Deluxe Edition.

Anonymous. *The Vinland Sagas*. 2008. Translated by Keneva Kunze, Editor Gisli Sigurdsson. Penguin Classics. London.

FitzHugh, William & Ward, Elizabeth (eds). 2000. *Vikings: The North Atlantic Saga*. Smithsonian Institution Press, Washington.

Ingstad, Helge & Anne. 2001. *The Viking: The Excavation of a Norse Settlement in L'Anse Aux Meadows, Newfoundland*. Checkmark Books, New York.

Jones, Gwyn. 2001. *A History of the Vikings*. Second Edition. Oxford University Press. Oxford.

McGovern, Thomas. 'The Archaeology of the Norse North Atlantic'. *Annual Review of Anthropology*. Vol. 19, 1990, pp 331–51.

Roesndahl, Else. 1998. *The Vikings: Revised Edition*. Penguin Books, London.

## The *Wager*

Anson, Commodore George. 1745. *A Voyage to the South Seas, And to Many Other Parts of the World*. R. Walker, Fleet St, London.

Bulkeley, John & Cummins, John. 1743. *A Voyage to the South Seas, in the Years 1740–41*. Publisher Jacob Robinson, London. (Bulkeley and Cummins spend much of this account trying to justify the unjustifiable. It is hard not to suspect they could feel a court martial and death by hanging waiting in the wings. The multiple oaths, and who signed them, are of particular interest.)

Byron, John. 1768. *The Narrative of the Honourable John Byron, Containing an Account of the Great Distresses Suffered by Himself and His Companions on the Coast of Patagonia*. S. Baker & G. Leigh, London.

Campbell, Alexander. 1747. *The Sequel to Bulkeley and Cummins's Voyage to the South Seas*. W. Owen Publisher. London. (Available online—www.patlibros.org)

Catsambis, Alexis, & Ford, Ben (eds). 2011. *The Oxford Handbook of Maritime Archaeology*. Oxford University Press, New York.

Edwards, Philip. 1994. *The Story of the Voyage: Sea-Narratives in Eighteenth-Century England*. Cambridge University Press, Cambridge.

Morris, Isaac. 1746. *Narrative of the Dangers and Distresses which Befel Isaac Morris and seven more of the crew belonging to the 'Wager'—Store Ship*. Bible & Ball. London. (Available online—www.patlibros.org)

Moss, Chris. 2008. *Patagonia: A Cultural History*. Oxford University Press, New York.

Rodger, N. A. M. 1996. *The Wooden World: An Anatomy of the Georgian Navy*. W. W. Norton & Co., New York.

## The lifeboat of the *William Brown*

Anonymous. 1842. *Trial of Alexander William Holmes one of the crew of the Ship William Brown for Manslaughter*. Philadelphia.

Brown, D. P. 1858. *Speech in Defence of Alexander William Holmes—Indicted for Manslaughter on the High Seas*. Robb, Pile & McElroy, Philadelphia.

Hayward, J. S. & Eckerson, J. D. 'Physiological responses and survival times predictions for humans in ice-water'. *Aviation, Space, & Environmental Medicine*, March 1984, 55 (3):206–11.

Hazard, Samuel (ed.). *Hazard's United States Commercial and Statistical Register*. Vol. 4, 1841, p. 371.

Koch, Tom. 2004. *The Wreck of the William Brown: A True Tale of Overcrowded Lifeboats and Murder at sea*. International Marine/ McGraw-Hill. Camden, ME.

'Captain Ball's Account—Dreadful Shipwreck'. *The Times* (London), 15 May, 1841. (From the *Havre Journal*.)

## Miscellaneous disasters, voyages and adventures

Anonymous. 1873. *The Loss of the Ship 'Northfleet': A Complete Account of All Connected with the Sad Disaster*. Waterlow & Sons, London.

Bailey, Maurice & Maralyn. 1992. *117 Days Adrift*. Sheridan House. New York.

Banks, Sir Joseph. *Series 3: The Endeavour Journal of Joseph Banks, 25 August 1768–12 July 1771*. Papers of Sir Joseph Banks, State Library of NSW. http://www2.sl.nsw.gov.au/banks/series_03/03_view.cfm

Beesley, Lawrence. 2005. *The Loss of the SS Titanic*. 1st World Library, Fairfield, IA.

Bugliois, Vincent & Gentry Curt. 1994. *Helter Skelter: The True Story of the Manson Murders*. W. W. Norton & Company Inc., New York.

Cook, Dr Frederick. 1909. *Through the First Antarctic Night 1898–1899*. Doubleday, Page & Company, New York.

Cook, Capt. James. *Cook's Endeavour Journal, Daily Entries, 1768–1771*. South Sea, 2004. http://nla.gov.au/nla.cs-ss-jrnl-cook-toc (An exact reproduction of Cook's journal, including his corrections. This version is far more interesting and reliable than many of the later versions which have been heavily edited, often combining Cook's version with Joseph Banks's version of events.)

Dary, David. 2004. *The Oregon Trail: An American Saga*. Oxford University Press, New York.

De Léry, Jean. 1992. *History of a Voyage to the Land of Brazil*. Translated by Janet Whatley. University of California Press, Berkley.

Flinders, Matthew. 1815. *A Voyage to Terra Australis*, vol. I. G. and W. Nicol, London.

Ghinsberg, Yossi. 2009. *Lost in the Jungle*. Skyhorse Publishing.

Giles, Ernest. 2004. *Australia Twice Traversed*. Kessinger Publishing, Montana.

Gilt Dragon Research Group. www.giltdragon.com.au

Gracie, Archibald. 1913. *The Truth about the Titanic*. J. J. Little & Ives, New York.

Harrison, Capt. David. 1766. *The Melancholy Narrative of the Distressful Voyage and Miraculous Deliverance of Captain David Harrison, of the Sloop Peggy*. Printed by James Harrison, London.

Harrison, Capt. David. *Copia of The Melancholy Narrative*, sworn by Captain David Harrison, Before Right Hon. George Nelson Esq, Lord Mayor of London and Robert Shank, Public Notary. London, April 1766.

Livingstone, David. 1857. *Missionary Travels and Researches in South Africa*. John Murray, London.

McGlashan, Charles F. 1879. *A History of the Donner Party: A Tragedy of the Sierras*. Crowley & McGlashan. Truckee, California.

Mancall, Peter C. 2009. *Fatal Journey: The Final Expedition of Henry Hudson*. Basic Books, New York.

Melville, George. 1885. *In the Lena Delta: A Narrative of the Search for Lieut.-Commander De Long and his Companions*. Longman Green & Co, London.

Mikkelsen, Ejnar. 2003. *Two Against the Ice*. Steerforth Press, Vermont.

Nash, Michael, 'Investigation of a survivor camp from the "Sydney Cove" shipwreck'. *Bulletin of the Australasian Institute for Maritime Archaeology*, 29: 9–24, 2005. (Maps and photographs make this in invaluable reference to the *Sydney Cove* shipwreck.)

Riley, Capt. James. 1817. *An Authentic Narrative of the Loss of the American Brig Commerce, Wrecked on the Western Coast of Africa, in the month of August, 1815*. T. & W. Mercein, New York.

Shackleton, Sir Ernest. 1999. *South: The Endurance Expedition*. Signet Books.

Sullenberger, Capt. Chesley, with Jeffery Zaslow. 2009. *Highest Duty: My Search for What Really Matters*. HarperLuxe, New York.

Tootell, Betty. 1985. *All Four Engines Have Failed: The True and Triumphant Story of Flight BA 009 and the Jakarta Incident*. André Deutsch Ltd, London.

Tyler, Daniel. 1881. *A Concise History of the Mormon Battalion in the Mexican War, 1846–1847*. Salt Lake City.

Worsley, Frank Arthur. 2000. *Endurance: An Epic of Polar Adventure*. W. W. Norton & Co., New York.

Patrick Breen Diary November 20, 1846–March 1, 1847, BANC MSS C-E 176, The Bancroft Library, University of California, Berkeley. http://www.oac.cdlib.org/view?docId=tf10000759;developer=local;style=oac4;doc.view=items

'A Horrible Tale—Letter to the Editor'. *Straits Times*, 14 November, 1874.

'Particulars of the Wreck of the Prison Ship "Neva"'. *Sydney Monitor*, July 18, 1835. http://trove.nla.gov.au/ndp/del/article/32149374

'The Loss of the Ship *Euxine* by Fire—Horrible Suffering of the Survivors'. *Singapore Daily Times*, November 16, 1874.

SV *Neva* (1835) www.wrecksite.edu (Technical information concerning the ship and the wreck location.)

**Science etc.**

Albiin, Nils & Erikkson, Anders. 1984. 'Fatal Accidental Hypothermia and Alcohol'. *Alcohol and Alcoholism*, Oxford Journals, vol. 19, issue 1, 1984.

Artwohl, Alexis. 'Perceptual and Memory Distortion During Officer-Involved Shooting'. *FBI Law Enforcement Bulletin*, Oct. 2002. (IACP Net Document No. 564080).

Artwohl, Alexis, 'Perceptual and Memory Distortion during Officer-Involved Shooting'. *FBI Law Enforcement Bulletin*, Oct 2002, (IACP Net Document No. 564080)

Asch, Solomon. 'Effects of Group Pressure Upon the Modification and Distortion of Judgements'. S. E. Asch, in H. Guetkow (ed.) *Groups, Leadership, and Men*, 1951.

Eisenberger, Naomi, et al. 'Does Rejection Hurt? An fMRI study of social exclusion'. (Eisenberger N., Lieberman MD, and Williams KD.) *Science*, 302, 290–2, 2003.

Elinder, Mikael, & Erixson, Oscar. 'Every Man for Himself: Gender, Norms and Survival in Maritime Disasters'. Department of Economics Uppsala University Working Paper 2012:8. April 2012.

Fong, Dr Kevin. 2013. *Extremes: Life, Death and the Limits of the Human Body*. Hodder & Stoughton Ltd, London.

Forsyth, Doneldson R. 2009. *Group Dynamics*. Fifth Edition. Cengage Learning, Belmont CA. (An invaluable book for anyone who wants to understand the mechanics of how groups function and malfunction.)

Fuman, K. I. 'Acute Hypervitaminosis A in Adults'. *American Journal of Clinical Nutrition* 26: June 1973.

Gilman, Jodi M. et al. 'Why We Like to Drink: A Functional Magnetic Imaging Study of the Rewarding and Anxiolytic Effects of Alcohol'. *Journal of Neuroscience*, April 30, 2008–28(18).

Gospic, Katarina, et al. 2011. 'Limbic Justice—Amygdala Involvement in the Immediate Rejection of the Ultimatum Game'. (Gospic K, Mohlin E, Fransson P, Petrovic P, Johannesson M, et al.) *PloS Biol* (9) May, 2011.

Grossman, Dave Lt Col. 2009. *On Killing: The Physiological Cost of Learning to Kill in War and Society*. Bay Back Books, Hachette Book Group, New York. (An excellent, accessible work on the subject.)

Hutchison, Ray & Dalke, Karen. 2011. *Thrill Killing in Wisconsin—Final Report to the Wisconsin Department of Natural Resources*. University of Wisconsin-Green Bay.

Kanas, N. & Manzey, D. (eds). 2008. *Space Psychology and Psychiatry, 2nd edition*. Microcosm Press, CA.

Keegan, John. 1978. *The Face of Battle*. Penguin Books, New York.

Kruuk , Hans. 'The Urge to Kill'. *New Scientist*, June 29, 1972, vol. 54, no. 802.

Kumar Parveen & Clark, Michael. 2009. *Clinical Medicine. Seventh Edition*,

Kundu, Rama. 2008. *Intertext: A Study of the Dialogue Between Texts*. Sarup & Sons, New Delhi.

LeDoux, Joseph. 1998. *The Emotional Brain: The Mysterious Underpinnings of Emotional Life*. Touchstone, New York.

Lorenz, Konrad. 1967. *On Aggression*. Translated by Marjorie Latzke. Methuen & Co. Ltd, London.

Marks, Isaac. 1987. *Fears, Phobias and Rituals: Panic, Anxiety and their Disorders*. Oxford University Press, New York.

Marshall, S. L. A. 2000. *Men Against Fire: The Problem of Battle Command*. University of Oklahoma Press.

McGrew, William, Marchant, L. F., Nishida, T. (eds). 1998. *Great Ape Societies*. Cambridge University Press.

McPhee, J. C. & Charles, J. B. (eds). 2010. *Human Health and Performance Risks of Space Exploration Missions: Evidence Reviewed by the NASA Human Research Program*. US National and Aeronautics and Space Administration.

Mujica-Parodi, L. et al. 2009. 'Chemosensory Cues to Conspecifis Emotional Stress Activated Amygdala in Humans'. *PLoS ONE* 4(7): e6415.

Poynter, Jane. 2006. *The Human Experiment: Two Years and Twenty Minutes Inside Biosphere II*. Thunder's Mouth Press, New York.

Raine, Adrian. 2013. *The Anatomy of Violence: The Biological Roots of Crime*. Random House, Inc. New York.

Rasmussen, John (ed.). 2009. *Man in Isolation and Confinement*. Transactions Publishers.

Ripley, Amanda. 2009. *The Unthinkable: Who Survives When Disaster Strikes—and Why*. Arrow Books, New York.

Rodahl, K. & Moore. T. 'The Vitamin A Content and Toxicity of Bears and Seals'. University of Cambridge, 1942.

Rothschild, Babette. 2000. *The Body Remembers: The Psychophysiology of Trauma and Trauma Treatment*. W. W. Norton & Company, Inc., New York.

Sandal, G.M., Vaernes R. et al. 'Psychological reactions during polar expeditions and isolation in hyperbaric chambers'. *Aviation, Space and Environmental Medicine Journal*. 1996, March;67 (3): 227–34.

Sindler, Amy J., Wellman, Nancy S. & Stier, O. B. 'Holocaust survivors report long-term effects on attitudes toward food'. *Journal of Nutrition, Education and Behavior.* 2004 Jul–Aug 36(4): 189–96.

Tiger, Lionel. 2005. *Men in Groups.* Transaction Publishers, New Brunswick.

Williamson, Ian & Sabath, Michael. 'Island Populations, Land Area and Climate: A Case Study of the Marshall Islands'. *Human Ecology,* (1982), vol. 10, issue 1.

'Ethnolichenology, part 1, A Brief Look at Lichen and People—Lichens as Food.' http://web.uvic.ca/~stucraw/part1.html#Lichens_as_food

'Understanding PTSD'. National Center for PTSD—Posttraumatic Stress Disorder. www.ptsd.va.gov

## Literature

Ballantyne, R. M. 2006. *The Coral Island.* 1st World Library, Fairfield. IA.

Bloom, Harold. 2004. *Bloom's Guides: William Golding's Lord of the Flies.* Chelsea House Publishing, Broomall, PA.

Brook, Peter. 1987. *The Shifting Point: Theatre, Film, Opera, 1946–1987.* Theatre Communications Group, Inc. New York.

Carey, John. 2009. *William Golding: The Man Who Wrote Lord of the Flies.* Faber and Faber, London.

Golding, Judy. 2012. *The Children of Lovers.* Faber and Faber, London.

Golding, William. 1988. *Lord of the Flies.* Faber and Faber, London.

Kermode, Frank. Interview with William Golding: *The Meaning of it All.* Broadcast August 28, 1959. BBC.

Melville, Herman (ed. Tony Tanner). 2008. *Moby Dick.* Oxford University Press, Oxford.

## General

Dikotter, Frank. 2010. *Mao's Great Famine: The History of China's Most Devastating Catastrophe, 1958–1962.* Walker Publishing Company Inc., New York.

Dwyer, Gwynne. 2004. *War: The Lethal Custom.* Carroll & Graf Publishers, New York.

Fleming, Fergus. 2001. *Barrow's Boys: A Stirring Story of Daring Fortitude and Outright Lunacy.* Granta Books. London.

Fleming, Fergus. 2001. *Ninety Degrees North: The Quest for the North Pole.* Granta Books, London.

Geiger, John. 2010. *The Third Man Factor: the Secret to Survival in Extreme Conditions.* Text Publishing, Melbourne.

Hughes, Robert. 1988. *The Fatal Shore.* Pan Books, London.

Lockhart, J. G. 1939. *True Tales of the Sea.* Quality Press.

Robinson, Michael. 2006. *The Coldest Crucible: Arctic Exploration and American Culture.* University of Chicago Press, London.

Simpson, A. W. Brian, 1994. *Cannibalism and the Common Law: A Victorian Yachting Tragedy.* The Hambledon Press, London.

Yang, Jisheng (translated by Stacy Mosher & Guo Jian). 2012. *Tombstone: The Great Chinese Famine, 1958–1962.* Farrar, Straus and Giroux. New York.

# Illustrations

15. Sir John Franklin reward poster, 1849. Sir George Gray Special Collections, Auckland Libraries. Reference number GMS 111.
16. De-fleshing cut on skeletal remains of Franklin expedition members. Courtesy Prof. Anne Keenleyside.
17. Dr John Rae. Artist: Stephen Pearce, Glenbow Archives NA-1252-2.
18. 'A feeling of freedom' booklet, 1978. Courtesy of The Jonestown Institute.
19. Jonestown, Guyana, mass suicide. Associated Press/via AAP, Ref: 78010103155.

# Index